Learn To Read English With Directions In Korean
Answer Key
Assessment
Black and White Edition

Assessment

ISBN 978-1-945738-77-7
© 2022 – Wendy A. Charles & Alexander J. Charles
All Rights Reserved
Baldwin, New York
www.intellastic.com

All rights reserved. No portion of this book may be reproduced, stored in a retrieval system, or transmitted in any form or by any means – electronic, mechanical, photocopy, recording, video presentation, private instruction, scanning or other – except for brief quotations in critical reviews or articles, without the prior written permission of the writers.

All Rights Reserved. Printed in the USA.

Answer Key

Table of Contents

Unit A

Lesson 1.1	Reading Words with the Letter A/a	1
Lesson 1.2	Reading Words with the Short Vowel "a" Sound	2
Lesson 1.2	Reading & Writing Words with the Short Vowel "a" Sound	3
Lesson 1.3	Reading Words with the Long Vowel "a" Sound	4
Lesson 1.3	Reading & Writing Words with the Long Vowel "a" Sound	5
Lessons 1.2 & 1.3	Reading Short Vowel and Long Vowel Words	6
Lesson 1.4	Reading Words with the "age" Letter Combination	7
Lesson 1.5	Reading Words with the "ai" Vowel Pair	8
Lesson 1.6	Reading Letter "a" Words with the Schwa Sound	9
Lesson 1.7	Reading Words with the "ar" Letter Combination	10
Lesson 1.7	Reading Words with the "ar" Letter Combination	11
Lesson 1.8	Reading Words with a Silent Letter "a"	12
Unit Review	Reading Words with Vowel "a" Sounds: /ă/, /ā/, /ə/ & Silent	13
Lesson 1.9	Reading Multisyllable Words	14
Lesson 1.9	Reading Multisyllable Words	15
Lesson 1.10	Proper and Common Nouns and Adjectives	16

Unit B

Lesson 2.1	Reading Words with the Letter B/b	17
Lesson 2.2	Reading Words with the "br" Letter Combination	18
Lesson 2.3	Reading Words with the "bl" Letter Combination	19
Lesson 2.3	Reading Words with the "ble" Letter Combination	20
Lesson 2.4	Reading Words with the "mb" Letter Combination	21
Lesson 2.4	Reading Words with the "bt" Letter Combination	22
Lesson 2.5	Reading Words with a Silent Letter "b"	23
Lesson 2.6	Reading Multisyllable Words	24
Lesson 2.6	Reading Multisyllable Words	25
Lesson 2.7	Proper and Common Nouns and Adjectives	26

Assessment

Unit C

Lesson 3.1	Reading Words with the Letter C/c	27
Lesson 3.1	Reading Words with the Hard Letter "c"	28
Lesson 3.2	Reading Words with the Soft Letter "c"	29
Lessons 3.1 & 3.2	Reading Hard Letter "c" and Soft Letter "c" Words	30
Lesson 3.3	Reading Words with the "cr" Letter Combination	31
Lesson 3.4	Reading Words with the "cl" Letter Combination	32
Lesson 3.4	Reading Words with the "cle" Letter Combination	33
Lesson 3.5	Reading Words with the "ct" Letter Combination	34
Lesson 3.6	Reading Soft Letter "c" Words	35
Lesson 3.6	Reading Soft Letter "c" Words	36
Lesson 3.7	Reading Words with the "ch" Letter Combination	37
Lesson 3.8	Reading Words with the "cc" Letter Combination	38
Lesson 3.9	Reading Words with a Silent Letter "c"	39
Lesson 3.10	Reading Multisyllable Words	40
Lesson 3.10	Reading Multisyllable Words	41
Lesson 3.11	Proper and Common Nouns and Adjectives	42

Unit D

Lesson 4.1	Reading Words with the Letter D/d	43
Lesson 4.2	Reading Letter "d" Words with the /d/ Sound & /j/ Sound	44
Lesson 4.2	Reading Words with the "dr" Letter Combination	45
Lesson 4.3	Reading Words with the "ed" Suffix/ Past Tense Verbs	46
Lesson 4.4	Reading Words with a Silent Letter "d"	47
Lesson 4.5	Reading Multisyllable Words	48
Lesson 4.5	Reading Multisyllable Words	49
Lesson 4.6	Proper and Common Nouns and Adjectives	50

Unit E

Lesson 5.1	Reading Words with the Letter E/e	51
Lesson 5.2	Reading Words with the Short Vowel "e" Sound	52
Lesson 5.2	Reading & Writing Words with the Short Vowel "e" Sound	53

Answer Key

Lesson 5.3	Reading Words with the Long Vowel "e" Sound	54
Lesson 5.3	Reading & Writing Words with the Long Vowel "e" Sound	55
Lessons 5.2 & 5.3	Reading Short Vowel and Long Vowel Words	56
Lesson 5.4	Reading Words with Letter "e" Vowel Pairs	57
Lesson 5.5	Reading Words with the Final Letter "e"	58
Lesson 5.6	Reading Letter "e" Words with the Schwa Vowel Sound	59
Lesson 5.7	Reading Words with the "er" Letter Combination	60
Lesson 5.8	Reading Words with the "eu" and "ew" Letter Combinations	61
Lesson 5.9	Reading Words with the "ey" Letter Combination	62
Lesson 5.10	Reading Words with a Silent Letter "e"	63
Unit Review	Reading Words with Vowel "e" Sounds: /ĕ/, /ē/, /ə/ & Silent	64
Lesson 5.11	Reading Multisyllable Words	65
Lesson 5.11	Reading Multisyllable Words	66
Lesson 5.12	Proper and Common Nouns and Adjectives	67

Unit F

Lesson 6.1	Reading Words with the Letter F/f	68
Lesson 6.2	Reading Words with the "fr" Letter Combination	69
Lesson 6.3	Reading Words with the "fl" Letter Combination	70
Lesson 6.3	Reading Words with the "fle" Letter Combination	71
Lesson 6.4	Reading Words with the "ft," "lf" and "ff" Letter Combinations	72
Lesson 6.5	Reading Words with a Silent Letter "f"	73
Lesson 6.6	Reading Singular and Plural forms of Words Ending in "-f" & "-fe"	74
Lesson 6.7	Reading Multisyllable Words	75
Lesson 6.7	Reading Multisyllable Words	76
Lesson 6.8	Proper and Common Nouns and Adjectives	77

Unit G

Lesson 7.1	Reading Words with the Letter G/g	78
Lesson 7.1	Reading Words with the Hard Letter "g"	79
Lesson 7.2	Reading Words with the Soft Letter G/g	80
Lessons 7.1 & 7.2	Reading Hard Letter "g" and Soft Letter "g" Words	81

Assessment

Lessons 7.1 & 7.2	Reading Hard Letter "g" and Soft Letter "g" Words	82
Lesson 7.3	Reading Words with the "gr" Letter Combination	83
Lesson 7.4	Reading Words with the "gl" Letter Combination	84
Lesson 7.4	Reading Words with the "gle" Letter Combination	85
Lesson 7.5	Reading Words with the "gh" Letter Combination	86
Lesson 7.6	Reading Words with the "gn" Letter Combination	87
Lesson 7.7	Reading Words with a Silent Letter "g"	88
Lesson 7.8	Reading Multisyllable Words	89
Lesson 7.8	Reading Multisyllable Words	90
Lesson 7.9	Proper and Common Nouns and Adjectives	91

Unit H

Lesson 8.1	Reading Words with the Letter H/h	92
Lesson 8.2	Reading Words with the Letter "h" Combinations: "sh," "wh," "ch," "th," "rh," "ph" and "gh"	93
Lesson 8.2	Reading Words with the Letter "h" Combinations: "sh," "wh," "ch," "th," "rh," "ph," "gh" and "sch"	94
Lesson 8.3	Reading Words with a Silent Letter "h"	95
Lesson 8.4	Reading Multisyllable Words	96
Lesson 8.4	Reading Multisyllable Words	97
Lesson 8.5	Proper and Common Nouns and Adjectives	98

Unit I

Lesson 9.1	Reading Words with the Letter I/i	99
Lesson 9.2	Reading Words with the Short Vowel "i" Sound	100
Lesson 9.2	Reading & Writing Words with the Short Vowel "i" Sound	101
Lesson 9.3	Reading Words with the Long Vowel "i" Sound	102
Lesson 9.3	Reading & Writing Words with the Long Vowel "i" Sound	103
Lessons 9.2 & 9.3	Reading Short Vowel and Long Vowel Words	104
Lesson 9.4	Reading Words with Letter "i" Vowel Pairs	105
Lesson 9.5	Reading Words with the Final Letter "i"	106
Lesson 9.6	Reading Letter "i" Words with the Schwa Vowel Sound	107

Answer Key

Lesson 9.7	Reading Words with the "ir" Letter Combination	108
Lesson 9.8	Reading Letter "i" Words with the Long Vowel "e" Sound	109
Lesson 9.9	Reading Words with a Silent Letter "i"	110
Unit Review	Reading Words with Vowel "i" Sounds: /ĭ/, /ī/, /ə/ & Silent	111
Lesson 9.10	Reading Multisyllable Words	112
Lesson 9.10	Reading Multisyllable Words	113
Lesson 9.11	Proper and Common Nouns and Adjectives	114

Unit J

Lesson 10.1	Reading Words with the Letter J/j	115
Lesson 10.2	Reading Multisyllable Words	116
Lesson 10.2	Reading Multisyllable Words	117
Lesson 10.3	Proper and Common Nouns and Adjectives	118

Unit K

Lesson 11.1	Reading Words with the Letter K/k	119
Lesson 11.2	Reading Words with the Letter "k" and "ck" Letter Combination	120
Lesson 11.3	Reading Words with the "kle" Letter Combination	121
Lesson 11.4	Reading Words with a Silent Letter "k"	122
Lesson 11.5	Reading Multisyllable Words	123
Lesson 11.5	Reading Multisyllable Words	124
Lesson 11.6	Proper and Common Nouns and Adjectives	125

Unit L

Lesson 12.1	Reading Words with the Letter L/l	126
Lesson 12.2	Reading Words with the Letter "l" Combinations: "bl," "pl" & "sl"	127
Lesson 12.3	Reading Words with a Silent Letter "l"	128
Lesson 12.4	Reading Multisyllable Words	129
Lesson 12.4	Reading Multisyllable Words	130
Lesson 12.5	Proper and Common Nouns and Adjectives	131

Assessment

Unit M

Lesson 13.1	Reading Words with the Letter M/m	132
Lesson 13.2	Reading Words with a Silent Letter "m"	133
Lesson 13.3	Reading Multisyllable Words	134
Lesson 13.3	Reading Multisyllable Words	135
Lesson 13.4	Proper and Common Nouns and Adjectives	136

Unit N

Lesson 14.1	Reading Words with the Letter N/n	137
Lesson 14.2	Reading Words with the "ng" Letter Combination	138
Lesson 14.3	Reading Words with a Silent Letter "n"	139
Lesson 14.4	Reading Multisyllable Words	140
Lesson 14.4	Reading Multisyllable Words	141
Lesson 14.5	Proper and Common Nouns and Adjectives	142

Unit O

Lesson 15.1	Reading Words with the Letter O/o	143
Lesson 15.2	Reading Words with the Short Vowel "o" Sound	144
Lesson 15.2	Reading & Writing Words with the Short Vowel "o" Sound	145
Lesson 15.3	Reading Words with the Long Vowel "o" Sound	146
Lesson 15.3	Reading & Writing Words with the Long Vowel "o" Sound	147
Lessons 15.2 & 15.3	Reading Short Vowel and Long Vowel Words	148
Lesson 15.4	Reading Words with Letter "o" Vowel Pairs	149
Lesson 15.5	Reading Words with the Final Letter "o"	150
Lesson 15.6	Reading Letter "o" Words with the Schwa Vowel Sound	151
Lesson 15.7	Reading Words with Vowel "o" Sounds: /ŏ/, /ō/ & /o͞o/	152
Lesson 15.8	Reading Words with the "or" Letter Combination	153
Lesson 15.8	Reading Words with the "or" Letter Combination	154
Lesson 15.9	Reading Words with a Silent Letter "o"	155
Unit Review	Reading Words with Vowel "o" Sounds: /ŏ/, /ō/, /ə/ & Silent	156
Lesson 15.10	Reading Multisyllable Words	157
Lesson 15.10	Reading Multisyllable Words	158

Answer Key

Lesson 15.11	Proper and Common Nouns and Adjectives	159
Unit P		
Lesson 16.1	Reading Words with the Letter P/p	160
Lesson 16.2	Reading Words with the "ph" Letter Combination	161
Lesson 16.3	Reading Words with the "pr" Letter Combination	162
Lesson 16.4	Reading Words with the "pl" Letter Combination	163
Lesson 16.4	Reading Words with the "ple" Letter Combination	164
Lesson 16.5	Reading Words with a Silent Letter "p"	165
Lesson 16.6	Reading Multisyllable Words	166
Lesson 16.6	Reading Multisyllable Words	167
Lesson 16.7	Proper and Common Nouns and Adjectives	168
Unit Q		
Lesson 17.1	Reading Words with the Letter Q/q	169
Lesson 17.2	Reading Words with the Letter "q" and "qu" Letter Combination	170
Lesson 17.2	Reading Words with the "qu" Letter Combination	171
Lesson 17.3	Reading Multisyllable Words	172
Lesson 17.3	Reading Multisyllable Words	173
Lesson 17.4	Proper and Common Nouns and Adjectives	174
Unit R		
Lesson 18.1	Reading Words with the Letter R/r	175
Lesson 18.2	Reading Words with the Letter "r" Combinations: "br," "cr," "dr," "fr," "gr," "pr" and "tr"	176
Lesson 18.3	Reading Multisyllable Words	177
Lesson 18.3	Reading Multisyllable Words	178
Lesson 18.4	Proper and Common Nouns and Adjectives	179
Unit S		
Lesson 19.1	Reading Words with the Letter S/s	180
Lesson 19.1	Reading Words with the Letter S/s	181

Assessment

Lesson 19.2	Reading Words with the "sion," "sial" & "scious" Suffixes	182
Lesson 19.3	Reading Words with the "sch" Letter Combination	183
Lesson 19.4	Reading Words with the "scr," "shr," "spr" & "str" Letter Combinations	184
Lesson 19.5	Reading Words with the "sl" & "sle" Letter Combinations	185
Lesson 19.5	Reading Words with the "sle" Letter Combination	186
Lesson 19.6	Reading Words with the "sm" Letter Combination	187
Lesson 19.7	Reading Words with the "ss" Letter Combination	188
Lesson 19.8	Reading Words with a Silent Letter "s"	189
Lesson 19.9	Reading Multisyllable Words	190
Lesson 19.9	Reading Multisyllable Words	191
Lesson 19.10	Proper and Common Nouns and Adjectives	192

Unit T

Lesson 20.1	Reading Words with the Letter T/t	193
Lesson 20.2	Reading Words with the "thm" Letter Combination	194
Lesson 20.3	Reading Words with the "tion," "tial" & "tious" Suffixes	195
Lesson 20.4	Reading Words with the "tr" Letter Combination	196
Lesson 20.5	Reading Words with the "tle" Letter Combination	197
Lesson 20.6	Reading Words with the Letter "t" Sounds	198
Lesson 20.7	Reading Words with a Silent Letter "t"	199
Lesson 20.8	Reading Multisyllable Words	200
Lesson 20.8	Reading Multisyllable Words	201
Lesson 20.9	Proper and Common Nouns and Adjectives	202

Unit U

Lesson 21.1	Reading Words with the Letter U/u	203
Lesson 21.2	Reading Words with the Short Vowel "u" Sound	204
Lesson 21.2	Reading & Writing Words with the Short Vowel "u" Sound	205
Lesson 21.3	Reading Words with the Long Vowel "u" Sound	206
Lesson 21.3	Reading & Writing Words with the Long Vowel "u" Sound	207
Lessons 21.2 & 21.3	Reading Short Vowel and Long Vowel Words	208
Lesson 21.4	Reading Words with Letter "u" Vowel Pairs	209

Lesson 21.5 — Reading Words with the Final Letter "u" — 210
Lesson 21.6 — Reading Letter "u" Words with the Schwa Vowel Sound — 211
Lesson 21.7 — Reading Words with the "ur" Letter Combination — 212
Lesson 21.8 — Reading Words with a Silent Letter "u" — 213
Unit Review — Reading Words with Vowel "u" Sounds: /ŭ/, /o͞o/, /ə/ & Silent — 214
Lesson 21.9 — Reading Multisyllable Words — 215
Lesson 21.9 — Reading Multisyllable Words — 216
Lesson 21.10 — Proper and Common Nouns and Adjectives — 217

Unit V

Lesson 22.1 — Reading Words with the Letter V/v — 218
Lesson 22.2 — Reading Multisyllable Words — 219
Lesson 22.2 — Reading Multisyllable Words — 220
Lesson 22.3 — Proper and Common Nouns and Adjectives — 221

Unit W

Lesson 23.1 — Reading Words with the Letter W/w — 222
Lesson 23.2 — Reading Words with a Vowel before the Letter "w" — 223
Lesson 23.3 — Reading Words with a Silent "w" and "wr" Letter Combination — 224
Lesson 23.3 — Reading Words with a Silent Letter "w" — 225
Lesson 23.4 — Reading Multisyllable Words — 226
Lesson 23.4 — Reading Multisyllable Words — 227
Lesson 23.5 — Proper and Common Nouns and Adjectives — 228

Unit X

Lesson 24.1 — Reading Words with the Letter X/x — 229
Lesson 24.1 — Reading Words with the Letter X/x — 230
Lesson 24.2 — Reading Multisyllable Words — 231
Lesson 24.2 — Reading Multisyllable Words — 232
Lesson 24.3 — Proper and Common Nouns and Adjectives — 233

Assessment

Unit Y

Lesson 25.1	Reading Words with the Letter Y/y	234
Lesson 25.1	Reading Words with the Letter Y/y	235
Lesson 25.2	Reading Words with a Vowel before the Letter "y"	236
Lesson 25.3	Reading Words with the "cy" Letter Combination	237
Lesson 25.4	Reading Words with the Final Letter "y"	238
Lesson 25.5	Reading Words with the "yr" Letter Combination	239
Lesson 25.6	Reading Letter "y" Words with the Schwa Sound	240
Lesson 25.7	Reading Words with a Silent Letter "y"	241
Lesson 25.8	Reading Multisyllable Words	242
Lesson 25.8	Reading Multisyllable Words	243
Lesson 25.9	Proper and Common Nouns and Adjectives	244

Unit Z

Lesson 26.1	Reading Words with the Letter Z/z	245
Lesson 26.1	Reading Words with the Letter Z/z	246
Lesson 26.2	Reading Words with a Silent Letter "z"	247
Lesson 26.3	Reading Multisyllable Words	248
Lesson 26.3	Reading Multisyllable Words	249
Lesson 26.4	Proper and Common Nouns and Adjectives	250

Appendix

Appendix 1.0	Introduction of the Letter A/a	251
Appendix 2.0	Introduction of the Letter B/b	252
Appendix 2.0	Letter Recognition B/b	253
Appendix 3.0	Introduction of the Letter C/c	254
Appendix 3.0	Letter Recognition C/c	255
Appendix 4.0	Introduction of the Letter D/d	256
Appendix 4.0	Letter Recognition D/d	257
Appendix 5.0	Introduction of the Letter E/e	258
Appendix 6.0	Introduction of the Letter F/f	259
Appendix 6.0	Letter Recognition F/f	260
Appendix 7.0	Introduction of the Letter G/g	261

Answer Key

Appendix 7.0	Letter Recognition G/g	262
Appendix 8.0	Introduction of the Letter H/h	263
Appendix 8.0	Letter Recognition H/h	264
Appendix 9.0	Introduction of the Letter I/i	265
Appendix 10.0	Introduction of the Letter J/j	266
Appendix 10.0	Letter Recognition J/j	267
Appendix 11.0	Introduction of the Letter K/k	268
Appendix 11.0	Letter Recognition K/k	269
Appendix 12.0	Introduction of the Letter L/l	270
Appendix 12.0	Letter Recognition L/l	271
Appendix 13.0	Introduction of the Letter M/m	272
Appendix 13.0	Letter Recognition M/m	273
Appendix 14.0	Introduction of the Letter N/n	274
Appendix 14.0	Letter Recognition N/n	275
Appendix 15.0	Introduction of the Letter O/o	276
Appendix 16.0	Introduction of the Letter P/p	277
Appendix 16.0	Letter Recognition P/p	278
Appendix 17.0	Introduction of the Letter Q/q	279
Appendix 17.0	Letter Recognition Q/q	280
Appendix 18.0	Introduction of the Letter R/r	281
Appendix 18.0	Letter Recognition R/r	282
Appendix 19.0	Introduction of the Letter S/s	283
Appendix 19.0	Letter Recognition S/s	284
Appendix 20.0	Introduction of the Letter T/t	285
Appendix 20.0	Letter Recognition T/t	286
Appendix 21.0	Introduction of the Letter U/u	287
Appendix 22.0	Introduction of the Letter V/v	288
Appendix 22.0	Letter Recognition V/v	289
Appendix 23.0	Introduction of the Letter W/w	290
Appendix 23.0	Letter Recognition W/w	291
Appendix 24.0	Introduction of the Letter X/x	292
Appendix 24.0	Letter Recognition X/x	293

Assessment

Appendix 25.0	Introduction of the Letter Y/y	294
Appendix 25.0	Letter Recognition Y/y	295
Appendix 26.0	Introduction of the Letter Z/z	296
Appendix 26.0	Letter Recognition Z/z	297

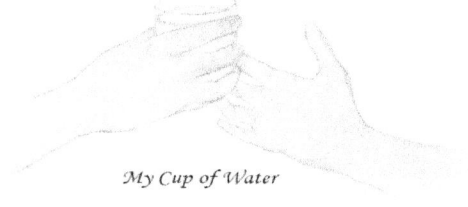

My Cup of Water

Answer Key

Name: _____ Date: ___/___/_____ Score: _____

Lesson 1.1

Reading Words with the Letter A/a

✓ Lesson Check Point

Directions: Read each target word. Find the letter "a" and put a check (✓) in the column that identifies its position: beginning, within or end.
지도: 각 대상 단어를 읽으십시오. 문자 "a"를 찾아 해당 위치를 나타내는 열에 확인 표시(✓)를 하십시오: 시작, 내부 또는 끝.

Target Words	Beginning (First Letter)	Within	End (Last Letter)
1. baker		✓	
2. sofa			✓
3. annex	✓		
4. gorilla			✓
5. apples	✓		

Directions: Read each target word. Read the words in the row and circle the word that has a different vowel "a" sound.
지도: 각 대상 단어를 읽으십시오. 행에 있는 단어를 읽고 모음 "a" 소리가 다른 단어에 동그라미를 치십시오.

Target Words				
6. flag	man	yam	cap	⟨take⟩
7. sad	clam	bag	⟨save⟩	brag
8. plan	rag	tag	pan	⟨made⟩
9. snap	⟨cake⟩	drag	add	has
10. trap	van	jazz	jam	⟨wave⟩

Learn To Read English With Directions In Korean   1   Copyrighted Material

Assessment

 Name: _____ Date: ___/___/_____ Score: _____

Lesson 1.2

Reading Words with the Short Vowel "a" Sound

✓ Lesson Check Point

 Directions: Read the words in the four boxes. Circle two words with the short vowel /ă/ sound. The anchor word for the short vowel /ă/ sound is <u>apple</u>.

지도: 네 개의 상자에 있는 단어를 읽으십시오. 짧은 모음 /ă/ 소리로 두 단어에 동그라미를 치십시오. 단모음 /ă/ 소리의 앵커 워드는 apple입니다.

| (flat) | tail |
| made | (fast) |

| safe | (dad) |
| spa | (sat) |

| Asia | pail |
| (ran) | (had) |

| plate | (sand) |
| (ask) | basic |

| wage | label |
| (cap) | (tab) |

| (slab) | (grab) |
| away | game |

 Directions: Read the words in the four boxes. Circle two words that rhyme. Rhyming words have the same ending sound, such as <u>tap</u> and <u>map</u>.

지도: 네 개의 상자에 있는 단어를 읽으십시오. 운이 맞는 두 단어에 동그라미를 치십시오. 운율이 있는 단어는 tap 및 map과 같이 끝 소리가 같습니다.

| ago | (tan) |
| (ran) | aunt |

| barn | (rat) |
| cake | (bat) |

| (mad) | all |
| (fad) | grape |

| (pass) | ball |
| jar | (class) |

| (past) | (last) |
| car | lake |

| fake | fall |
| (glad) | (bad) |

Learn To Read English With Directions In Korean

Answer Key

Name: _____ Date: ___/___/_____ Score: _____

Lesson 1.2

Reading & Writing Words with the Short Vowel "a" Sound

✓ Lesson Check Point

Directions: Read each sentence and underline three words with the short vowel /ă/ sound. Then, write the underlined words on the lines below. The anchor word for the short vowel /ă/ sound is <u>apple</u>.

지도: 각 문장을 읽고 세 단어에 짧은 모음 /ă/ 소리에 밑줄을 긋습니다. 그런 다음 밑줄 친 단어를 아래 줄에 쓰십시오. 단모음 /ă/ 소리의 기준어는 appple입니다.

Model

<u>Ann</u> raised her <u>hand</u> in <u>class</u>.

    Ann   hand   class

1. Today, <u>Dan</u> <u>sat</u> on <u>Pam's</u> sofa.

    Dan   sat   Pam's

2. Kate <u>and</u> Dave <u>have</u> two <u>cats</u>.

    and   have   cats

3. Dora <u>cannot</u> <u>stand</u> with the <u>band</u>.

    cannot   stand   band

4. My <u>dad</u> did not put <u>gas</u> in Nora's <u>cab</u>.

    dad   gas   cab

5. The <u>campers</u> <u>ran</u> in the rain with the <u>flags</u>.

    campers   ran   flags

Assessment

 Name: _____ Date: ___/___/_____ Score: _____

Lesson 1.3

Reading Words with the Long Vowel "a" Sound

✓ Lesson Check Point

 Directions: Read the words in the four boxes. Circle two words with the long vowel /ā/ sound. The anchor word for the long vowel /ā/ sound is <u>ape</u>.

지도: 네 개의 상자에 있는 단어를 읽으십시오. 장모음 /ā/ 소리로두단어에 동그라미를 치십시오. 장모음 /ā/ 소리의 기준어는 ape입니다.

(fail)	clan		van	flat		sap	(train)
rat	(day)		(rate)	(bait)		(tale)	jam

gap	swam		(tray)	(tail)		lap	(sale)
(way)	(fade)		jam	ham		nag	(mail)

 Directions: Read the words in the four boxes. Circle two words that rhyme. Rhyming words have the same ending sound, such as <u>wait</u> and <u>date</u>.

지도: 네 개의 상자에 있는 단어를 읽으십시오. 운이 맞는 두 단어에 동그라미를 치십시오. 운율이 있는 단어는 wait 및 date와 같이 끝 소리가 같습니다.

cab	(race)		(strain)	(rain)		bran	(lay)
(lace)	rag		jazz	grab		fat	(way)

(late)	brag		(fade)	Sam		tab	tan
gaps	(mate)		(made)	man		(wait)	(rate)

Answer Key

Name: _____ Date: ___/___/_____ Score: _____

Lesson 1.3

Reading & Writing Words with the Long Vowel "a" Sound

✓ Lesson Check Point

Directions: Read each sentence and underline three words with the long vowel /ā/ sound. Then, write the underlined words on the lines below. The anchor word for the long vowel /ā/ sound is <u>ape</u>.

지도: 각 문장을 읽고 장모음 /ā/ 소리로 세 단어에 밑줄을 긋습니다. 그런 다음 밑줄 친 단어를 아래 줄에 쓰십시오. 장모음 /ā/ 소리의 기준어는 ape입니다.

Model

Ann has <u>grapes</u> and <u>cake</u> on her <u>plate</u>.

    grapes   cake   plate

1. Al saw the <u>snake's</u> <u>tail</u> in the <u>cave</u>.

    snake's   tail   cave

2. Ann said, "It is not <u>safe</u> to <u>skate</u> in the <u>rain</u>."

    safe   skate   rain

3. We <u>ate</u> the <u>glazed</u> <u>cake</u> in the afternoon.

    ate   glazed   cake

4. <u>Kate</u> said, "Papa, the square <u>plates</u> are on <u>sale</u>."

    Kate   plates   sale

5. Last night, <u>David</u> and I were on the <u>same</u> <u>plane</u>.

    David   same   plane

Learn To Read English With Directions In Korean   Copyrighted Material

Assessment

Name: _____ Date: ___/___/_____ Score: _____

Review Lessons 1.2 & 1.3

Reading Short Vowel and Long Vowel Words

 Directions: Read the target words in the word box. In the first column, write the words that have the short vowel /ă/ sound, as in the word <u>apple</u>. In the second column, write the words that have the long vowel /ā/ sound, as in the word <u>ape</u>.

지도: 단어 상자에 있는 대상 단어를 읽습니다. 첫 번째 열에는 apple이라는 단어에서와 같이 단모음 /ă/ 소리가 나는 단어를 씁니다. 두 번째 열에는 장모음이 포함된 단어를 쓰십시오 /ā/ 소리, 단어 ape에서와 같이.

Target Word Box				
shack	made	rack	stay	camp
bag	plan	day	jazz	glass
tape	cave	stand	gate	pain
slam	plate	rain	lake	grab

Letter "a" has the /ă/ sound as in the word <u>apple</u>

- shack
- bag
- slam
- plan
- rack
- stand
- jazz
- camp
- glass
- grab

Letter "a" has the /ā/ sound as in the word <u>ape</u>

- tape
- made
- cave
- plate
- day
- rain
- stay
- gate
- lake
- pain

Answer Key

Name: _____ Date: ___/___/_____ Score: _____

Lesson 1.4

Reading Words with the "age" Letter Combination

 Lesson Check Point

 Directions: Read each target word. Find the "age" letter combination and put a check (✓) in the column that correctly identifies its sounds.
지도: 각 대상 단어를 읽으십시오. "age" 문자 조합을 찾아 해당 소리를 올바르게 식별하는 열에 체크(✓)를 하십시오.

Target Words	"age" has the /ā/ + /j/ sounds as in the word stage	"age" has the /ĭ/ + /j/ sounds as in the word package	"age" has the /ä/ + /j/ or /ä/ + /zh/ sounds as in the word massage
1. fuselage			✓
2. discouraged		✓	
3. sabotage			✓
4. backstage	✓		
5. engaged	✓		

 Directions: Read each sentence and underline the word that has an "age" letter combination that has the /ĭ/ + /j/ sounds, as in the word package.
지도: 각 문장을 읽고 단어 package에서와 같이 /ĭ/ + /j/ 소리가나는 "age" 문자 조합이 있는 단어에 밑줄을 긋습니다.

6. Yesterday, they <u>salvaged</u> the plane's fuselage.

7. The backstage <u>managers</u> asked the teenagers to sing loudly.

8. The lizards by the <u>cottage</u> are camouflaged on the green leaves.

9. She <u>encouraged</u> the teenagers to look at the animals in the cage.

10. My agent's text <u>message</u> said the entourage is not allowed backstage.

Assessment

 Name: _____ Date: ___/___/_____ Score: _____

Lesson 1.5

Reading Words with the "ai" Vowel Pair

✓ Lesson Check Point

 Directions: Read each target word. Circle the word in the column that has the same "ai" sound as the target word.
지도: 각 대상 단어를 읽으십시오. 목표 단어와 같은"ai" 소리가 나는 열의 단어에 동그라미를 치십시오.

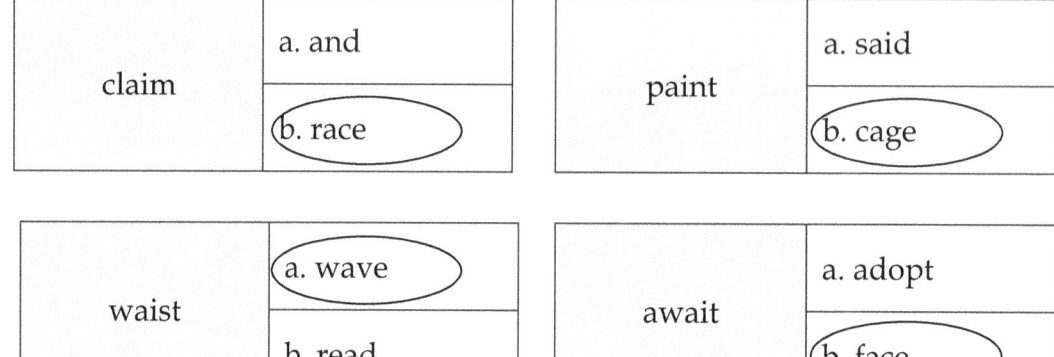

 Directions: Read each target word. Put a check (✓) under the correct column heading.
지도: 각 대상 단어를 읽으십시오. 올바른 열 제목 아래에 체크(✓)를 하십시오.

Target Words	Words have the long "a" sound as in the word <u>sail</u>	Words do not have the long "a" sound
1. rain	✓	
2. plaid		✓
3. said		✓
4. wait	✓	

Answer Key

 Name: _____ Date: ___/___/_____ Score: _____

Lesson 1.6

Reading Letter "a" Words with the Schwa Vowel Sound

✓ Lesson Check Point

 Directions: Read each target word. Circle the word in the column that has the same "a" sound as the target word.
지도: 각 대상 단어를 읽으십시오. 대상 단어와 동일한"a"소리가 나는 열의 단어에 동그라미를 치십시오.

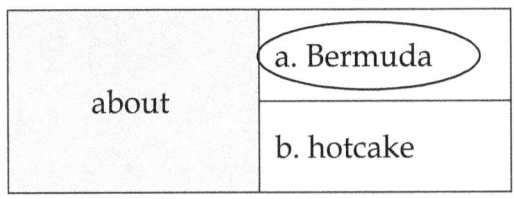

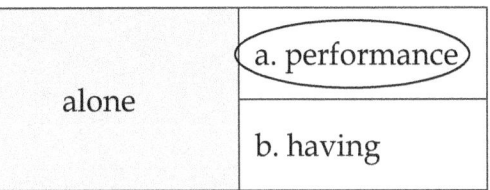

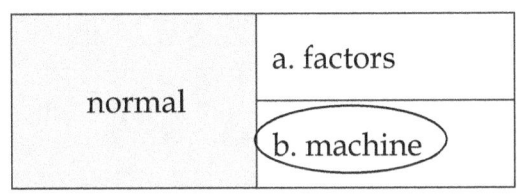

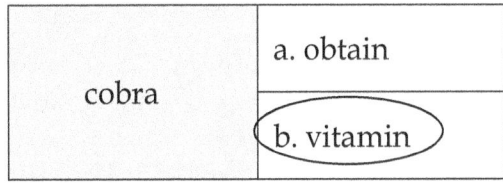

 Directions: Read each sentence and underline the letter "a" word that has the schwa vowel /ə/ sound. The anchor word for the letter "a" schwa vowel sound is sofa.
지도: 각 문장을 읽고 슈와 모음 /ə/ 소리가 있는 문자"a" 단어에 밑줄을 긋습니다. 문자"a" 슈와 모음 소리의 앵커 단어는 sofa입니다.

1. On Sunday, Dale will take a train to <u>Canada</u>.

2. The <u>scholars</u> in my class are obviously smart.

3. Annie saw beautiful, black snakes in <u>Jamaica</u>.

4. The awesome artist, Alexander, is very <u>popular</u>.

5. We were late for Mr. Anderson's <u>grammar</u> class.

6. The reggae <u>performances</u> in the park were awesome.

Assessment

 Name: _____ Date: ___/___/_____ Score: _____

Lesson 1.7

Reading Words with the "ar" Letter Combination

✓ Lesson Check Point

 Directions: Read each target word. Circle the word in the column that has the same "a" + "r" sounds as the target word.
지도: 각 대상 단어를 읽으십시오. 해당 열에 있는 단어에 동그라미를치십시오. 대상 단어와 동일한"a" + "r" 소리가 있습니다.

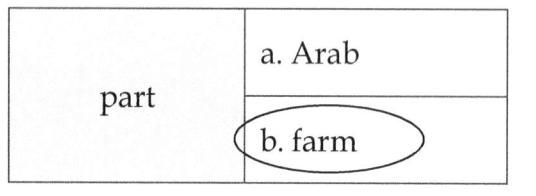
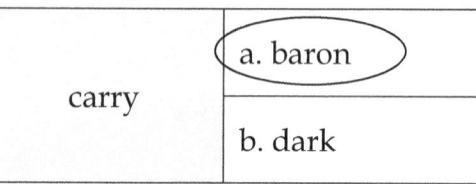
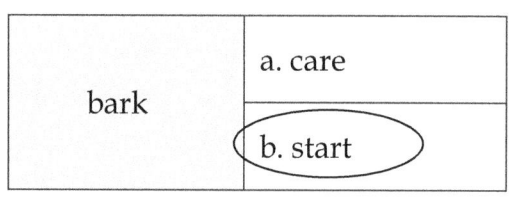
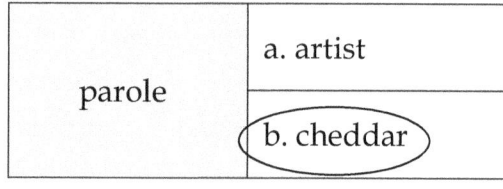

 Directions: Read each target word. Put a check (✓) under the correct column heading.
지도: 각 대상 단어를 읽으십시오. 올바른 열 제목 아래에 체크(✓)를하십시오.

Target Words	"ar" has the /ă/ + /r/ sounds as in the word <u>baron</u>	"ar" has the /ə/ + /r/ sounds as in the word <u>dollar</u>	"ar" has the /ä/ + /r/ sounds as in the word <u>car</u>	"ar" has the /ô/ + /r/ sounds as in the word <u>war</u>
1. part			✓	
2. carry	✓			
3. bark			✓	
4. parole		✓		

Answer Key

 Name: _____ Date: ___/___/_____ Score: _____

Lesson 1.7

Reading Words with the "ar" Letter Combination

Dictionary Skills/ Vocabulary

✓ Lesson Check Point

 Directions: Read each target word and its definition. Write the target word on the line in front of its meaning. Use a dictionary or the Internet to check your answers.
지도: 각 대상 단어와 그 정의를 읽으십시오. 의미 앞 줄에 대상단어를 쓰십시오. 사전이나 인터넷을 사용하여 답을 확인하십시오.

Target Word Box				
guards	year	cheddar	triangular	hangar

1. __hangar__   a structure used for housing aircrafts
2. __guards__   people who protect, oversee and defend
3. __year__   a period of time that consists of 365 or 366 days
4. __triangular__   shape with three sides, three corners and three angles
5. __cheddar__   a flavor of cheese that ranges from mild to extra sharp

 Directions: Read each sentence and write the target word that correctly completes the sentence.
지도: 각 문장을 읽고 다음과 같은 목표 단어를 쓰십시오. 장을 올바르게 완성합니다.

6. We measured the angles of three __triangular__ figures.
7. The armed __guards__ are stationed throughout the airport.
8. Arnold received a four __year__ scholarship to the university.
9. At the park, I will have __cheddar__ cheese sandwiches for lunch.
10. The airplane in the __hangar__ is being repaired by the engineers.

Assessment

 Name: _____ Date: ___/___/_____ Score: _____

Lesson 1.8

Reading Words with a Silent Letter "a"

✓ Lesson Check Point

 Directions: Read the target words in the word box. Write the words that have a silent letter "a" in the first column. Write the words that do not have a silent letter "a" in the second column.

지도: 단어 상자에 있는 대상 단어를 읽습니다. 첫 번째 열에 묵음 문자"a"가 있는 단어를 쓰십시오. 두 번째 열에 묵음 문자"a"가 없는 단어를 쓰십시오.

Target Word Box				
answer	beating	zealous	reaping	heater
faces	ago	alarms	sweat	back
Eastern	heads	bands	boats	always
have	stand	oats	cars	eating

Letter "a" is silent

- Eastern
- beating
- heads
- zealous
- oats
- reaping
- sweat
- boats
- heater
- eating

Letter "a" has a letter "a" sound

- answer
- faces
- have
- ago
- stand
- bands
- alarms
- cars
- back
- always

Answer Key

 Name: _____ Date: ___/___/_____ Score: _____

Unit Review - A/a

Reading Words with Vowel "a" Sounds: /ă/, /ā/, /ə/ & Silent

✓ Lesson Check Point

 Directions: Read each target word. Circle the word in the column that has the same "a" sound as the target word.
지도: 각 대상 단어를 읽으십시오. 대상 단어와 동일한 "a" 소리가 나는 열의 단어에 동그라미를 치십시오.

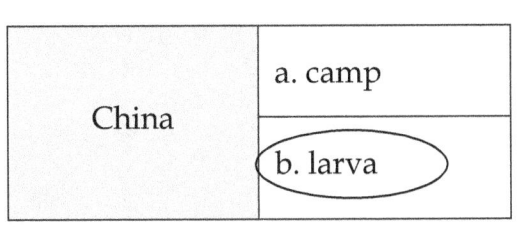

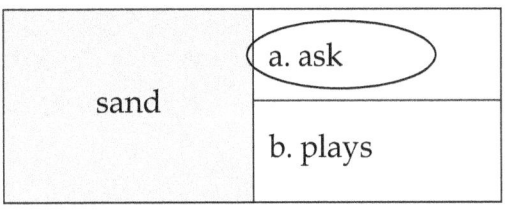

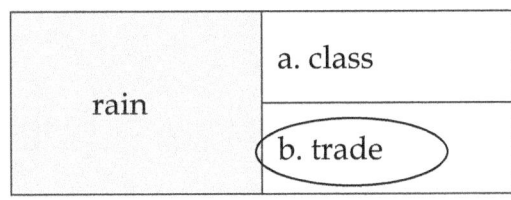

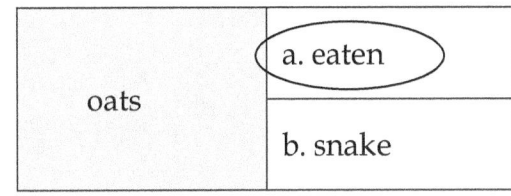

 Directions: Read each target word. Put a check (✓) under the correct column heading.
지도: 각 대상 단어를 읽으십시오. 올바른 열 제목 아래에 체크(✓)를 하십시오.

Target Words	"a" has the /ă/ sound as in the word <u>apple</u>	"a" has the /ā/ sound as in the word <u>ate</u>	"a" has the /ə/ sound as in the word <u>sofa</u>	"a" is silent as in the word <u>boat</u>
1. China			✓	
2. sand	✓			
3. rain		✓		
4. oats				✓

Learn To Read English With Directions In Korean

Assessment

 Name: _____ Date: ___/___/_____ Score: _____

The Reading Challenge

Lesson 1.9

Reading Multisyllable Words

✓ Lesson Check Point

 Directions: Read and divide each target word into syllables. Write each word and place a hyphen (-) between the syllables in the second column. Write the number of syllables in the third column. Use a dictionary or the Internet to check your answers.

지도: 각 대상 단어를 읽고 음절로 나눕니다. 각 단어를 쓰고 두 번째 열의 음절 사이에 하이픈(-)을 넣습니다. 세 번째 열에 음절 수를 쓰십시오. 사전이나 인터넷을 사용하여 답을 확인하십시오.

Target Words	Words Divided into Syllables	Number of Syllables
1. distant	dis-tant	2
2. jubilant	ju-bi-lant	3
3. mishap	mis-hap	2
4. burlap	bur-lap	2
5. doormat	door-mat	2
6. transplant	trans-plant	2
7. brainwash	brain-wash	2
8. demanding	de-mand-ing	3
9. vibrantly	vi-brant-ly	3
10. landing	land-ing	2

Answer Key

Name: _____ Date: ___/___/_____ Score: _____

The Reading Challenge

Lesson 1.9

Reading Multisyllable Words

✓ Lesson Check Point

 Directions: Read each target word. Circle the word in the row that is divided correctly into syllables. Use a dictionary or the Internet to check your answers.

지도: 각 대상 단어를 읽으십시오. 음절로 올바르게 나누어진 행에 있는 단어에 동그라미를 치십시오. 사전이나 인터넷을 사용하여 답을 확인하십시오.

Model

| important | **a. im-por-tant** ⭕ | b. im-port-ant | c. im-porta-nt |

| 1. bureaucrat | **a. bu-reau-crat** ⭕ | b. bur-eau-crat | c. bur-eauc-rat |

| 2. thermostat | a. therm-os-tat | b. ther-mos-tat | **c. ther-mo-stat** ⭕ |

| 3. atmosphere | **a. at-mos-phere** ⭕ | b. atm-o-sphere | c. at-mosp-here |

| 4. handicap | a. han-dic-ap | b. hand-ic-ap | **c. hand-i-cap** ⭕ |

| 5. tolerant | a. to-ler-ant | b. tol-e-rant | **c. tol-er-ant** ⭕ |

| 6. pelican | a. pel-ic-an | **b. pel-i-can** ⭕ | c. pe-li-can |

| 7. radiant | a. rad-i-ant | **b. ra-di-ant** ⭕ | c. ra-dia-nt |

| 8. hesitant | a. hes-it-ant | b. he-sit-ant | **c. hes-i-tant** ⭕ |

Assessment

Name: _____ Date: ___/___/_____ Score: _____

Lesson 1.10

Reading and Writing

Proper and Common Nouns and Adjectives

✓ Lesson Check Point

Directions: Read the words in the word box. Put an (X) on the line next to each word that is written incorrectly. Remember that all proper nouns and proper adjectives are capitalized. Use a dictionary or the Internet to check your answers.

지도: 단어 상자에 있는 단어를 읽으십시오. 잘못 쓰여진 각 단어 옆의 줄에 (X)를 표시하십시오. 모든 고유 명사와 고유 형용사는 대문자임을 기억하십시오. 사전이나 인터넷을 사용하여 답을 확인하십시오.

Word Box					
__	Arabian	X	albania	__	Australia
__	announcer	X	atlantic Ocean	__	article
X	Algebra	__	anchor	X	Anthill
X	april	__	Angola	X	After

Directions: Read each unedited sentence and underline the word that is written incorrectly. Write each sentence correctly on the line.

지도: 편집되지 않은 각 문장을 읽고 잘못 쓰여진 단어에 밑줄을긋습 니다. 각 문장을 줄에 올바르게 쓰십시오..。

Model
Andrew has a view of the <u>atlantic</u> Ocean from his apartment.
<u>Andrew has a view of the Atlantic Ocean from his apartment.</u>

1. <u>alex's</u> cats are Angora cats.
<u>Alex's cats are Angora cats.</u>

2. Anna ate an apple and an <u>Avocado</u>.
<u>Anna ate an apple and an avocado.</u>

3. Mr. Aspen is an <u>Assistant</u> at Apple, Inc.
<u>Mr. Aspen is an assistant at Apple, Inc.</u>

4. I read an <u>Article</u> about Africa and Asia.
<u>I read an article about Africa and Asia.</u>

Answer Key

Name: _____ Date: ___/___/_____ Score: _____

Lesson 2.1

Reading Words with the Letter B/b

✓ Lesson Check Point

Directions: Read each target word. Find the letter "b" and put a check (✓) in the column that identifies its position: beginning, within or end.
지도: 각 대상 단어를 읽으십시오. 문자"b"를 찾아 위치를 나타내는열: 시작, 내부 또는 끝에 체크(✓)를 하십시오.

Target Words	Beginning (First Letter)	Within	End (Last Letter)
1. lab			✓
2. habit		✓	
3. biker	✓		
4. lubricate		✓	
5. honeycomb			✓

Directions: Read each sentence and underline the words that begin with the letter "b." Write all the underlined words in alphabetical order on the lines below.
지도: 각 문장을 읽고"b"로 시작하는 단어에 밑줄을 긋습니다. 밑줄친모든단어를 아래 줄에 알파벳 순서로 쓰십시오.

6. <u>Beef</u> is not good <u>bait</u> for fish.

7. The <u>baseballs</u> are on the <u>bench</u>.

8. Ann has a <u>blog</u> about <u>baskets</u>.

9. The <u>baker</u> <u>baked</u> a good cake.

10. My <u>book</u> is about <u>birds</u> and cats.

<u>bait</u>　　　　　　　<u>baked</u>　　　　　　　<u>baker</u>
<u>baseballs</u>　　　　 <u>baskets</u>　　　　　 <u>Beef</u>
<u>bench</u>　　　　　　<u>birds</u>　　　　　　　<u>blog</u>
　　　　　　　　　　　<u>book</u>

Assessment

 Name: _____ Date: ___/___/_____ Score: _____

Lesson 2.2

Reading Words with the "br" Letter Combination

Dictionary Skills/ Vocabulary

✓ Lesson Check Point

 Directions: Read each target word and its definition. Write the letter of the definition on the line of each target word. Use a dictionary or the Internet to check your answers.

지도: 각 대상 단어와 그 정의를 읽으십시오. 각 대상 단어의 행에 정의의 문자를 씁니다. 사전이나 인터넷을 사용하여 답을 확인하십시오.

Target Words	Definitions
1. <u>b</u> braids	a. a gentle wind
2. <u>d</u> brave	b. to weave strands together
3. <u>a</u> breeze	c. the color of dirt and a tree bark
4. <u>e</u> brother	d. description of a courageous person
5. <u>c</u> brown	e. a male person who has the same parent(s) as another person

 Directions: Read each sentence. Underline the word in the parentheses that correctly completes each sentence. Then, write the underlined word on the line.

지도: 각 문장을 읽으십시오. 각 문장을 올바르게 완성하는 괄호 안에 있는 단어에 밑줄을 긋습니다. 그런 다음 밑줄 친 단어를 줄에 쓰십시오.

6. My ____brother's____ name is Brian. (braids, <u>brother's</u>)

7. Brad's favorite color is _____brown_____. (brags, <u>brown</u>)

8. Bridgette ____braids____ her hair every day. (<u>braids</u>, brave)

9. Bret is the ____brave____ boy who saved the baby. (<u>brave</u>, breeze)

10. When I opened the window, I felt a cool ____breeze____. (brags, <u>breeze</u>)

Answer Key

 Name: _____ Date: ___/___/_____ Score: _____

Lesson 2.3

Reading Words with the "bl" Letter Combination

Dictionary Skills/ Vocabulary

✓ Lesson Check Point

 Directions: Read each target word and its definition. Write the target word on the line in front of its meaning. Use a dictionary or the Internet to check your answers.
지도: 각 대상 단어와 그 정의를 읽으십시오. 의미 앞 줄에 대상단어를 쓰십시오. 사전이나 인터넷을 사용하여 답을 확인하십시오.

Target Word Box				
black	blank	blend	bloom	blue

1. <u>bloom</u>   the opening of a flower bud
2. <u>black</u>   the color of tar and the night sky
3. <u>blend</u>   the process of mixing things together
4. <u>blue</u>   the color of the sky on a clear sunny day
5. <u>blank</u>   a surface that does not have any words, images or marks

 Directions: Read each sentence. Underline the word in the parentheses that correctly completes each sentence. Then, write the underlined word on the line.
지도: 각 문장을 읽으십시오. 각 문장을 올바르게 완성하는 괄호 안에 있는 단어에 밑줄을 긋습니다. 그런 다음 밑줄 친 단어를 줄에 쓰십시오.

6. Bill's bike is _____<u>blue</u>_____. (blend, <u>blue</u>)

7. My boots are _____<u>black</u>_____. (<u>black</u>, bloom)

8. My art book has ___<u>blank</u>___ pages. (<u>blank</u>, bloom)

9. The flowers _____<u>bloom</u>_____ by the brook. (<u>bloom</u>, blue)

10. I will ___<u>blend</u>___ the berries in the blender. (blank, <u>blend</u>)

Assessment

 Name: _____ Date:___/___/_____ Score: _____

Lesson 2.3

Reading Words with the "ble" Letter Combination

✓ Lesson Check Point

 Directions: Read each target word. Find the "ble" letter combination and put a check (✓) in the column that identifies its position: beginning, within or end.

지도: 각 대상 단어를 읽으십시오. "ble" 문자 조합을 찾아 위치를 식별하는 열에 체크(✓)를 하십시오: 시작, 내부 또는 끝.

Target Words	Beginning (First 3 Letters)	Within	End (Last 3 Letters)
1. seasonable			✓
2. bleep	✓		
3. nibbler		✓	
4. bleaker	✓		
5. assembler		✓	

 Directions: Read each target word. Put a check (✓) in the "yes" column if the "ble" letter combination has the /b/ + /ə/ + /l/ sounds. Put a check (✓) in the "no" column if the "ble" letter combination does not have the /b/ + /ə/ + /l/ sounds.

지도: 각 대상 단어를 읽으십시오. "ble" 문자 조합에/b/ + /ə/ + /l/소리가 있는 경우"yes" 열에 체크(✓)를 하십시오. "ble" 문자 조합에/b/ + /ə/ + /l/소리가 없으면"no"열에 체크(✓)를 하십시오.

Target Words	Yes	No
6. syllable	✓	
7. ramble	✓	
8. bleak		✓
9. tumble	✓	
10. blending		✓

Answer Key

 Name: _____ Date: ___/___/_____ Score: _____

Lesson 2.4

Reading Words with the "mb" Letter Combination

✓ Lesson Check Point

 Directions: Read each target word. Circle the word in the column that has the same "mb" sound(s) as the target word.
지도: 각 대상 단어를 읽으십시오. 대상 단어와 동일한"mb" 소리가 있는 열의 단어에 동그라미를 치십시오.

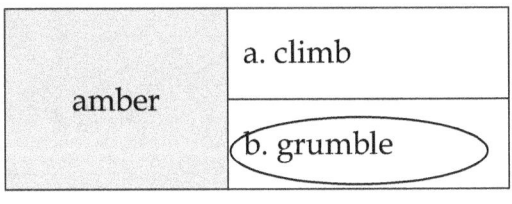
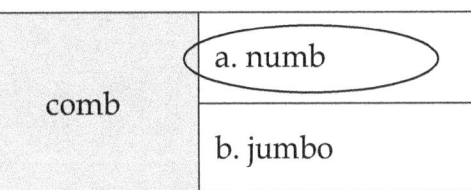
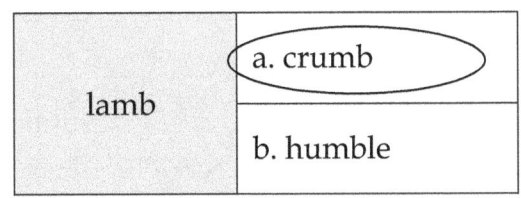
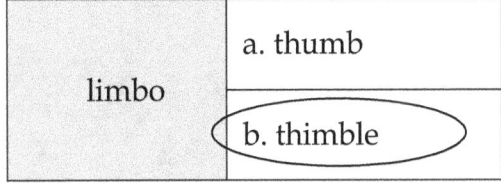

 Directions: Read each target word. In the second column, write the number of letters in the word. In the third column, write the number of letters heard in the word.
지도: 각 대상 단어를 읽으십시오. 두 번째 열에는 단어의 글자 수를 씁니다. 세 번째 열에는 단어에서 들리는 글자 수를 쓰십시오.

Target Words	Number of letters in the word	Number of letters heard
1. amber	5	5
2. comb	4	3
3. lamb	4	3
4. limbo	5	5

Assessment

 Name: _____ Date: ___/___/_____ Score: _____

Lesson 2.4

Reading Words with the "bt" Letter Combination

✓ Lesson Check Point

 Directions: Read each target word. Circle the word in the column that has the same "bt" sound(s) as the target word.
지도: 각 대상 단어를 읽으십시오. 대상 단어와 동일한 "bt" 소리가 있는 열의 단어에 동그라미를 치십시오.

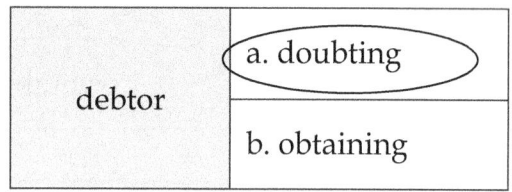
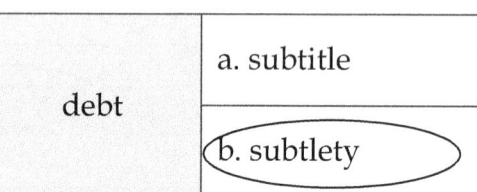
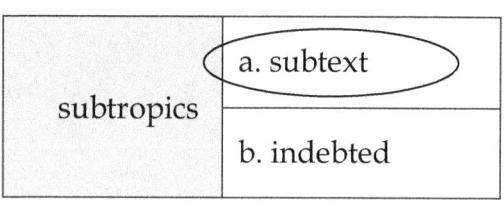
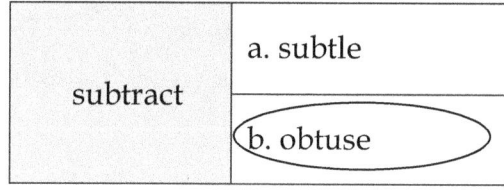

 Directions: Read each target word. In the second column, write the number of letters in the word. In the third column, write the number of letters heard in the word.
지도: 각 대상 단어를 읽으십시오. 두 번째 열에는 단어의 글자 수를 씁니다. 세 번째 열에는 단어에서 들리는 글자 수를 쓰십시오.

Target Words	Number of letters in the word	Number of letters heard
1. debtor	6	5
2. debt	4	3
3. subtropics	10	10
4. subtract	8	8

Answer Key

Name: _____ Date: ___/___/_____ Score: _____

Lesson 2.5

Reading Words with a Silent "b"

✓ Lesson Check Point

Directions: Read the target words in the word box. Write the words that have a silent letter "b" in the first column. Write the words that do not have a silent letter "b" in the second column.

지도: 단어 상자에 있는 대상 단어를 읽습니다. 첫 번째 열에 묵음 문자"b"가 있는 단어를 쓰십시오. 두 번째 열에 묵음 문자"b"가 없는 단어를 쓰십시오.

Target Word Box				
comb	Arabic	subpoena	debtors	basketball
herb	lamb	obtain	doubting	subtleness
cobweb	debt	thumb	plumber	curb
bubbles	cab	bathtub	disturb	superb

Letter "b" is silent	Letter "b" has the /b/ sound
comb	herb
bubbles	cobweb
lamb	Arabic
debt	cab
subpoena	obtain
thumb	bathtub
debtors	disturb
doubting	basketball
plumber	curb
subtleness	superb

Learn To Read English With Directions In Korean

Assessment

 Name: _____ Date:___/___/_____ Score:_____

The Reading Challenge

Lesson 2.6

Reading Multisyllable Words

✓ Lesson Check Point

 Directions: Read and divide each target word into syllables. Write each word and place a hyphen (-) between the syllables in the second column. Write the number of syllables in the third column. Use a dictionary or the Internet to check your answers.

지도: 각 대상 단어를 읽고 음절로 나눕니다. 각 단어를 쓰고 두 번째 열의 음절 사이에 하이픈(-)을 넣습니다. 세 번째 열에 음절 수를 쓰십시오. 사전이나 인터넷을 사용하여 답을 확인하십시오.

Target Words	Words Divided into Syllables	Number of Syllables
1. anybody	an-y-bod-y	4
2. tugboat	tug-boat	2
3. subtracting	sub-tract-ing	3
4. sandbox	sand-box	2
5. banana	ba-nan-a	3
6. bankroll	bank-roll	2
7. suburb	sub-urb	2
8. barbecue	bar-be-cue	3
9. becoming	be-com-ing	3
10. centerboard	cen-ter-board	3

Answer Key

Name: _____ Date: ___/___/_____ Score: _____

The Reading Challenge

Lesson 2.6

Reading Multisyllable Words

✓ Lesson Check Point

Directions: Read each target word. Circle the word in the row that is divided correctly into syllables. Use a dictionary or the Internet to check your answers.
지도: 각 대상 단어를 읽으십시오. 음절로 올바르게 나누어진 행에 있는 단어에 동그라미를 치십시오. 사전이나 인터넷을 사용하여 답을 확인 하십시오.

Model

| because | **a. be-cause** ⭕ | b. beca-use | c. b-ecause |

| 1. backyard | a. ba-ckyard | b. backy-ard | **c. back-yard** ⭕ |

| 2. Bahamas | **a. Ba-ha-mas** ⭕ | b. Baha-mas | c. Bah-amas |

| 3. bagel | a. bag-el | b. b-agel | **c. ba-gel** ⭕ |

| 4. bedtime | a. be-dtime | **b. bed-time** ⭕ | c. bedt-ime |

| 5. belonging | a. belong-ing | b. be-lo-nging | **c. be-long-ing** ⭕ |

| 6. between | **a. be-tween** ⭕ | b. bet-ween | c. betw-een |

| 7. byproduct | a. by-pro-duct | **b. by-prod-uct** ⭕ | c. by-produ-ct |

| 8. bifocal | a. bif-o-cal | **b. bi-fo-cal** ⭕ | c. bi-foc-al |

Learn To Read English With Directions In Korean

Assessment

Name: _____ Date:___/___/_____ Score:_____

Lesson 2.7

Reading and Writing

Proper and Common Nouns and Adjectives

✓ Lesson Check Point

Directions: Read the words in the word box. Put an (X) on the line next to each word that is written incorrectly. Remember that all proper nouns and proper adjectives are capitalized. Use a dictionary or the Internet to check your answers.

지도: 단어 상자에 있는 단어를 읽으십시오. 잘못 쓰여진 각 단어 옆의 줄에 (X)를 표시하십시오. 모든 고유 명사와 고유 형용사는 대문자임을 기억하십시오. 사전이나 인터넷을 사용하여 답을 확인하십시오.

Word Box					
___	brother	_X_	Dr. brown	___	Boston
_X_	bolivia	___	bubbles	_X_	british
_X_	Baby	___	Burma	___	Brussels
___	baking	_X_	bahamas	_X_	Bridge

Directions: Read each unedited sentence and underline the word that is written incorrectly. Write each sentence correctly on the line.

지도: 편집되지 않은 각 문장을 읽고 잘못 쓰여진 단어에 밑줄을 긋습 니다. 각 문장을 줄에 올바르게 쓰십시오.

Model
<u>brandon's</u> books are about big boats.
<u>Brandon's books are about big boats.</u>

1. <u>bobby</u> will borrow Ben's banjo.
<u>Bobby will borrow Ben's banjo.</u>

2. The brown brick <u>Building</u> is a bank.
<u>The brown brick building is a bank.</u>

3. The breadbasket has <u>Big</u> buns and bread.
<u>The breadbasket has big buns and bread.</u>

4. You can buy belts and brushes from <u>benny</u>.
<u>You can buy belts and brushes from Benny.</u>

Answer Key

Name: _____ Date: ___/___/___ Score: _____

Lesson 3.1

Reading Words with the Letter C/c

✓ Lesson Check Point

Directions: Read each target word. Find the letter "c" and put a check (✓) in the column that identifies its position: beginning, within or end.
지도: 각 대상 단어를 읽으십시오. 문자"c"를 찾아 위치를 나타내는 열: 시작, 내부 또는 끝에 체크(✓)를 하십시오.

Target Words	Beginning (First Letter)	Within	End (Last Letter)
1. picture		✓	
2. music			✓
3. economy		✓	
4. control	✓		
5. microbe		✓	

Directions: Read each sentence and underline the words that begin with the letter "c." Write all the underlined words in alphabetical order on the lines below.
지도: 각 문장을 읽고"c"로 시작하는 단어에 밑줄을 긋습니다. 밑줄 친 모든 단어를 아래 줄에 알파벳 순서로 쓰십시오.

6. <u>Cats</u> do not like <u>cheese</u>.

7. The <u>cheesecake</u> is very <u>cold</u>.

8. Annie has <u>cocoa</u> on her <u>chin</u>.

9. Bob said, "The <u>cab</u> is parked by the <u>cabin</u>."

10. The <u>coconut</u> tart was baked with <u>cranberries</u>.

<u>cab</u>	<u>cabin</u>	<u>Cats</u>
<u>cheese</u>	<u>cheesecake</u>	<u>chin</u>
<u>cocoa</u>	<u>coconut</u>	<u>cold</u>
	<u>cranberries</u>	

Assessment

Name: _____ Date:___/___/_____ Score:_____

Lesson 3.1

Reading Words with the Hard Letter "c"

✓ Lesson Check Point

Directions: Read each target word. Put a check (✓) under the correct column heading.
지도: 각 대상 단어를 읽으십시오. 올바른 열 제목 아래에 체크(✓)를 하십시오.

Target Words	Hard "c" has the /k/ sound as in the word <u>cat</u>	Soft "c" has the /s/ sound as in the word <u>cell</u>
1. comic	✓	
2. created	✓	
3. balance		✓
4. camels	✓	
5. civilian		✓

Directions: Read each sentence and underline the words that have the hard "c" sound, as in the word <u>cat</u>. Write all the underlined words in alphabetical order on the lines below.
지도: 각 문장을 읽고 단어 cat에서와 같이 단단한"c" 소리가 나는 단어에 밑줄을 긋습니다. 아래 줄에 밑줄 친 단어를 알파벳 순서로 모두 쓰십시오.

6. <u>Craig</u> ate my cinnamon cherry <u>cake</u>.

7. I ate cheese at the <u>Canadian</u> <u>cafeteria</u>.

8. The <u>carrots</u> in the ceramic bowl are <u>crunchy</u>.

9. All the cheerful <u>campers</u> are in the big <u>cabin</u>.

10. The <u>characters</u> in my book like to eat cheap <u>candy</u>.

<u>cabin</u>   <u>cafeteria</u>   <u>cake</u>

<u>campers</u>   <u>Canadian</u>   <u>candy</u>

<u>carrots</u>   <u>characters</u>   <u>Craig</u>

                     <u>crunchy</u>

Answer Key

Name: _____ Date:___/___/_____ Score:_____

Lesson 3.2

Reading Words with the Soft Letter "c"

✓ Lesson Check Point

Directions: Read each target word. Put a check (✓) under the correct column heading.
지도: 각 대상 단어를 읽으십시오. 올바른 열 제목 아래에 체크(✓)를하십시오.

Target Words	Hard "c" has the /k/ sound as in the word cat	Soft "c" has the /s/ sound as in the word cell
1. pencil		✓
2. ice		✓
3. cage	✓	
4. brace		✓
5. cute	✓	

Directions: Read each sentence and underline the words that have the soft "c" sound, as in the word cell. Write all the underlined words in alphabetical order on the lines below.
지도: 각 문장을 읽고 cell이라는 단어에서처럼 부드러운"c" 소리가 나는 단어에 밑줄을 긋습니다. 아래 줄에 밑줄 친 단어를 알파벳 순서로 모두 쓰십시오.

6. The cooks have <u>fancy</u> <u>ceramic</u> pots.

7. I took a cab to the <u>cinema</u> in the <u>city</u>.

8. The country performer <u>danced</u> in a <u>circle</u>.

9. The <u>cyclist</u> has a cranberry-colored <u>bicycle</u>.

10. Mom <u>placed</u> vanilla <u>icing</u> on the coconut crumb cake.

bicycle	ceramic	cinema
circle	city	cyclist
danced	fancy	icing
	placed	

Assessment

Name: _____ Date: ___/___/_____ Score: _____

Review Lessons 3.1 & 3.2

Reading Hard Letter "c" and Soft Letter "c" Words

 Directions: Read the target words in the word box. In the first column, write the words with the letter "c" that have the /k/ sound, as in the word <u>cat</u>. In the second column, write the words with the letter "c" that have the /s/ sound, as in the word <u>cell</u>.

지도: 단어 상자에 있는 대상 단어를 읽으십시오. 첫 번째 열에는 cat라는 단어에서와 같이 /k/ 소리가 나는 문자"c"가 있는 단어를 씁니다. 두 번째 열에는 cell이라는 단어에서와 같이 /s/ 소리가 나는 문자"c"가 있는 단어를 씁니다.

Target Word Box				
faces	celery	coil	cider	cool
candy	cellar	fancy	code	come
ace	cute	cook	cent	place
curly	civil	cap	cure	bouncy

Hard letter "c" has the /k/ sound as in the word <u>cat</u>

- coil
- cool
- candy
- code
- come
- cute
- cook
- curly
- cap
- cure

Soft letter "c" has the /s/ sound as in the word <u>cell</u>

- faces
- celery
- cider
- cellar
- fancy
- ace
- cent
- place
- civil
- bouncy

Answer Key

Name: _____ Date:___/___/_____ Score: _____

Lesson 3.3

Reading Words with the "cr" Letter Combination

Dictionary Skills/ Vocabulary

✓ Lesson Check Point

Directions: Read each target word and its definition. Write the letter of the definition on the line of each target word. Use a dictionary or the Internet to check your answers.

지도: 각 대상 단어와 그 정의를 읽으십시오. 각 대상 단어의 행에 정의의 문자를 씁니다. 사전이나 인터넷을 사용하여 답을 확인하십시오.

Target Words	Definitions
1. _c_ cream	a. an insect that makes noises by rubbing its wings
2. _e_ crib	b. the firm, outer part of a loaf of bread or a pie
3. _a_ cricket	c. something made from milk; a dairy product
4. _d_ crop	d. harvested fruits, grains and/or vegetables
5. _b_ crust	e. a baby's bed with high sides

Directions: Read each sentence. Underline the word in the parentheses that correctly completes each sentence. Then, write the underlined word on the line.

지도: 각 문장을 읽으십시오. 각 문장을 올바르게 완성하는 괄호 안에 있는 단어에 밑줄을 긋습니다. 그런 다음 밑줄 친 단어를 줄에 쓰십시오.

6. The _____crust_____ of my pie crumbles. (<u>crust</u>, cream)

7. The baby's _____crib_____ is very clean. (<u>crib</u>, crop)

8. The farmer has a large _____crop_____ of corn. (crust, <u>crop</u>)

9. I can hear the _____crickets_____ by the cabin. (crust, <u>crickets</u>)

10. I like to put _____cream_____ on my cranberries. (<u>cream</u>, crop)

Assessment

Name: _____ Date: ___/___/_____ Score: _____

Lesson 3.4

Reading Words with the "cl" Letter Combination

Dictionary Skills/ Vocabulary

✓ Lesson Check Point

Directions: Read each target word and its definition. Write the target word on the line in front of its meaning. Use a dictionary or the Internet to check your answers.

지도: 각 대상 단어와 그 정의를 읽으십시오. 의미 앞 줄에 대상단어를 쓰십시오. 사전이나 인터넷을 사용하여 답을 확인하십시오.

Target Word Box				
class	classmates	climbed	clinic	closed

1. closed   the position of something that is not open
2. classmates   students who are in the same class
3. climbed   to have moved upward
4. class   a group of students instructed by a teacher
5. clinic   a place where patients receive medical treatment

Directions: Read each sentence. Underline the word in the parentheses that correctly completes each sentence. Then, write the underlined word on the line.

지도: 각 문장을 읽으십시오. 각 문장을 올바르게 완성하는 괄호 안에 있는 단어에 밑줄을 긋습니다. 그런 다음 밑줄 친 단어를 줄에 쓰십시오.

6. Chad _____closed_____ the cab door. (class, closed)

7. The campers _____climbed_____ up the cliff. (climbed, classmates)

8. I enrolled in a chemistry ___class___ at Cleveland College. (class, clinic)

9. My doctor works at the children's ___clinic___. (climbed, clinic)

10. Chad and Cindy are ___classmates___ at school. (classmates, closed)

Answer Key

 Name: _____ Date: ___/___/_____ Score: _____

Lesson 3.4

Reading Words with the "cle" Letter Combination

✓ Lesson Check Point

 Directions: Read each target word. Find the "cle" letter combination and put a check (✓) in the column that identifies its position: beginning, within or end.

지도: 각 대상 단어를 읽으십시오. "cle" 문자 조합을 찾아 위치를 식별하는 열에 체크(✓)를 하십시오: 시작, 내부 또는 끝.

Target Words	Beginning (First 3 Letters)	Within	End (Last 3 Letters)
1. clean	✓		
2. clerk	✓		
3. clerical	✓		
4. uncle			✓
5. encirclement		✓	

 Directions: Read each target word. Put a check (✓) in the "yes" column if the "cle" letter combination has the /k/ + /ə/ + /l/ sounds. Put a check (✓) in the "no" column if the "cle" letter combination does not have the /k/ + /ə/ + /l/ sounds.

지도: 각 대상 단어를 읽으십시오. "cle" 문자 조합에 /k/ + /ə/ + /l/ 소리가있으 면 "yes" 열에 체크(✓)를 하십시오. "cle" 문자 조합에 /k/ + /ə/ + /l/ 소리가없으 면 "no" 열에 체크(✓)를 하십시오.

Target Words	Yes	No
6. clean		✓
7. clerk		✓
8. clerical		✓
9. uncle	✓	
10. encirclement	✓	

Assessment

Name: _____ Date: ___/___/_____ Score: _____

Lesson 3.5

Reading Words with the "ct" Letter Combination

✓ Lesson Check Point

Directions: Read each target word. Circle the word in the column that has the same "ct" sound(s) as the target word.
지도: 각 대상 단어를 읽으십시오. 대상 단어와 동일한 "ct" 소리가 있는 열의 단어에 동그라미를 치십시오.

| actor | a. (impact) |
| | b. indict |

| direct | a. victual |
| | b. (effects) |

| convict | a. connection |
| | b. (inspect) |

| Connecticut | a. (indict) |
| | b. factor |

Directions: Read each target word. Put a check (✓) under the correct column heading.
지도: 각 대상 단어를 읽으십시오. 올바른 열 제목 아래에 체크(✓)를 하십시오.

Target Words	"ct" has the /k/ + /t/ sounds as in the word <u>fact</u>	"ct" has the silent "c" + /t/ sound as in the word <u>indict</u>
1. actor	✓	
2. direct	✓	
3. convict	✓	
4. Connecticut		✓

Answer Key

 Name: _____ Date: ___/___/_____ Score: _____

Lesson 3.6

Reading Soft Letter "c" Words

✓ Lesson Check Point

 Directions: Read each target word. Circle the word in the column that has the same "cean," "cian," "cial," "cious" or "cient" sound as the target word.

지도: 각 대상 단어를 읽으십시오. 대상 단어와 동일한 "cean," "cian," "cial," "cious" 또는 "cient" 소리가 나는 열의 단어에 동그라미를 치십시오.

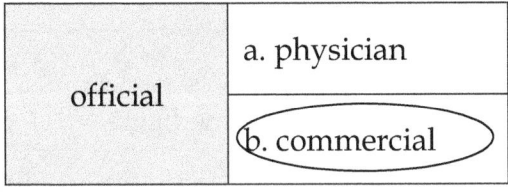
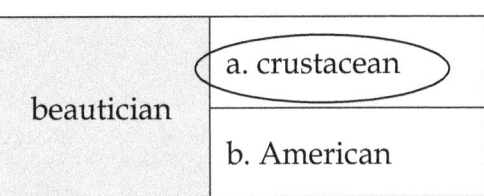
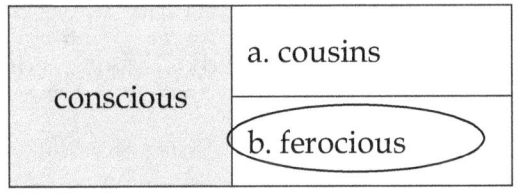
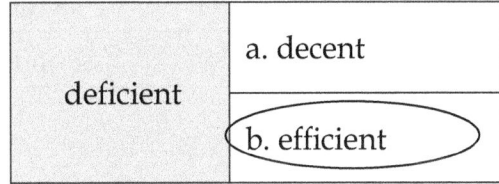

 Directions: Read each target word. Put a check (✓) in the column that identifies the same "cean," "cian," "cial," "cious" or "cient" sound within the target word.

지도: 각 대상 단어를 읽으십시오. 대상 단어 내에서 동일한 "cean," "cian," "cial," "cious" 또는 "cient" 소리를 식별하는 열에 체크(✓)를 하십시오.

Target Words	"cean" has the /sh/+/ə/+/n/ sounds as in the word <u>ocean</u>	"cial" has the /sh/+/ə/+/l/ sounds as in the word <u>special</u>	"cious" has the /sh/+/ə/+/s/ sounds as in the word <u>delicious</u>	"cient" has the /sh/+/ə/+/n/+/t/ sounds as in the word <u>ancient</u>
1. official		✓		
2. beautician	✓			
3. conscious			✓	
4. deficient				✓

Learn To Read English With Directions In Korean

Assessment

Name: _____ Date: ___/___/_____ Score: _____

Lesson 3.6

Reading Soft Letter "c" Words

Directions: Read the target words in the word box. In the first column, write the words with the letter "c" that have the /s/ sound, as in the word <u>cell</u>. In the second column, write the words with the letter "c" that have the /sh/ sound, as in the word <u>ocean</u>.

지도: 단어 상자에 있는 대상 단어를 읽으십시오. 첫 번째 열에는 cell이라는 단어에서와 같이 /s/ 소리가 나는 문자"c"가 있는 단어를 씁니다. 두 번째 열에는 다음과 같은 문자"c"가 포함된 단어를 쓰십시오. /sh/ 소리, ocean이라는 단어에서처럼.

Target Word Box				
proficient	voice	electrician	medicine	place
princess	official	pencil	capricious	judicious
artificial	lacy	dance	recipe	mercy
physician	sentence	clinician	pediatrician	commercial

Soft letter "c" has the /s/ sound as in the word <u>cell</u>

- princess
- voice
- lacy
- sentence
- pencil
- dance
- medicine
- place
- recipe
- mercy

Soft letter "c" has the /sh/ sound as in the word <u>ocean</u>

- proficient
- artificial
- physician
- official
- electrician
- clinician
- capricious
- judicious
- pediatrician
- commercial

Answer Key

 Name: _____ Date: ___/___/_____ Score: _____

Lesson 3.7

Reading Words with the "ch" Letter Combination

✓ Lesson Check Point

 Directions: Read each target word. Circle the word in the column that has the same "ch" sound as the target word.
지도: 각 대상 단어를 읽으십시오. 대상 단어와 같은"ch" 소리가 나는 열의 단어에 동그라미를 치십시오.

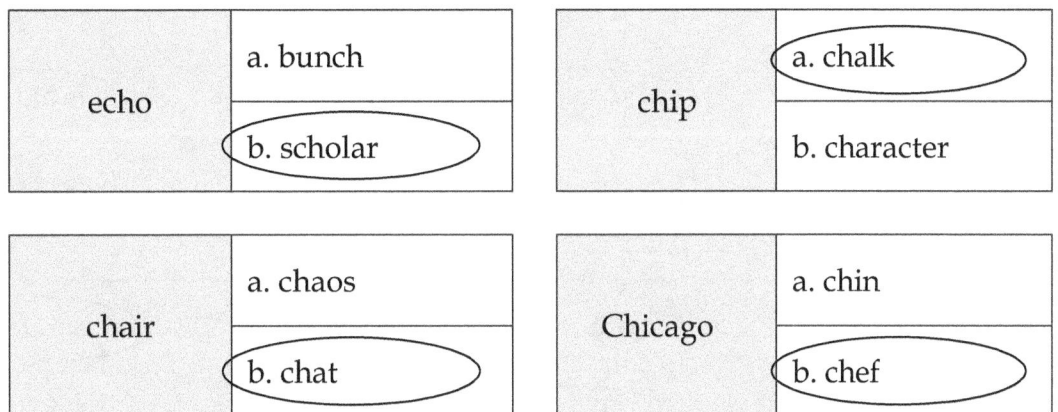

 Directions: Read each target word. Put a check (✓) under the correct column heading.
지도: 각 대상 단어를 읽으십시오. 올바른 열 제목 아래에 체크(✓)를하십시오.

Target Words	"ch" has the /ch/ sound as in the word <u>chain</u>	"ch" has the /sh/ sound as in the word <u>chef</u>	"ch" has the /k/ sound as in the word <u>chaos</u>	"ch" is silent as in the word <u>yacht</u>
1. echo			✓	
2. chip	✓			
3. chair	✓			
4. Chicago		✓		

Assessment

 Name: _____ Date: ___/___/_____ Score: _____

Lesson 3.8

Reading Words with the "cc" Letter Combination

✓ Lesson Check Point

 Directions: Read each target word. Circle the word in the column that has the same "cc" sound(s) as the target word.
지도: 각 대상 단어를 읽으십시오. 대상 단어와 동일한 "cc" 소리가 나는 열의 단어에 동그라미를 치십시오.

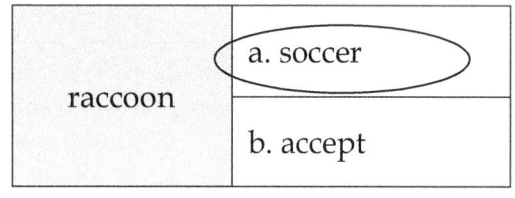
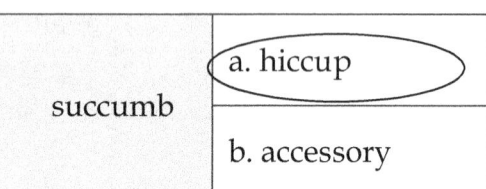
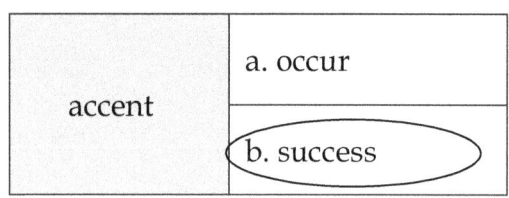
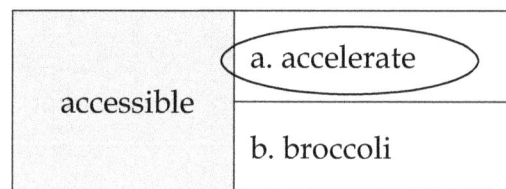

 Directions: Read each target word. Put a check (✓) under the correct column heading.
지도: 각 대상 단어를 읽으십시오. 올바른 열 제목 아래에 체크(✓)를 하십시오.

Target Words	"cc" has the /k/ sound as in the word <u>soccer</u>	"cc" has the /k/ + /s/ sounds as in the word <u>accept</u>
1. raccoon	✓	
2. succumb	✓	
3. accent		✓
4. accessible		✓

Answer Key

Name: _____ Date: ___/___/_____ Score: _____

Lesson 3.9

Reading Words with a Silent Letter "c"

 Lesson Check Point

Directions: Read the target words in the word box. Write the words that have a silent letter "c" in the first column. Write the words that do not have a silent letter "c" in the second column.

지도: 단어 상자에 있는 대상 단어를 읽으십시오. 첫 번째 열에 묵음 문자"c"가 있는 단어를 쓰십시오. 두 번째 열에 묵음 문자"c"가 없는 단어를 쓰십시오.

Target Word Box				
recycle	science	exclude	campers	scene
corpuscle	kneecap	scuff	adolescent	yacht
local	increase	conscience	wildcats	scenery
comment	muscle	distance	scissors	scenario

Letter "c" is silent

- corpuscle
- science
- muscle
- conscience
- adolescent
- scissors
- scene
- yacht
- scenario
- scenery

Letter "c" has the /k/, /s/ or /sh/ sound

- recycle
- local
- comment
- increase
- exclude
- scuff
- distance
- campers
- kneecap
- wildcats

Assessment

Name: _____   Date: ___/___/_____   Score: _____

The Reading Challenge

Lesson 3.10

Reading Multisyllable Words

✓ Lesson Check Point

Directions: Read and divide each target word into syllables. Write each word and place a hyphen (-) between the syllables in the second column. Write the number of syllables in the third column. Use a dictionary or the Internet to check your answers.

지도: 각 대상 단어를 읽고 음절로 나눕니다. 각 단어를 쓰고 두 번째 열의 음절 사이에 하이픈(-)을 넣습니다. 세 번째 열에 음절 수를 쓰십시오. 사전이나 인터넷을 사용하여 답을 확인하십시오.

Target Words	Words Divided into Syllables	Number of Syllables
1. cavity	cav-i-ty	3
2. cabinet	cab-i-net	3
3. chlorine	chlo-rine	2
4. category	cat-e-go-ry	4
5. conception	con-cep-tion	3
6. ceremony	cer-e-mo-ny	4
7. cardinal	car-di-nal	3
8. continue	con-tin-ue	3
9. chandelier	chan-de-lier	3
10. cauliflower	cau-li-flow-er	4

Answer Key

Name: _____ Date: ___/___/_____ Score: _____

The Reading Challenge

Lesson 3.10

Reading Multisyllable Words

✓ Lesson Check Point

Directions: Read each target word. Circle the word in the row that is divided correctly into syllables. Use a dictionary or the Internet to check your answers.

지도: 각 대상 단어를 읽으십시오. 음절로 올바르게 나누어진 행에 있는 단어에 동그라미를 치십시오. 사전이나 인터넷을 사용하여 답을 확인하십시오.

Model

| calculus | a. calcu-lus | (b. cal-cu-lus) | c. cal-culus |

1. clerical	(a. cler-i-cal)	b. cle-ri-cal	c. cle-ric-al
2. circulate	a. cir-cul-ate	b. ci-rcul-ate	(c. cir-cu-late)
3. character	a. cha-ra-cter	(b. char-ac-ter)	c. char-act-er
4. Chicago	a. Chic-a-go	(b. Chi-ca-go)	c. Chi-cag-o
5. circular	(a. cir-cu-lar)	b. ci-rcu-lar	c. circu-lar
6. conclude	(a. con-clude)	b. con-clu-de	c. co-nclu-de
7. chestnut	a. che-st-nut	b. chest-n-ut	(c. chest-nut)
8. centipede	(a. cen-ti-pede)	b. cent-i-pede	c. ce-nti-pede

Learn To Read English With Directions In Korean

Assessment

Name: _____ **Date:** ___/___/_____ **Score:** _____

Lesson 3.11

Reading and Writing

Proper and Common Nouns and Adjectives

✓ Lesson Check Point

Directions: Read the words in the word box. Put an (X) on the line next to each word that is written incorrectly. Remember that all proper nouns and proper adjectives are capitalized. Use a dictionary or the Internet to check your answers.

지도: 단어 상자에 있는 단어를 읽으십시오. 잘못 쓰여진 각 단어 옆의 줄에 (X)를 표시하십시오. 모든 고유 명사와 고유 형용사는 대문자임을 기억하십시오. 사전이나 인터넷을 사용하여 답을 확인하십시오.

Word Box					
X	Center	__	classical	X	Chapter
__	Connecticut	__	Canada	__	chain
__	carpet	X	Coffee	X	chinese
X	canada	X	celtic	__	classroom

Directions: Read each unedited sentence and underline the word that is written incorrectly. Write each sentence correctly on the line.

지도: 편집되지 않은 각 문장을 읽고 잘못 쓰여진 단어에 밑줄을 긋습 니다. 각 문장을 줄에 올바르게 쓰십시오.

Model
The <u>Camp</u> in Cleveland is closed.
The camp in Cleveland is closed.

1. Carson City is not close to <u>chicago</u>.
Carson City is not close to Chicago.

2. <u>champion</u> breakfast cereal is chewy.
Champion breakfast cereal is chewy.

3. Chloe said, "Columbus is a <u>Capital</u> city."
Chloe said, "Columbus is a capital city."

4. Mrs. Charles' <u>Class</u> is studying storybook characters.
Mrs. Charles' class is studying storybook characters.

Answer Key

 Name: _____ Date:___/___/_____ Score:_____

Lesson 4.1

Reading Words with the Letter D/d

✓ **Lesson Check Point**

 Directions: Read each target word. Find the letter "d" and put a check (✓) in the column that identifies its position: beginning, within or end.
지도: 각 대상 단어를 읽으십시오. 문자"d"를 찾아 위치를 나타내는 열에 체크(✓)를 하십시오: 시작, 내부 또는 끝.

Target Words	Beginning (First Letter)	Within	End (Last Letter)
1. mud			✓
2. dream	✓		
3. landing		✓	
4. period			✓
5. medal		✓	

 Directions: Read each sentence and underline the words that begin with the letter "d." Write all the underlined words in alphabetical order on the lines below.
지도: 각 문장을 읽고 문자"d"로 시작하는 단어에 밑줄을 긋습니다. 아래 줄에 밑줄 친 단어를 알파벳 순서로 모두 쓰십시오.

6. Andy <u>drew</u> a <u>dog</u> and a cat.

7. <u>Dan</u> always reads about <u>dinosaurs</u>.

8. <u>Dr.</u> Brown <u>delivered</u> Betty's baby boy.

9. The chicken <u>drumstick</u> costs one <u>dollar</u>.

10. Annie and Charles went to the <u>desert</u> for a <u>day</u>.

Dan	day	delivered
desert	dinosaurs	dog
dollar	Dr.	drew
	drumstick	

Assessment

Name: _____ Date:___/___/_____ Score:_____

Lesson 4.2

Reading Letter "d" Words with the /d/ Sound & /j/ Sound

✓ **Lesson Check Point**

Directions: Read each target word. Circle the word in the column that has the same "d" sound as the target word.
지도: 각 대상 단어를 읽으십시오. 대상 단어와 "d" 소리가 같은 열의 단어에 동그라미를 치십시오.

| induct | a. sedulous |
| | b. extend (circled) |

| glandular | a. decide |
| | b. educable (circled) |

| schedule | a. completed |
| | b. modulate (circled) |

| ladder | a. cordial |
| | b. middle (circled) |

Directions: Read each target word. Put a check (✓) under the correct column heading.
지도: 각 대상 단어를 읽으십시오. 올바른 열 제목 아래에 체크(✓)를 하십시오.

Target Words	"d" has the /d/ sound as in the word <u>doctor</u>	"d" has the /j/ sound as in the word <u>educate</u>
1. induct	✓	
2. glandular		✓
3. schedule		✓
4. ladder	✓	

Learn To Read English With Directions In Korean

Answer Key

Name: _____ Date:___/___/_____ Score:_____

Lesson 4.2

Reading Words with the "dr" Letter Combination

Dictionary Skills/ Vocabulary

✓ Lesson Check Point

Directions: Read each target word and its definition. Write the letter of the definition on the line of each target word. Use a dictionary or the Internet to check your answers.
지도: 각 대상 단어와 그 정의를 읽으십시오. 각 대상 단어의 행에 정의의 문자를 씁니다. 사전이나 인터넷을 사용하여 답을 확인하십시오.

Target Words	Definitions
1. _b_ drain	a. to have made a picture with a pencil or crayon
2. _e_ drawer	b. to allow liquid to gradually flow away
3. _a_ drew	c. the process of making a hole with a tool
4. _c_ drill	d. feeling sleepy or tired
5. _d_ drowsy	e. a boxlike pull-out section in furniture

Directions: Read each sentence. Underline the word in the parentheses that correctly completes each sentence. Then, write the underlined word on the line.
지도: 각 문장을 읽으십시오. 각 문장을 올바르게 완성하는 괄호 안에 있는 단어에 밑줄을 긋습니다. 그런 다음 밑줄 친 단어를 줄에 쓰십시오.

6. I will ____drain____ the water into the sink. (<u>drain</u>, drill)

7. Daisy puts her dresses in the ____drawer____. (<u>drawer</u>, drain)

8. Dot and Dan will ____drill____ a hole in the door. (<u>drill</u>, drowsy)

9. Dan went to bed because he was ____drowsy____. (drawer, <u>drowsy</u>)

10. The boys ____drew____ pictures of ducks and dogs. (drain, <u>drew</u>)

Learn To Read English With Directions In Korean   45   Copyrighted Material

Assessment

 Name: _____ Date:___/__/_____ Score: _____

Lesson 4.3

Reading Words with the "ed" Suffix/ Past Tense Verbs

✓ **Lesson Check Point**

 Directions: Read each target word. Circle the word in the column that has the same "ed" sound(s) as the target word.

지도: 각 대상 단어를 읽으십시오. 대상 단어와 동일한"ed" 소리(들)가있는열의 단어에 동그라미를 치십시오.

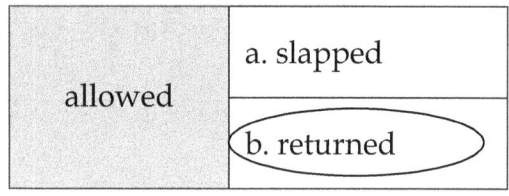

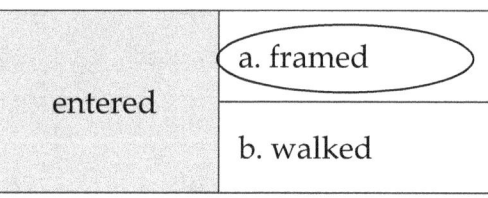

 Directions: Read each target word. Put a check (✓) under the correct column heading.

지도: 각 대상 단어를 읽으십시오. 올바른 열 제목 아래에 체크(✓)를 하십시오.

Target Words	"ed" has the /ĭ/ + /d/ sounds as in the word <u>rested</u>	"ed" has the /d/ sound as in the word <u>hugged</u>	"ed" has the /t/ sound as in the word <u>tipped</u>
1. allowed		✓	
2. shaped			✓
3. waited	✓		
4. entered		✓	

Answer Key

 Name: _____ Date:___/___/_____ Score:_____

Lesson 4.4

Reading Words with a Silent Letter "d"

✓ **Lesson Check Point**

 Directions: Read the target words in the word box. Write the words that have a silent letter "d" in the first column. Write the words that do not have a silent letter "d" in the second column.

지도: 단어 상자에 있는 대상 단어를 읽으십시오. 첫 번째 열에 묵음문자 "d"가 있는 단어를 쓰십시오. 두 번째 열에 묵음 문자"d"가 없는 단어를 쓰십시오.

Target Word Box				
shed	dislodge	third	adjust	landscape
adjunct	handsome	duck	date	grudge
side	dress	hedge	handrail	ready
bridge	handkerchief	doctors	Wednesday	judge

Letter "d" is silent

- adjunct
- bridge
- dislodge
- handsome
- hedge
- adjust
- judge
- grudge
- Wednesday
- handkerchief

Letter "d" has the /d/ sound

- shed
- side
- dress
- third
- duck
- doctors
- date
- handrail
- ready
- landscape

Unit D Lesson 4.4

Assessment

Name: _____ Date: ___/___/_____ Score: _____

The Reading Challenge

Lesson 4.5

Reading Multisyllable Words

✓ **Lesson Check Point**

Directions: Read and divide each target word into syllables. Write each word and place a hyphen (-) between the syllables in the second column. Write the number of syllables in the third column. Use a dictionary or the Internet to check your answers.

지도: 각 대상 단어를 읽고 음절로 나눕니다. 각 단어를 쓰고 두 번째 열의 음절 사이에 하이픈(-)을 넣습니다. 세 번째 열에 음절 수를 쓰십시오. 사전이나 인터넷을 사용하여 답을 확인하십시오.

Target Words	Words Divided into Syllables	Number of Syllables
1. development	de-vel-op-ment	4
2. demonstrator	dem-on-stra-tor	4
3. despondent	de-spon-dent	3
4. digital	dig-i-tal	3
5. duplication	du-pli-ca-tion	4
6. digestion	di-ges-tion	3
7. derivation	der-i-va-tion	4
8. durable	du-ra-ble	3
9. delinquency	de-lin-quen-cy	4
10. doctoral	doc-tor-al	3

Answer Key

Name: _____ Date: ___/___/_____ Score: _____

The Reading Challenge

Lesson 4.5

Reading Multisyllable Words

✓ Lesson Check Point

Directions: Read each target word. Circle the word in the row that is divided correctly into syllables. Use a dictionary or the Internet to check your answers.
지도: 각 대상 단어를 읽으십시오. 음절로 올바르게 나누어진 행에 있는 단어에 동그라미를 치십시오. 사전이나 인터넷을 사용하여 답을 확인하십시오.

Model

| dictionary | a. di-ction-ary | **b. dic-tion-ar-y** ⭕ | c. dic-tiona-ry |

| 1. decision | **a. de-ci-sion** ⭕ | b. dec-i-sion | c. de-cis-ion |

| 2. disciple | a. di-sci-ple | b. disc-i-ple | **c. dis-ci-ple** ⭕ |

| 3. decagram | a. de-ca-gram | **b. dec-a-gram** ⭕ | c. de-cag-ram |

| 4. dynamite | a. dyn-a-mite | b. dy-nam-ite | **c. dy-na-mite** ⭕ |

| 5. democrat | **a. dem-o-crat** ⭕ | b. de-mo-crat | c. de-mocr-at |

| 6. dynasty | a. dyn-as-ty | b. dy-nast-y | **c. dy-nas-ty** ⭕ |

| 7. decimal | a. de-cim-al | **b. dec-i-mal** ⭕ | c. de-ci-mal |

| 8. document | **a. doc-u-ment** ⭕ | b. do-cum-ent | c. do-cume-nt |

Unit D
Lesson 4.5

Learn To Read English With Directions In Korean   49   Copyrighted Material

Assessment

Name: _____ Date: ___/___/_____ Score: _____

Lesson 4.6

Reading and Writing

Proper and Common Nouns and Adjectives

✓ **Lesson Check Point**

Directions: Read the words in the word box. Put an (X) on the line next to each word that is written incorrectly. Remember that all proper nouns and proper adjectives are capitalized. Use a dictionary or the Internet to check your answers.

지도: 단어 상자에 있는 단어를 읽으십시오. 잘못 쓰여진 각 단어 옆의 줄에 (X)를 표시하십시오. 모든 고유 명사와 고유 형용사는 대문자임을 기억하십시오. 사전이나 인터넷을 사용하여 답을 확인하십시오.

Word Box					
__	Delaware	X	danish	__	dresses
X	Dependent	X	Dishes	X	Diner
__	dense	__	doormat	__	Dominican
X	december	__	Denver	X	dr.

Directions: Read each unedited sentence and underline the word that is written incorrectly. Write each sentence correctly on the line.

지도: 편집되지 않은 각 문장을 읽고 잘못 쓰여진 단어에 밑줄을긋습 니다. 각 문장을 줄에 올바르게 쓰십시오.

Model
Dan said, "My daughter's name is <u>donna</u>."
<u>Dan said, "My daughter's name is Donna."</u>

1. The dictionary belongs to <u>dean</u> Douglas.
<u>The dictionary belongs to Dean Douglas.</u>

2. Dakota dreams about ducks in the <u>Desert</u>.
<u>Dakota dreams about ducks in the desert.</u>

3. Bobby said, "<u>diana's</u> desk is by the front door."
<u>Bobby said, "Diana's desk is by the front door."</u>

4. <u>denver</u> Diner sells one dozen donuts for one dollar.
<u>Denver Diner sells one dozen donuts for one dollar.</u>

Answer Key

 Name: _____ Date: ___/___/_____ Score: _____

Lesson 5.1

Reading Words with the Letter E/e

✓ Lesson Check Point

 Directions: Read each target word. Find the letter "e" and put a check (✓) in the column that identifies its position: beginning, within or end.
지도: 각 대상 단어를 읽으십시오. 문자"e"를 찾아 체크 표시(✓)위치를식별하는 열에서 시작, 내부 또는 끝.

Target Words	Beginning (First Letter)	Within	End (Last Letter)
1. multiple			✓
2. after		✓	
3. evict	✓		
4. enchant	✓		
5. indicate			✓

 Directions: Read each target word. Read the words in the row and circle the word that has a different vowel "e" sound.
지도: 각 대상 단어를 읽으십시오. 줄에 있는 단어를 읽고 모음"e" 소리가 다른 단어에 동그라미를 치세요.

Target Words				
6. neck	bend	tell	(be)	pest
7. flesh	(me)	vest	yell	felt
8. blend	went	(she)	fresh	tent
9. press	fell	then	cell	(he)
10. spend	nest	(we)	mend	bled

Assessment

Name: _____ Date: ___/___/_____ Score: _____

Lesson 5.2

Reading Words with the Short Vowel "e" Sound

✓ Lesson Check Point

Directions: Read the words in the four boxes. Circle two words with the short vowel /ĕ/ sound. The anchor word for the short vowel /ĕ/ sound is egg.

지도: 네 개의 상자에 있는 단어를 읽으십시오. 짧은 모음 /ĕ/ 소리로 두 단어에 동그라미를 치십시오. 단모음 /ĕ/ 소리의 앵커 워드는 egg입니다.

(trend)	leak	(tent)	reap	(mend)	(beck)
zero	(bent)	(flesh)	east	scene	lease

lean	(bled)	heap	peace	theme	(knelt)
seek	(end)	(dent)	(mesh)	(wedge)	peas

Directions: Read the words in the four boxes. Circle two words that rhyme. Rhyming words have the same ending sound, such as set and wet.

지도: 네 개의 상자에 있는 단어를 읽으십시오. 운이 맞는 두 단어에 동그라미를 치십시오. 운율이 있는 단어는 set 및 wet와 같이 끝 소리가 같습니다.

(leg)	grease	(rent)	(sent)	eat	(fled)
me	(beg)	fleas	east	see	(sled)

(spent)	tea	scene	(wed)	real	beam
(cent)	help	(led)	steak	(cell)	(fell)

Answer Key

Name: _____ Date: ___/___/_____ Score: _____

Lesson 5.2

Reading & Writing Words with the Short Vowel "e" Sound

✓ Lesson Check Point

Directions: Read each sentence and underline three words with the short vowel /ĕ/ sound. Then, write the underlined words on the lines below. The anchor word for the short vowel /ĕ/ sound is egg.

지도: 각 문장을 읽고 세 단어에 짧은 모음 /ĕ/ 소리에 밑줄을 긋습니다. 그런 다음 밑줄 친 단어를 아래 줄에 쓰십시오. 단모음 /ĕ/ 소리의 기준어는 egg입니다.

Model

She placed her <u>legs</u> on the <u>wet</u> <u>deck</u>.

    legs   wet   deck

1. On Tuesday, we <u>met</u> <u>Ted</u> at the <u>shed</u>.

    met   Ted   shed

2. My <u>pet</u> is <u>next</u> to the neatly made <u>bed</u>.

    pet   next   bed

3. On Tuesday, <u>Ken's</u> <u>jet</u> did not <u>set</u> off.

    Ken's   jet   set

4. At camp, the <u>men</u> made the <u>best</u> <u>eggs</u>.

    men   best   eggs

5. <u>Ed's</u> little, <u>red</u> <u>sled</u> is on the car seat.

    Ed's   red   sled

Assessment

 Name: _____ Date: ___/___/_____ Score: _____

Lesson 5.3

Reading Words with the Long Vowel "e" Sound

✓ Lesson Check Point

 Directions: Read the words in the four boxes. Circle two words with the long vowel /ē/ sound. The anchor word for the long vowel /ē/ sound is <u>me</u>.

지도: 네 개의 상자에 있는 단어를 읽으십시오. 장모음 /ē/ 소리로두단어에 동그라미를 치십시오. 장모음 /ē/ 소리의 기준어는 me입니다.

dell	(zeal)	(peak)	melt	(seize)	cress
wear	(reap)	head	(bee)	(meet)	sell

their	(see)	(wheat)	(free)	(neat)	met
(each)	swell	pear	pelt	(steel)	fled

 Directions: Read the words in the four boxes. Circle two words that rhyme. Rhyming words have the same ending sound, such as <u>beep</u> and <u>reap</u>.

지도: 네 개의 상자에 있는 단어를 읽으십시오. 운이 맞는 두 단어에동그라미를 치십시오. 운율이 있는 단어는 beep 및 reap과 같이 끝 소리가같습니다.

led	(mean)	smelt	eight	learn	(beat)
hear	(dean)	(heal)	(peel)	(feet)	jets

(glean)	(clean)	(heap)	drench	(real)	gem
trench	vein	dear	(leap)	(seal)	tear

Answer Key

Name: _____ Date: ___/___/_____ Score: _____

Lesson 5.3

Reading & Writing Words with the Long Vowel "e" Sound

✓ Lesson Check Point

Directions: Read each sentence and underline three words with the long vowel /ē/ sound. Then, write the underlined words on the lines below. The anchor word for the long vowel /ē/ sound is <u>me</u>.

지도: 각 문장을 읽고 장모음 /ē/ 소리로 세 단어에 밑줄을 긋습니다. 그런 다음 밑줄 친 단어를 아래 줄에 쓰십시오. 장모음 /ē/ 소리의 기준어는 <u>me</u> 입니다.

Model

<u>We</u> are <u>reading</u> an article entitled, "<u>Eagles</u> Bird of Prey."

   We   reading   Eagles
 _____   _____   _____

1. Ed's <u>hockey</u> <u>team</u> reigns <u>supreme</u>.

  hockey   team   supreme
 _____   _____   _____

2. The <u>lead</u> <u>teacher</u> wrote interesting <u>themes</u> on the board.

  lead   teacher   themes
 _____   _____   _____

3. The <u>athletes</u> on the <u>Swedish</u> <u>team</u> are in good health.

  athletes   Swedish   team
 _____   _____   _____

4. For good health, <u>people</u> should <u>eat</u> and <u>sleep</u> well.

  people   eat   sleep
 _____   _____   _____

5. I noticed that the <u>green</u> <u>leaves</u> are falling off the <u>trees</u>.

  green   leaves   trees
 _____   _____   _____

Assessment

Name: _____ Date: ___/___/_____ Score: _____

Review Lessons 5.2 & 5.3

Reading Short Vowel and Long Vowel Words

Directions: Read the target words in the word box. In the first column, write the words that have the short vowel /ĕ/ sound, as in the word <u>egg</u>. In the second column, write the words that have the long vowel /ē/ sound, as in the word <u>me</u>.

지도: 단어 상자에 있는 대상 단어를 읽으십시오. 첫 번째 칸에는 egg라는 단어처럼 단모음 /ĕ/ 소리가 나는 단어를 씁니다. 두 번째 칸에는 me라는 단어처럼 장모음 /ē/ 소리가 나는 단어를 쓰세요.

Target Word Box				
receive	sketch	clever	legacy	deceive
edit	eagle	eating	scheme	them
when	scream	Chinese	eggshell	compete
people	vest	sending	concrete	medal

Letter "e" has the /ĕ/ sound as in the word <u>egg</u>

- edit
- when
- sketch
- vest
- clever
- sending
- legacy
- eggshell
- them
- medal

Letter "e" has the /ē/ sound as in the word <u>me</u>

- receive
- people
- eagle
- scream
- eating
- Chinese
- scheme
- concrete
- deceive
- compete

Answer Key

 Name: _____ Date:___/___/_____ Score:_____

Lesson 5.4

Reading Words with Letter "e" Vowel Pairs

✓ Lesson Check Point

 Directions: Read each target word. Circle the word in the column that has the same vowel "ea," "ee," "ei," "eo" or "eu" sound as the target word.
지도: 각 대상 단어를 읽으십시오. 같은 모음"ea," "ee," "ei," "eo" 또는 "eu"가 대상 단어와 동일한 열의 단어에 동그라미를 치십시오.

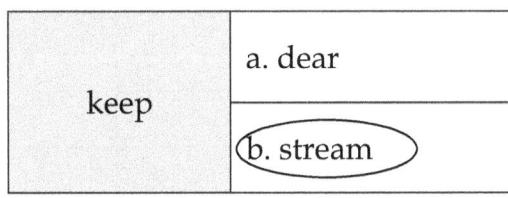
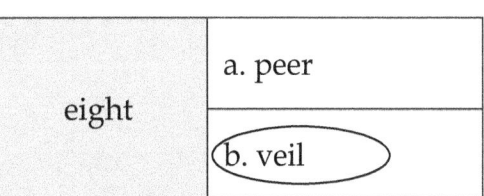
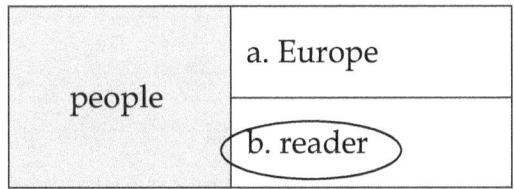
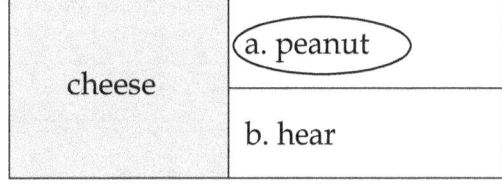

 Directions: Read each target word. Put a check (✓) under the correct column heading.
지도: 각 대상 단어를 읽으십시오. 올바른 열 제목 아래에 체크(✓)를 하십시오.

Target Words	Words have the long "e" sound as in the word <u>tea</u>	Words do not have the long "e" sound
1. keep	✓	
2. eight		✓
3. people	✓	
4. cheese	✓	

Assessment

Name: _____ Date: ___/___/_____ Score: _____

Lesson 5.5

Reading Words with the Final Letter "e"

✓ Lesson Check Point

Directions: Read each target word. Find the letter "e" and put a check (✓) in the column that identifies its position within the syllable.
지도: 각 대상 단어를 읽으십시오. 문자"e"를 찾아 체크 표시(✓)음 절 내에서 위치를 식별하는 열에서.

Target Words	"e" is at the end of a one syllable word	"e" is at the end of the first syllable	"e" is at the end of a multi-syllable word
1. dispute			✓
2. she	✓		
3. hero		✓	
4. we	✓		
5. began		✓	

Directions: Read each target word. Put a check (✓) under the correct column heading.
지도: 각 대상 단어를 읽으십시오. 올바른 열 제목 아래에 체크(✓)를 하십시오.

Target Words	"e" has the /ĕ/ sound as in the word <u>egg</u>	"e" has the /ē/ sound as in the word <u>me</u>	"e" has the /ə/ sound as in the word <u>item</u>	"e" is silent as in the word <u>great</u>
6. label			✓	
7. medical	✓			
8. seedling		✓		
9. cake				✓
10. tenant	✓			

Answer Key

 Name: _____ Date: ___/___/_____ Score: _____

Lesson 5.6

Reading Letter "e" Words with the Schwa Vowel Sound

✓ Lesson Check Point

 Directions: Read each target word. Circle the word in the column that has the same "e" sound as the target word.

지도: 각 대상 단어를 읽으십시오. 목표 단어와 같은"e" 소리가 나는 열의 단어에 동그라미를 치십시오.

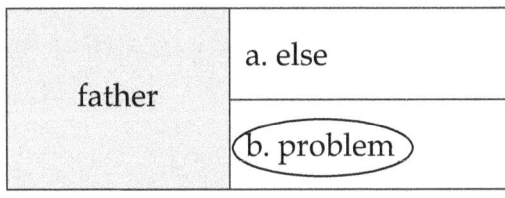
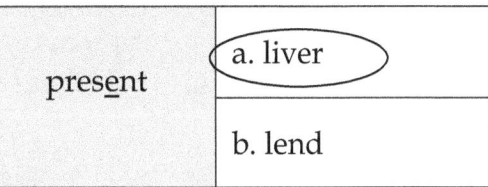
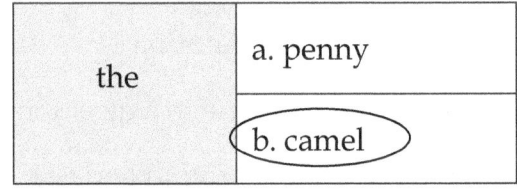
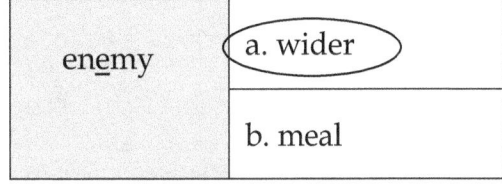

 Directions: Read each sentence and underline the letter "e" word that has the schwa vowel /ə/ sound. The anchor word for the letter "e" schwa vowel sound is <u>item</u>.

지도: 각 문장을 읽고 슈와 모음 /ə/ 소리가 있는 문자"e" 단어에 밑줄을 긋습니다. "e" 슈와 모음 소리의 앵커 단어는 item입니다.

1. We lived in <u>Belize</u> for five years.

2. My toy <u>elephants</u> are stuffed with cotton fibers.

3. Our education <u>system</u> focuses on teaching students.

4. My instructor said, "This year, I have a <u>marvelous</u> class!"

5. Mr. Eastman made nine food <u>deliveries</u> along our coastline.

6. We read an <u>interesting</u> short story entitled "Two Kinds" by Amy Tan.

Assessment

Name: _____ Date: ___/___/_____ Score: _____

Lesson 5.7

Reading Words with the "er" Letter Combination

Dictionary Skills/ Vocabulary

✓ Lesson Check Point

Directions: Read each target word and its definition. Write the letter of the definition on the line of each target word. Use a dictionary or the Internet to check your answers.
지도: 각 대상 단어와 그 정의를 읽으십시오. 각 대상 단어의 행에 정의의 문자를 씁니다. 사전이나 인터넷을 사용하여 답을 확인하십시오.

Target Words	Definitions
1. _c_ cherry	a. a written form of communication
2. _d_ terrible	b. a verbal or written response to a question
3. _e_ periscope	c. a sweet fruit that is small, round and red
4. _a_ letter	d. something very bad or unacceptable
5. _b_ answer	e. a viewing instrument that has a system of lenses

Directions: Read each sentence and write the target word that correctly completes the sentence.
지도: 각 문장을 읽고 문장을 올바르게 완성하는 목표 단어를 쓰십시오.

6. Jerry's milkshake has whipped cream and a ___cherry___ on top.

7. Sherry received a business ___letter___ in the mail.

8. The clerk used his new ___periscope___ for entertainment.

9. My sister said the correct ___answer___ to the difficult question.

10. The shaky ladder against the house is in a ___terrible___ place.

Answer Key

 Name: _____ Date: ___/___/_____ Score: _____

Lesson 5.8

Reading Words with the "eu" and "ew" Letter Combinations

✓ Lesson Check Point

 Directions: Read each sentence and underline the word that has a silent letter "e."
지도: 각 문장을 읽고 묵음 문자"e"가 있는 단어에 밑줄을 긋습니다.

Model
My father said, "The apricot streusel is very tasty."

1. Ben read the eulogy at Mr. Edward's funeral.
2. The domestic cat was neutered by the veterinarian.
3. The driver skillfully maneuvers his red car in the parking lot.
4. Helen Evans, the author of the award-winning book, has a pseudonym.

 Directions: Read each sentence and underline the word with an "eu" or "ew" letter combination that has the long vowel /y$\overline{oo}$/ or /$\overline{oo}$/ sound, as in the words feud and flew.
지도: 각 문장을 읽고 단어 feud 그리고 flew에서와 같이 장모음 /y$\overline{oo}$/ 또는 /$\overline{oo}$/ 소리가 있는"eu" 또는"ew" 문자 조합으로 단어에 밑줄을 긋습니다.

5. Last summer, Edward grew rather quickly.
6. Emily accidentally lost her gold and silver jewelry.
7. My mother is sewing a red dress for Mrs. Andrews.
8. The major family dispute was over a pot of beef stew.
9. It was difficult for the judge to maintain a neutral position.
10. The successful battle was directed by Lieutenant Edmonds.

Assessment

Name: _____ Date: ___/___/_____ Score: _____

Lesson 5.9

Reading Words with the "ey" Letter Combination

Directions: Read each target word. Put a check (✓) under the correct column heading.
지도: 각 대상 단어를 읽으십시오. 올바른 열 제목 아래에 체크(✓)를 하십시오.

Target Words	"ey" has the long /ē/ sound as in the word <u>honey</u>	"ey" has the long /ā/ sound as in the word <u>hey</u>
1. kidney	✓	
2. grey		✓
3. they		✓
4. volley	✓	

Directions: Read each sentence and underline the word with the "ey" letter combination. Put a check (✓) under the correct column heading.
지도: 각 문장을 읽고 "ey" 문자 조합으로 단어에 밑줄을 긋습니다. 올바른 열 제목 아래에 체크(✓)를 하십시오.

	"ey" has the long /ē/ sound as in the word <u>honey</u>	"ey" has the long /ā/ sound as in the word <u>hey</u>
5. The students must <u>obey</u> the rules.		✓
6. The eagle is looking for its <u>prey</u>.		✓
7. <u>Bradley</u> is eating cheese for lunch.	✓	
8. <u>They</u> are eager to go to Europe.		✓
9. Jeffery has a <u>hockey</u> game this evening.	✓	
10. Shama saw four fat <u>monkeys</u> at the zoo.	✓	

Answer Key

 Name: _____ Date: ___/___/_____ Score: _____

Lesson 5.10

Reading Words with a Silent Letter "e"

✓ Lesson Check Point

 Directions: Read the target words in the word box. Write the words that have a silent letter "e" in the first column. Write the words that do not have a silent letter "e" in the second column.

지도: 단어 상자에 있는 대상 단어를 읽으십시오. 첫 번째 열에 묵음 문자"e"가 있는 단어를 쓰십시오. 두 번째 열에 묵음 문자"e"가 없는 단어를 쓰십시오.

Target Word Box				
issues	dependent	partake	clues	computer
restore	screen	effect	sideways	element
eating	elephants	made	seagulls	beneath
space	teapot	rake	pine	ending

Letter "e" is silent

- issues
- restore
- space
- partake
- made
- rake
- clues
- sideways
- pine
- screen

Letter "e" has a letter "e" sound

- eating
- dependent
- elephants
- teapot
- effect
- seagulls
- computer
- element
- beneath
- ending

Assessment

Name: _____ Date:___/___/_____ Score:_____

Unit Review - E/e

Reading Words with Vowel "e" Sounds: /ĕ/, /ē/, /ə/ & Silent

✓ Lesson Check Point

Directions: Read each target word. Circle the word in the column that has the same "e" sound as the target word.
지도: 각 대상 단어를 읽으십시오. 목표 단어와 같은 "e" 소리가 나는 열의 단어에 동그라미를 치십시오.

| marvel | a. legged |
| | b. item ⭕ |

| trade | a. blue ⭕ |
| | b. smell |

| elephant | a. legacy ⭕ |
| | b. east |

| navel | a. Belize ⭕ |
| | b. paycheck |

Directions: Read each target word. Put a check (✓) under the correct column heading.
지도: 각 대상 단어를 읽으십시오. 올바른 열 제목 아래에 체크(✓)를 하십시오.

Target Words	"e" has the /ĕ/ sound as in the word **egg**	"e" has the /ē/ sound as in the word **me**	"e" has the /ə/ sound as in the word **item**	"e" is silent as in the word **great**
1. marvel			✓	
2. trade				✓
3. elephant	✓			
4. navel			✓	

Answer Key

The Reading Challenge

Lesson 5.11

Reading Multisyllable Words

✓ Lesson Check Point

 Directions: Read and divide each target word into syllables. Write each word and place a hyphen (-) between the syllables in the second column. Write the number of syllables in the third column. Use a dictionary or the Internet to check your answers.

지도: 각 대상 단어를 읽고 음절로 나눕니다. 각 단어를 쓰고 두 번째 열의 음절 사이에 하이픈(-)을 넣습니다. 세 번째 열에 음절 수를 쓰십시오. 사전이나 인터넷을 사용하여 답을 확인하십시오.

Target Words	Words Divided into Syllables	Number of Syllables
1. problem	prob-lem	2
2. systemic	sys-tem-ic	3
3. retelling	re-tell-ing	3
4. featuring	fea-tur-ing	3
5. heartfelt	heart-felt	2
6. peacock	pea-cock	2
7. leaflet	leaf-let	2
8. kitchen	kitch-en	2
9. fifteen	fif-teen	2
10. golden	gold-en	2

Assessment

 Name: _____ Date:___/___/_____ Score:_____

The Reading Challenge

Lesson 5.11

Reading Multisyllable Words

✓ Lesson Check Point

 Directions: Read each target word. Circle the word in the row that is divided correctly into syllables. Use a dictionary or the Internet to check your answers.
지도: 각 대상 단어를 읽으십시오. 음절로 올바르게 나누어진 행에 있는 단어에 동그라미를 치십시오. 사전이나 인터넷을 사용하여 답을 확인하십시오.

Model

| megabyte | a. me-ga-byte | b. meg-a-byte ⭕ | c. me-gaby-te |

1. amending	a. am-end-ing	b. a-mend-ing ⭕	c. am-en-ding
2. extending	a. ex-tend-ing ⭕	b. ex-ten-ding	c. e-xten-ding
3. systemic	a. sy-stem-ic	b. sys-te-mic	c. sys-tem-ic ⭕
4. condescend	a. con-de-scend ⭕	b. cond-e-scend	c. con-des-cend
5. depended	a. de-pen-ded	b. de-pend-ed ⭕	c. dep-end-ed
6. expanding	a. ex-pand-ing ⭕	b. ex-pan-ding	c. exp-and-ing
7. apartment	a. a-partme-nt	b. ap-art-ment	c. a-part-ment ⭕
8. suspending	a. su-spend-ing	b. sus-pend-ing ⭕	c. sus-pen-ding

Answer Key

Name: _____ Date: ___/___/_____ Score: _____

Lesson 5.12

Reading and Writing

Proper and Common Nouns and Adjectives

✓ Lesson Check Point

Directions: Read the words in the word box. Put an (X) on the line next to each word that is written incorrectly. Remember that all proper nouns and proper adjectives are capitalized. Use a dictionary or the Internet to check your answers.
지도: 단어 상자에 있는 단어를 읽으십시오. 잘못 쓰여진 각 단어 옆의 줄에 (X)를 표시하십시오. 모든 고유 명사와 고유 형용사는 대문자임을 기억하십시오. 사전이나 인터넷을 사용하여 답을 확인하십시오.

Word Box					
__	East Germany	__	Estonia	X	Element
__	eliminate	X	easter	__	equator
X	Mt. everest	X	Email	__	embark
X	Efficient	__	entrance	X	england

Directions: Read each unedited sentence and underline the word that is written incorrectly. Write each sentence correctly on the line.
지도: 편집되지 않은 각 문장을 읽고 잘못 쓰여진 단어에 밑줄을긋습 니다. 각 문장을 줄에 올바르게 쓰십시오.

Model
All my friends are <u>Excited</u> about the class trip to Europe.
<u>All my friends are excited about the class trip to Europe.</u>

1. Eloise took a picture of the <u>eiffel</u> Tower.
<u>Eloise took a picture of the Eiffel Tower.</u>

2. In Europe, people like to eat <u>Eggs</u> for breakfast.
<u>In Europe, people like to eat eggs for breakfast.</u>

3. Eve is reading books about how <u>eskimos</u> survive in the Arctic.
<u>Eve is reading books about how Eskimos survive in the Arctic.</u>

4. Early in the morning, Beth and I will go to the <u>english</u> Channel.
<u>Early in the morning, Beth and I will go to the English Channel.</u>

Assessment

Name: _____ Date: ___/___/_____ Score: _____

Lesson 6.1

Reading Words with the Letter F/f

✓ Lesson Check Point

Directions: Read each target word. Find the letter "f" and put a check (✓) in the column that identifies its position: beginning, within or end.
지도: 각 대상 단어를 읽으십시오. 문자 "f"를 찾아 체크 표시(✓)위치를 식별하는 열에서 시작, 내부 또는 끝.

Target Words	Beginning (First Letter)	Within	End (Last Letter)
1. informed		✓	
2. fox	✓		
3. roof			✓
4. proof			✓
5. enforced		✓	

Directions: Read each sentence and underline the words that begin with the letter "f." Write all the underlined words in alphabetical order on the lines below.
지도: 각 문장을 읽고 "f"로 시작하는 단어에 밑줄을 긋습니다. 밑줄친 모든 단어를 아래 줄에 알파벳 순서로 쓰십시오.

6. <u>Fish</u> do not have <u>feet</u>.

7. <u>Frank</u> has two big <u>frogs</u>.

8. My <u>file</u> <u>folder</u> is in the cabinet.

9. The <u>fruits</u> in the bowls are <u>firm</u>.

10. You can eat <u>food</u> with your <u>fingers</u>.

file	fingers	firm
Fish	food	folder
feet	Frank	frogs
	fruits	

Answer Key

📖 Name: _____ Date:___/___/_____ Score:_____

Lesson 6.2

Reading Words with the "fr" Letter Combination

Dictionary Skills/ Vocabulary

✓ Lesson Check Point

Directions: Read each target word and its definition. Write the letter of the definition on the line of each target word. Use a dictionary or the Internet to check your answers.
지도: 각 대상 단어와 그 정의를 읽으십시오. 각 대상 단어의 행에 정의의 문자를 씁니다. 사전이나 인터넷을 사용하여 답을 확인하십시오.

Target Words	Definitions
1. _d_ fractions	a. the state of being physically free
2. _e_ free	b. thin, long pieces of fried potato
3. _a_ freedom	c. icing on a dessert
4. _b_ fries	d. math concept; part of a whole
5. _c_ frosting	e. receiving something without payment or cost

Directions: Read each sentence. Underline the word in the parentheses that correctly completes each sentence. Then, write the underlined word on the line.
지도: 각 문장을 읽으십시오. 각 문장을 올바르게 완성하는 괄호 안에 있는 단어에 밑줄을 긋습니다. 그런 다음 밑줄 친 단어를 줄에 쓰십시오.

6. I am learning to add ____fractions____ in class. (<u>fractions</u>, free)

7. I ate fried chicken and ____fries____ for lunch. (<u>fries</u>, frosting)

8. The nonfiction books are ____free____ of charge. (fractions, <u>free</u>)

9. I spread a thin layer of ____frosting____ on the cake. (fries, <u>frosting</u>)

10. Frederick Douglass fought for the ____freedom____ of enslaved people. (free, <u>freedom</u>)

Assessment

Name: _____ Date:___/___/_____ Score: _____

Lesson 6.3

Reading Words with the "fl" Letter Combination

Dictionary Skills/ Vocabulary

✓ Lesson Check Point

Directions: Read each target word and its definition. Write the target word on the line in front of its meaning. Use a dictionary or the Internet to check your answers.
지도: 각 대상 단어와 그 정의를 읽으십시오. 의미 앞 줄에대상단어를 쓰십시오. 사전이나 인터넷을 사용하여 답을 확인하십시오.

Target Word Box				
flash	fleet	flexible	float	flooded

1. _fleet_   vehicles owned or operated as a unit
2. _float_   to stay on top of liquid without sinking
3. _flooded_   a place full of water that is normally dry
4. _flexible_   something that can bend easily without breaking
5. _flash_   a device on a camera that provides light to brighten a picture

Directions: Read each sentence. Underline the word in the parentheses that correctly completes each sentence. Then, write the underlined word on the line.
지도: 각 문장을 읽으십시오. 각 문장을 올바르게 완성하는 괄호 안에 있는 단어에 밑줄을 긋습니다. 그런 다음 밑줄 친 단어를 줄에 쓰십시오.

6. Fred's black belt is flat and _____flexible_____. (fleet, <u>flexible</u>)

7. Flower lilies _____float_____ on top of the water. (<u>float</u>, flash)

8. The camera's built-in _____flash_____ is broken. (fleet, <u>flash</u>)

9. My dad's company has a new _____fleet_____ of buses. (<u>fleet</u>, float)

10. On Friday, my den was _____flooded_____ with water. (flashed, <u>flooded</u>)

Answer Key

 Name: _____ Date:___/___/_____ Score:_____

Lesson 6.3

Reading Words with the "fle" Letter Combination

✓ Lesson Check Point

 Directions: Read each target word. Find the "fle" letter combination and put a check (✓) in the column that identifies its position: beginning, within or end.

지도: 각 대상 단어를 읽으십시오. "fle" 문자 조합을 찾아해당 위치를식 별 하는열에 체크(✓)를 하십시오: 시작, 내부 또는 끝.

Target Words	Beginning (First 3 Letters)	Within	End (Last 3 Letters)
1. flea	✓		
2. baffle			✓
3. unfledged		✓	
4. flexible	✓		
5. raffle			✓

 Directions: Read each target word. Put a check (✓) in the "yes" column if the "fle" letter combination has the /f/ + /ə/ + /l/ sounds. Put a check (✓) in the "no" column if the "fle" letter combination does not have the /f/ + /ə/ + /l/ sounds.

지도: 각 대상 단어를 읽으십시오. "fle" 문자 조합에/f/ + /ə/ + /l/ 소리가있으면 "yes" 열에 체크(✓)를 하십시오. "fle" 문자 조합에/f/ + /ə/ + /l/ 소리가"no" 아 니오" 열에 체크(✓)를 하십시오.

Target Words	Yes	No
6. flea		✓
7. baffle	✓	
8. unfledged		✓
9. flexible		✓
10. raffle	✓	

Assessment

Name: _____ Date: ___/___/_____ Score: _____

Lesson 6.4

Reading Words with the "ft," "lf" and "ff" Letter Combinations

Dictionary Skills/ Vocabulary

✓ Lesson Check Point

Directions: Read each target word and its definition. Write the letter of the definition on the line of each target word. Use a dictionary or the Internet to check your answers.
지도: 각 대상 단어와 그 정의를 읽으십시오. 각 대상 단어의 행에 정의의 문자를 씁니다. 사전이나 인터넷을 사용하여 답을 확인하십시오.

Target Words	Definitions
1. _c_ gift	a. a place where clerical work is conducted
2. _a_ office	b. the opposite of the right
3. _b_ left	c. something that is freely given
4. _e_ coffee	d. adequate; enough
5. _d_ sufficient	e. hot or cold drink made from coffee beans

Directions: Read each sentence and write the target word that correctly completes the sentence.
지도: 각 문장을 읽고 다음과 같은 목표 단어를 쓰십시오. 장을 올바르게 완성합니다.

6. I write notes with my _____left_____ hand.

7. I always drink _____coffee_____ with a toasted bagel.

8. Fred received a nice _____gift_____ for his birthday.

9. My boss had a business meeting in the _____office_____.

10. We have a _____sufficient_____ amount of money to buy our books.

Answer Key

 Name: _____ Date: ___/___/_____ Score: _____

Lesson 6.5

Reading Words with a Silent Letter "f"

✓ Lesson Check Point

 Directions: Read the target words in the word box. Write the words that have a silent letter "f" in the first column. Write the words that do not have a silent letter "f" in the second column.

지도: 단어 상자에 있는 대상 단어를 읽으십시오. 첫 번째 열에 묵음문자 "f"가 있는 단어를 쓰십시오. 두 번째 열에 묵음 문자"f"가 없는 단어를 쓰십시오.

Target Word Box				
off	stiffen	surf	life	Africa
belief	fillet	cliff	suffering	profess
staff	afford	benefit	muffin	ruffle
jiffy	bluffing	feather	prefer	confuse

Letter "f" is silent

- off
- stiffen
- cliff
- suffering
- staff
- afford
- muffin
- ruffle
- jiffy
- bluffing

Letter "f" has the /f/ sound

- surf
- life
- Africa
- belief
- fillet
- profess
- benefit
- feather
- prefer
- confuse

Assessment

L Name: _____ Date: ___/___/_____ Score: _____

Lesson 6.6

Reading Singular and Plural forms of Words Ending in "-f" & "-fe"

✓ Lesson Check Point

Directions: Read each target word. Put a check (✓) in the second column if the plural form of the target word ends with "-ves." Put a check (✓) in the third column if the plural form of the target word ends with "-s" or "-es."
지도: 각 대상 단어를 읽으십시오. 대상 단어의 복수형이 "-ves"로 끝나는 경우 두 번째 열에 체크(✓)를 하십시오. 대상 단어의 복수형이 "-s" 또는 "-es."로 끝나는 경우 세 번째 열에 체크(✓)를 하십시오.

Target Words	The plural form of the target word ends with "-ves"	The plural form of the target word ends with "-s" or "-es"
1. wife	✓	
2. wolf	✓	
3. proof		✓
4. chef		✓
5. life	✓	

Directions: Read each sentence. Complete each sentence by writing the plural form of the word on the line.
지도: 각 문장을 읽으십시오. 단어의 복수형을 줄에 써서 각 문장을 완성하세요.

6. The cow has four ___hooves___. (hoof)

7. I received four ___elves___ as a gift. (elf)

8. The baker is baking two ___loaves___ of bread. (loaf)

9. The ___knives___ in the kitchen are sharp. (knife)

10. At night, I heard the ___wolves___ howling. (wolf)

Answer Key

Name: _____ Date: ___/___/_____ Score: _____

The Reading Challenge

Lesson 6.7

Reading Multisyllable Words

 Lesson Check Point

 Directions: Read and divide each target word into syllables. Write each word and place a hyphen (-) between the syllables in the second column. Write the number of syllables in the third column. Use a dictionary or the Internet to check your answers.

지도: 각 대상 단어를 읽고 음절로 나눕니다. 각 단어를 쓰고 두 번째 열의 음절 사이에 하이픈(-)을 넣습니다. 세 번째 열에 음절 수를 쓰십시오. 사전이나 인터넷을 사용하여 답을 확인하십시오.

Target Words	Words Divided into Syllables	Number of Syllables
1. fabric	fab-ric	2
2. family	fam-i-ly	3
3. factory	fac-to-ry	3
4. flamingo	fla-min-go	3
5. featuring	fea-tur-ing	3
6. feeling	feel-ing	2
7. formulate	for-mu-late	3
8. flavoring	fla-vor-ing	3
9. fingerprints	fin-ger-prints	3
10. faithfulness	faith-ful-ness	3

Assessment

Name: _____ Date: ___/___/_____ Score: _____

The Reading Challenge

Lesson 6.7

Reading Multisyllable Words

✓ Lesson Check Point

Directions: Read each target word. Circle the word in the row that is divided correctly into syllables. Use a dictionary or the Internet to check your answers.
지도: 각 대상 단어를 읽으십시오. 음절로 올바르게 나누어진 행에 있는 단어에 동그라미를 치십시오. 사전이나 인터넷을 사용하여 답을 확인하십시오.

Model

| factory | a. fac-tor-y | b. fac-to-ry ⭕ | c. fa-cto-ry |

1. factual	a. fa-ctu-al	b. fact-u-al	c. fac-tu-al ⭕
2. federal	a. fe-der-al	b. fed-er-al ⭕	c. fed-e-ral
3. finishing	a. fin-ish-ing ⭕	b. fi-nish-ing	c. fin-is-hing
4. fascinate	a. fas-ci-nate ⭕	b. fasc-i-nate	c. fa-scin-ate
5. feminine	a. fe-min-ine	b. fem-i-nine ⭕	c. fem-in-ine
6. fixation	a. fi-xat-ion	b. fix-a-tion ⭕	c. fi-xa-tion
7. favorite	a. fav-o-rite	b. fa-vo-rite	c. fa-vor-ite ⭕
8. foundation	a. foun-da-tion ⭕	b. found-a-tion	c. foun-dat-ion

Answer Key

Name: _____ Date: ___/___/_____ Score: _____

Lesson 6.8

Reading and Writing

Proper and Common Nouns and Adjectives

✓ Lesson Check Point

Directions: Read the words in the word box. Put an (X) on the line next to each word that is written incorrectly. Remember that all proper nouns and proper adjectives are capitalized. Use a dictionary or the Internet to check your answers.

지도: 단어 상자에 있는 단어를 읽으십시오. 잘못 쓰여진 각 단어 옆의 줄에 (X)를 표시하십시오. 모든 고유 명사와 고유 형용사는 대문자임을 기억하십시오. 사전이나 인터넷을 사용하여 답을 확인하십시오.

Word Box					
X	Family	__	freshmen	X	french
__	flesh	X	finnish	__	fellow
X	Factory	__	fences	__	Florida
X	Fasten	__	Frankfort	X	Fraction

Directions: Read each unedited sentence and underline the word that is written incorrectly. Write each sentence correctly on the line.

지도: 편집되지 않은 각 문장을 읽고 잘못 쓰여진 단어에 밑줄을긋습 니다. 각 문장을 줄에 올바르게 쓰십시오.

Model
Fiji is my <u>Florist's</u> favorite holiday destination.
<u>Fiji is my florist's favorite holiday destination.</u>

1. Fred and <u>florence</u> are from France.
<u>Fred and Florence are from France.</u>

2. Flossy, the florist, has a high <u>Fever</u>.
<u>Flossy, the florist, has a high fever.</u>

3. Five flowers are <u>Floating</u> in the first fountain.
<u>Five flowers are floating in the first fountain.</u>

4. Fran is reading a book entitled "<u>fitness</u> Framework."
<u>Fran is reading a book entitled "Fitness Framework."</u>

Learn To Read English With Directions In Korean

Assessment

J. Name: _____ Date: ___/___/_____ Score: _____

Lesson 7.1

Reading Words with the Letter G/g

✓ Lesson Check Point

Directions: Read each target word. Find the letter "g" and put a check (✓) in the column that identifies its position: beginning, within or end.
지도: 각 대상 단어를 읽으십시오. 문자"g"를 찾아 체크 표시(✓)위치를 식별하는 열에서 시작, 내부 또는 끝.

Target Words	Beginning (First Letter)	Within	End (Last Letter)
1. triangle		✓	
2. gifted	✓		
3. writing			✓
4. grandson	✓		
5. clipping			✓

Directions: Read each sentence and underline the words that begin with the letter "g." Write all the underlined words in alphabetical order on the lines below.
지도: 각 문장을 읽고 문자"g"로 시작하는 단어에 밑줄을 긋습니다. 밑줄 친 모든 단어를 아래 줄에 알파벳 순서로 쓰십시오.

6. The <u>goats</u> ran across the <u>golf</u> course.

7. The <u>generous</u> man <u>gave</u> everyone a new car.

8. The <u>governor</u> attends all the <u>general</u> meetings.

9. <u>Gregg</u> used a <u>glass</u> cleaner to clean the windows.

10. Andy chews bubble <u>gum</u> while playing board <u>games</u>.

games_____   gave_____   general_____
generous_____   glass_____   goats_____
golf_____   governor_____   Gregg_____
                   gum_____

J. Learn To Read English With Directions In Korean

Answer Key

Name: _____ Date: ___/___/_____ Score: _____

Lesson 7.1

Reading Words with the Hard Letter "g"

✓ Lesson Check Point

Directions: Read each target word. Put a check (✓) under the correct column heading.

지도: 각 대상 단어를 읽으십시오. 올바른 열 제목 아래에 체크(✓)를하십시오.

Target Words	Hard "g" has the /g/ sound as in the word <u>gum</u>	Soft "g" has the /j/ sound as in the word <u>gem</u>
1. golf	✓	
2. glow	✓	
3. ginger		✓
4. goats	✓	
5. grabs	✓	

Directions: Read each sentence and underline the words that have the hard "g" sound. The anchor word for the hard "g" sound is <u>gum</u>. Write all the underlined words in alphabetical order on the lines below.

지도: 각 문장을 읽고 단단한"g" 소리가 나는 단어에 밑줄을 긋습니다. 단단한"g" 소리의 기준어는 gum입니다. 밑줄 친 모든 단어를 아래 줄에알파벳 순서로 쓰십시오.

6. Gina said, "<u>Golf</u> is <u>great</u>!"

7. In Georgia, the <u>grass</u> <u>grows</u> quickly.

8. <u>Grandmother's</u> gems look like <u>glaciers</u>.

9. The <u>glass</u> bottle is filled with <u>ground</u> ginger.

10. Generally, the boys in my <u>group</u> are always <u>gossiping</u>.

<u>Golf</u>   <u>gossiping</u>   <u>glaciers</u>
<u>glass</u>   <u>Grandmother's</u>   <u>grass</u>
<u>great</u>   <u>ground</u>   <u>group</u>
                <u>grows</u>

Assessment

Name: _____ Date: ___/___/_____ Score: _____

Lesson 7.2

Reading Words with the Soft Letter "g"

Directions: Read each target word. Put a check (✓) under the correct column heading.

지도: 각 대상 단어를 읽으십시오. 올바른 열 제목 아래에 체크(✓)를 하십시오.

Target Words	Soft "g" has the /j/ or /zh/ sound as in the words gem & massage	Hard "g" has the /g/ sound as in the word gum	Both soft "g" and hard "g" sounds as in the word gauge
1. gift		✓	
2. grain		✓	
3. large	✓		
4. allergy	✓		
5. gigantic			✓

Directions: Read each sentence and underline the words that have the soft "g" sound. The anchor word for the soft "g" sound is gem. Write all the underlined words in alphabetical order on the lines below.

지도: 각 문장을 읽고 부드러운"g" 소리가 나는 단어에 밑줄을 긋습니다. 부드러운"g" "g" 소리의 기준어는 gem입니다. 밑줄 친 모든 단어를 아래 줄에 알파벳 순서로 쓰십시오.

6. My grandmother, Gina, was a famous gymnast.

7. The graduates studied geometry and geophysics.

8. My guests and I ate gyros after gymnastics class.

9. Gregg said, "The dirty gym floor has lots of germs."

10. In Georgia, the girls grew giant grapes in the garden.

geometry   geophysics   Georgia
germs   giant   Gina
gym   gymnast   gymnastics
                  gyros

Answer Key

Name: _____ Date: ___/___/_____ Score: _____

Review Lessons 7.1 & 7.2

Reading Hard Letter "g" and Soft Letter "g" Words

Directions: Read each target word. Put a check (✓) under the correct column heading.
지도: 각 대상 단어를 읽으십시오. 올바른 열 제목 아래에 체크(✓)를하십시오.

Target Words	Soft "g" has the /j/ or /zh/ sound as in the words gem & massage	Hard "g" has the /g/ sound as in the word gum	Both soft "g" and hard "g" sounds as in the word gauge
1. tiger		✓	
2. grades		✓	
3. gorgeous			✓
4. intelligent	✓		
5. gymnastics	✓		

Directions: Read each sentence and underline the words that have the hard "g" sound. The anchor word for the hard "g" sound is gum. Write all the underlined words in alphabetical order on the lines below.
지도: 각 문장을 읽고 단단한"g" 소리가 나는 단어에 밑줄을 긋습니다. 단단한"g" 소리의 기준어는 gum입니다. 밑줄 친 모든 단어를 아래 줄에 알파벳 순서로 쓰십시오.

6. I ate a gyro and drank <u>green</u> tea in the <u>garden</u>.

7. Mr. <u>Grant</u> is the infamous <u>governor</u> of Georgia.

8. My <u>grandparents</u> attended General <u>Grammar</u> School.

9. Although Gekenna is from <u>Ghana</u>, he speaks <u>Greek</u> fluently.

10. In the morning, the giraffes and <u>goats</u> were eating the <u>grass</u>.

<u>garden</u>	<u>Ghana</u>	<u>goats</u>
<u>governor</u>	<u>Grammar</u>	<u>grandparents</u>
<u>Grant</u>	<u>grass</u>	<u>Greek</u>
	<u>green</u>	

Assessment

Name: _____ Date: ___/___/_____ Score: _____

Review Lessons 7.1 & 7.2

Reading Hard Letter "g" and Soft Letter "g" Words

Directions: Read the target words in the word box. In the first column, write the words with the letter "g" that have the /g/ sound, as in the word <u>gum</u>. In the second column, write the words with the letter "g" that have the /j/ sound, as in the word <u>gem</u>.

지도: 단어 상자에 있는 대상 단어를 읽으십시오. 첫 번째 열에는 단어 gum 에서와 같이 /g/ 소리가 나는 문자 "g"가 있는 단어를 씁니다. 두 번째 열에 "g"가 포함된 단어를 쓰십시오. /j/ 소리, gem이라는 단어에서와 같이.

Target Word Box				
gymnast	grant	give	pigeon	glove
giraffe	get	grow	garden	gel
gift	guest	arrange	giant	got
imagine	apologize	college	goat	cage

Hard letter "g" has the /g/ sound as in the word <u>gum</u>

- get
- got
- give
- glove
- grow
- goat
- gift
- guest
- grant
- garden

Soft letter "g" has the /j/ sound as in the word <u>gem</u>

- gel
- cage
- giraffe
- pigeon
- arrange
- giant
- imagine
- apologize
- college
- gymnast

Answer Key

Name: _____ Date: ___/___/_____ Score: _____

Lesson 7.3

Reading Words with the "gr" Letter Combination

Dictionary Skills/Vocabulary

 Lesson Check Point

 Directions: Read each target word and its definition. Write the letter of the definition on the line of each target word. Use a dictionary or the Internet to check your answers.
지도: 각 대상 단어와 그 정의를 읽으십시오. 각 대상 단어의 행에 정의의 문자를 씁니다. 사전이나 인터넷을 사용하여 답을 확인하십시오.

Target Words	Definitions
1. _c_ graduate	a. sweet purple or green fruit that grows on a vine
2. _d_ gradually	b. the hard outer surface of the earth's crust
3. _a_ grapes	c. to earn a diploma or degree from a school
4. _e_ graph	d. happens over a slow period of time
5. _b_ ground	e. a diagram that shows data

 Directions: Read each sentence. Underline the word in the parentheses that correctly completes each sentence. Then, write the underlined word on the line.
지도: 각 문장을 읽으십시오. 각 문장을 올바르게 완성하는 괄호 안에 있는 단어에 밑줄을 긋습니다. 그런 다음 밑줄 친 단어를 줄에 쓰십시오.

6. My grandson ran and fell on the _____ground_____. (graph, <u>ground</u>)

7. Today, I completed my bar _____graph_____ in class. (graduate, <u>graph</u>)

8. I will ___graduate___ from a graphic design program. (<u>graduate</u>, ground)

9. Greg will ___gradually___ learn to make griddlecakes. (graph, <u>gradually</u>)

10. My grandparents ate ___grapes___ and grapefruits. (<u>grapes</u>, gradually)

Assessment

Name: _____ Date: ___/___/_____ Score: _____

Lesson 7.4

Reading Words with the "gl" Letter Combination

Dictionary Skills/ Vocabulary

✓ Lesson Check Point

Directions: Read each target word and its definition. Write the target word on the line in front of its meaning. Use a dictionary or the Internet to check your answers.

지도: 각 대상 단어와 그 정의를 읽으십시오. 의미 앞 줄에대상단어를 쓰십시오. 사전이나 인터넷을 사용하여 답을 확인하십시오.

Target Word Box				
glad	glaring	glasses	gloomy	gloves

1. _gloves_   protective coverings for hands
2. _gloomy_   feeling sad or depressed
3. _glaring_   looking at someone with anger
4. _glasses_   containers used to hold liquids
5. _glad_   to be happy or pleased about something or someone

Directions: Read each sentence. Underline the word in the parentheses that correctly completes each sentence. Then, write the underlined word on the line.

지도: 각 문장을 읽으십시오. 각 문장을 올바르게 완성하는 괄호 안에 있는 단어에 밑줄을 긋습니다. 그런 다음 밑줄 친 단어를 줄에 쓰십시오.

6. The captain was ____glad____ to see the lighthouse. (gloomy, <u>glad</u>)

7. The angry boys were ____glaring____ at each other. (glasses, <u>glaring</u>)

8. During the fight, the boxers must wear ____gloves____. (<u>gloves</u>, glaring)

9. The drinking ____glasses____ are in the cabinet. (<u>glasses</u>, gloves)

10. Usually, I feel ____gloomy____ on dark, cloudy days. (<u>gloomy</u>, glaring)

Answer Key

 Name: _____ Date:___/___/_____ Score:_____

Lesson 7.4

Reading Words with the "gle" Letter Combination

✓ Lesson Check Point

 Directions: Read each target word. Find the "gle" letter combination and put a check (✓) in the column that identifies its position: beginning, within or end.
지도: 각 대상 단어를 읽으십시오. "gle" 문자 조합을 찾아 위치를 식별하는 열에 체크(✓)를 하십시오: 시작, 내부 또는 끝.

Target Words	Beginning (First 3 Letters)	Within	End (Last 3 Letters)
1. angled		✓	
2. Glenn	✓		
3. jungle			✓
4. gleam	✓		
5. goggle			✓

 Directions: Read each target word. Put a check (✓) in the "yes" column if the "gle" letter combination has the /g/ + /ə/ + /l/ sounds. Put a check (✓) in the "no" column if the "gle" letter combination does not have the /g/ + /ə/ + /l/ sounds.
지도: 각 대상 단어를 읽으십시오. "gle" 문자 조합에/g/ + /ə/ + /l/소리가있으면 "yes"열에 체크(✓)를 하십시오. "gle" 문자 조합에/g/ + /ə/ + /l/소리가없으면 "no" 열에 체크(✓)를 하십시오.

Target Words	Yes	No
6. angled	✓	
7. Glenn		✓
8. jungle	✓	
9. gleam		✓
10. goggle	✓	

Assessment

 Name: _____ Date: ___/___/_____ Score: _____

Lesson 7.5

Reading Words with the "gh" Letter Combination

✓ Lesson Check Point

 Directions: Read each target word. Circle the word in the column that has the same "gh" sound as the target word.
지도: 각 대상 단어를 읽으십시오. 대상 단어와 같은 "gn" 소리가 나는 열의 단어에 동그라미를 치십시오.

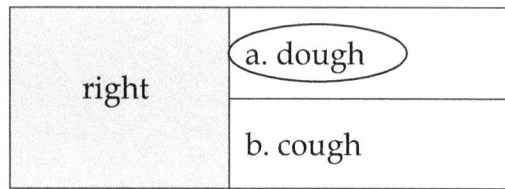
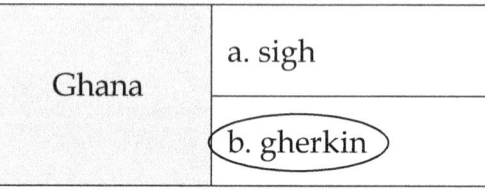
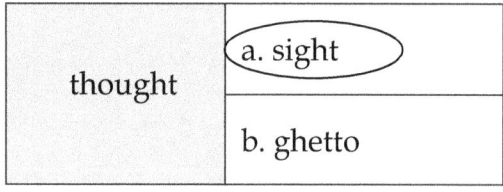
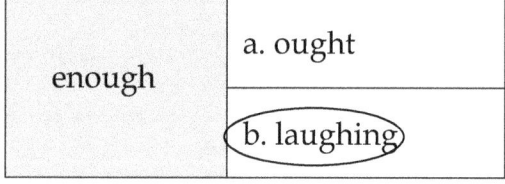

 Directions: Read each target word. Put a check (✓) under the correct column heading.
지도: 각 대상 단어를 읽으십시오. 올바른 열 제목 아래에 체크(✓)를 하십시오.

Target Words	"gh" has the /g/ sound as in the word <u>ghetto</u>	"gh" has the /f/ sound as in the word <u>laugh</u>	"gh" is silent as in the word <u>light</u>
1. right			✓
2. Ghana	✓		
3. thought			✓
4. enough		✓	

Answer Key

 Name: _____ Date:____/____/_____ Score: _____

Lesson 7.6

Reading Words with the "gn" Letter Combination

✓ Lesson Check Point

 Directions: Read each target word. Circle the word in the column that has the same "gn" sound(s) as the target word.
지도: 각 대상 단어를 읽으십시오. 대상 단어와 같은 "gn" 소리가 나는 열의 단어에 동그라미를 치십시오.

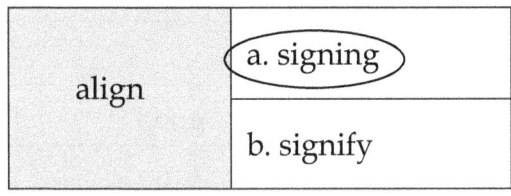
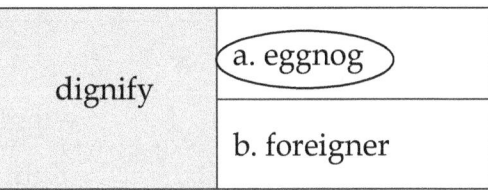
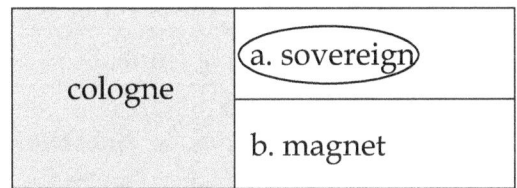
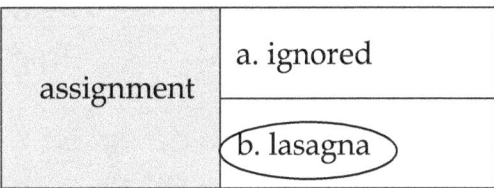

align — a. signing (circled) / b. signify

dignify — a. eggnog (circled) / b. foreigner

cologne — a. sovereign (circled) / b. magnet

assignment — a. ignored / b. lasagna (circled)

 Directions: Read each target word. Put a check (✓) under the correct column heading.
지도: 각 대상 단어를 읽으십시오. 올바른 열 제목 아래에 체크(✓)를 하십시오.

Target Words	"gn" has the /g/ + /n/ sounds as in the word <u>ignite</u>	"gn" has the silent "g" + /n/ sound as in the word <u>sign</u>
1. align		✓
2. dignify	✓	
3. cologne		✓
4. assignment		✓

Assessment

 Name: _____ Date:___/___/_____ Score:_____

Lesson 7.7

Reading Words with a Silent Letter "g"

✓ Lesson Check Point

 Directions: Read the target words in the word box. Write the words that have a silent letter "g" in the first column. Write the words that do not have a silent letter "g" in the second column.

지도: 단어 상자에 있는 대상 단어를 읽으십시오. 첫 번째 열에 묵음문자 "g"가 있는 단어를 쓰십시오. 두 번째 열에 묵음 문자"g"가 없는 단어를 쓰십시오.

Target Word Box				
sign	wiggle	juggle	good	though
signal	light	campaign	gum	align
cologne	resign	gorillas	nag	right
greed	frog	games	gymnast	dog

Letter "g" is silent	Letter "g" has the /g/ or /j/ sound
sign	dog
wiggle	gum
juggle	frog
right	good
light	nag
though	greed
align	signal
cologne	games
resign	gorillas
campaign	gymnast

Answer Key

 Name: _____ Date: ___/___/_____ Score: _____

The Reading Challenge

Lesson 7.8

Reading Multisyllable Words

✓ Lesson Check Point

 Directions: Read and divide each target word into syllables. Write each word and place a hyphen (-) between the syllables in the second column. Write the number of syllables in the third column. Use a dictionary or the Internet to check your answers.

지도: 각 대상 단어를 읽고 음절로 나눕니다. 각 단어를 쓰고 두 번째 열의 음절 사이에 하이픈(-)을 넣습니다. 세 번째 열에 음절 수를 쓰십시오. 사전이나 인터넷을 사용하여 답을 확인하십시오.

Target Words	Words Divided into Syllables	Number of Syllables
1. graduate	grad-u-ate	3
2. gingerly	gin-ger-ly	3
3. getaway	get-a-way	3
4. gigantic	gi-gan-tic	3
5. golden	gold-en	2
6. gourmet	gour-met	2
7. galvanize	gal-van-ize	3
8. grapevine	grape-vine	2
9. generate	gen-er-ate	3
10. garbanzo	gar-ban-zo	3

Assessment

 Name: _____ Date: ___/___/_____ Score: _____

The Reading Challenge

Lesson 7.8

Reading Multisyllable Words

✓ Lesson Check Point

 Directions: Read each target word. Circle the word in the row that is divided correctly into syllables. Use a dictionary or the Internet to check your answers.

지도: 각 대상 단어를 읽으십시오. 음절로 올바르게 나누어진 행에 있는 단어에 동그라미를 치십시오. 사전이나 인터넷을 사용하여 답을 확인하십시오.

Model

| galaxy | a. ga-lax-y | b. gal-ax-y ⭕ | c. gal-a-xy |

1. groundwork	a. gro-undwo-rk	b. ground-work ⭕	c. grou-ndwor-k
2. glorify	a. glo-ri-fy ⭕	b. glor-i-fy	c. glo-rif-y
3. governor	a. gov-er-nor ⭕	b. gov-ern-or	c. go-ver-nor
4. granola	a. gr-ano-la	b. gra-nol-a	c. gra-no-la ⭕
5. gymnastics	a. gym-nas-tics ⭕	b. gy-mnast-ics	c. gym-nast-ics
6. guarantee	a. gua-rant-ee	b. guar-an-tee ⭕	c. guar-ant-ee
7. grandchild	a. gr-andch-ild	b. gr-and-child	c. grand-child ⭕
8. guidance	a. gui-dance	b. guid-an-ce	c. guid-ance ⭕

Answer Key

Name: _____ Date: ___/___/_____ Score: _____

Lesson 7.9

Reading and Writing

Proper and Common Nouns and Adjectives

✓ Lesson Check Point

Directions: Read the words in the word box. Put an (X) on the line next to each word that is written incorrectly. Remember that all proper nouns and proper adjectives are capitalized. Use a dictionary or the Internet to check your answers.

지도: 단어 상자에 있는 단어를 읽으십시오. 잘못 쓰여진 각 단어 옆의 줄에 (X)를 표시하십시오. 모든 고유 명사와 고유 형용사는 대문자임을 기억하십시오. 사전이나 인터넷을 사용하여 답을 확인하십시오.

Word Box		
X guyanese	X Ghetto	__ Gibraltar
__ gondola	__ governor	__ garage
__ German	X Graduate	X Gladiator
X garry	__ gorilla	X great Britain

Directions: Read each unedited sentence and underline the word that is written incorrectly. Write each sentence correctly on the line.

지도: 편집되지 않은 각 문장을 읽고 잘못 쓰여진 단어에 밑줄을 긋습 니다. 각 문장을 줄에 올바르게 쓰십시오.

Model
Ginger and <u>gene</u> are going to Georgetown, Guyana.
<u>Ginger and Gene are going to Georgetown, Guyana.</u>

1. Dr. <u>graham</u> graduated from Georgetown College.
<u>Dr. Graham graduated from Georgetown College.</u>

2. Grandfather was a general in <u>great</u> Britain's army.
<u>Grandfather was a general in Great Britain's army.</u>

3. Mr. and Mrs. Getter lived in the <u>Ghetto</u> for years.
<u>Mr. and Mrs. Getter lived in the ghetto for years.</u>

4. The governor is an active member of our <u>Government</u>.
<u>The governor is an active member of our government.</u>

Assessment

L Name: _____ Date: ___/___/_____ Score: _____

Lesson 8.1

Reading Words with the Letter H/h

✓ Lesson Check Point

Directions: Read each target word. Find the letter "h" and put a check (✓) in the column that identifies its position: beginning, within or end.
지도: 각 대상 단어를 읽으십시오. 문자"h"를 찾아 체크 표시(✓)위치를 식별하는 열에서 시작, 내부 또는 끝.

Target Words	Beginning (First Letter)	Within	End (Last Letter)
1. hair	✓		
2. verandah			✓
3. helping	✓		
4. cheetah			✓
5. Fahrenheit		✓	

Directions: Read each sentence and underline the words that begin with the letter "h." Write all the underlined words in alphabetical order on the lines below.
지도: 각 문장을 읽고"h"로 시작하는 단어에 밑줄을 긋습니다. 밑줄 친 모든 단어를 아래 줄에 알파벳 순서로 쓰십시오.

6. David's farm sells <u>hens</u> and <u>hogs</u>.

7. <u>Hattie</u> likes to dance to <u>hip-hop</u> music.

8. The <u>hermit</u> crab cannot climb up the <u>hill</u>.

9. Danny flew <u>his</u> <u>helicopter</u> to the regional airport.

10. My <u>hairstylist</u>, Gina, works in <u>Harlem</u>, New York.

hairstylist   Harlem   Hattie
helicopter   hens   hermit
hill   his   hip-hop
                     hogs

L Learn To Read English With Directions In Korean   Copyrighted Material

Answer Key

 Name: _____ Date: ___/___/_____ Score: _____

Lesson 8.2

Reading Words with the Letter "h" Combinations:
"sh," "wh," "ch," "th," "rh," "ph" and "gh"

✓ Lesson Check Point

 Directions: Read the target words in the word box. Identify the words with the following letter combinations: "sh," "wh," "ch," "th," "rh," "ph" and "gh." Write the word on the line that shows the position of the letter combination: beginning, within or end.

지도: 단어 상자에 있는 대상 단어를 읽으십시오. "sh," "wh," "ch," "th," "rh," "ph" 및"gh" 문자 조합으로 단어를 식별합니다. 문자 조합의 위치를 나타내는 줄에 단어를 쓰십시오: 시작, 내부 또는 끝.

Target Word Box				
pathway	photos	things	pinwheel	cough
graph	diarrhea	rhyme	myrrh	blemished
with	triumphant	shave	Ghana	impeach
whale	cherries	caught	teachers	accomplish

		Beginning	Within	End
sh		1. shave	2. blemished	3. accomplish
wh		4. whale	5. pinwheel	
ch		6. cherries	7. teachers	8. impeach
th		9. things	10. pathway	11. with
rh		12. rhyme	13. diarrhea	14. myrrh
ph		15. photos	16. triumphant	17. graph
gh		18. Ghana	19. caught	20. cough

Assessment

Name: _____ Date:___/___/_____ Score:_____

Lesson 8.2

Reading Words with the Letter "h" Combinations:
"sh," "wh," "ch," "th," "rh," "ph," "gh" and "sch"

✓ Lesson Check Point

Directions: Read the target words in the word box. Identify the words with the following letter combinations: "sh," "wh," "ch," "th," "rh," "ph," "gh" and "sch." Write the target word that correctly completes each sentence on the line.

지도: 단어 상자에 있는 대상 단어를 읽습니다: "sh," "wh," "ch," "th," "rh," "ph," "gh" 및 "sch"의 문자 조합으로 단어를 식별합니다. 각 문장을 올바르게 완성하는 대상 단어를 줄에 쓰십시오.

Target Word Box		
whistling	enough	scheduled
show	graph	Rhinos
physics		anchor
wheelchair		phone

1. __Rhinos_____ are large animals with two horns.

2. The captain threw the boat's ____anchor_____ overboard.

3. Mr. Sherman called his brother on the _____phone_____.

4. Shelly and Bobby are _____whistling_____ to the loud music.

5. The clown brought ____enough____ balloons for all the children.

6. They used the survey information to draw a bar ____graph____.

7. The students are ____scheduled____ to start school at nine o'clock.

8. After breaking his leg, Charles had to use a ____wheelchair____.

9. All the children are performing in the school's talent ____show____.

10. Chemistry and ____physics____ are required undergraduate courses.

Answer Key

 Name: _____ Date:___/___/_____ Score:_____

Lesson 8.3

Reading Words with a Silent Letter "h"

✓ Lesson Check Point

 Directions: Read the target words in the word box. Write the words that have a silent letter "h" in the first column. Write the words that do not have a silent letter "h" in the second column.

지도: 단어 상자에 있는 대상 단어를 읽습니다. 첫 번째 열에 묵음문자 "h"가 있는 단어를 쓰십시오. 두 번째 열에 묵음 문자"h"가 없는 단어를 쓰십시오.

Target Word Box				
exhaust	hour	hurting	helpful	statehood
inhale	rhubarb	why	honesty	Thailand
heir	unhook	exhaustion	rehearsal	ghost
hope	hammer	hairy	inhabitant	vehicle

Letter "h" is silent

- why
- heir
- hour
- ghost
- vehicle
- exhaust
- honesty
- Thailand
- rhubarb
- exhaustion

Letter "h" has the /h/ sound

- inhale
- hope
- hairy
- unhook
- hurting
- hammer
- helpful
- rehearsal
- inhabitant
- statehood

Assessment

 Name: _____ Date: ___/___/_____ Score: _____

The Reading Challenge

Lesson 8.4

Reading Multisyllable Words

✓ Lesson Check Point

 Directions: Read and divide each target word into syllables. Write each word and place a hyphen (-) between the syllables in the second column. Write the number of syllables in the third column. Use a dictionary or the Internet to check your answers.

지도: 각 대상 단어를 읽고 음절로 나눕니다. 각 단어를 쓰고 두 번째 열의 음절 사이에 하이픈(-)을 넣습니다. 세 번째 열에 음절 수를 쓰십시오. 사전이나 인터넷을 사용하여 답을 확인하십시오.

Target Words	Words Divided into Syllables	Number of Syllables
1. hesitate	hes-i-tate	3
2. horizon	ho-ri-zon	3
3. healthy	health-y	2
4. hospital	hos-pi-tal	3
5. helpful	help-ful	2
6. hypocrite	hyp-o-crite	3
7. honestly	hon-est-ly	3
8. heavenly	heav-en-ly	3
9. hamburger	ham-bur-ger	3
10. headquarters	head-quar-ters	3

Answer Key

Name: _____ Date: ___/___/_____ Score: _____

The Reading Challenge

Lesson 8.4

Reading Multisyllable Words

✓ Lesson Check Point

Directions: Read each target word. Circle the word in the row that is divided correctly into syllables. Use a dictionary or the Internet to check your answers.
지도: 각 대상 단어를 읽으십시오. 음절로 올바르게 나누어진 행에 있는 단어에 동그라미를 치십시오. 사전이나 인터넷을 사용하여 답을 확인하십시오.

Model

| heroic | a. he-roi-c | b. her-o-ic | c. he-ro-ic ⭕ |

1. habitual	a. hab-it-u-al	b. ha-bit-u-al ⭕	c. hab-i-tu-al
2. honesty	a. hon-es-ty ⭕	b. ho-nest-y	c. hon-e-sty
3. Hispanic	a. Hi-span-ic	b. His-pa-nic	c. His-pan-ic ⭕
4. Halifax	a. Hal-if-ax	b. Hal-i-fax ⭕	c. Ha-li-fax
5. helium	a. hel-i-um	b. hel-iu-m	c. he-li-um ⭕
6. hamburger	a. hamb-ur-ger	b. ham-burg-er ⭕	c. ham-bur-ger
7. history	a. his-tor-y	b. his-to-ry ⭕	c. hi-stor-y
8. handlebar	a. han-dle-bar ⭕	b. hand-leb-ar	c. hand-le-bar

Learn To Read English With Directions In Korean

Assessment

L Name: _____ Date: ___/___/_____ Score: _____

Lesson 8.5

Reading and Writing

Proper and Common Nouns and Adjectives

✓ Lesson Check Point

Directions: Read the words in the word box. Put an (X) on the line next to each word that is written incorrectly. Remember that all proper nouns and proper adjectives are capitalized. Use a dictionary or the Internet to check your answers.

지도: 단어 상자에 있는 단어를 읽으십시오. 잘못 쓰여진 각 단어 옆의 줄에 (X)를 표시하십시오. 모든 고유 명사와 고유 형용사는 대문자임을 기억하십시오. 사전이나 인터넷을 사용하여 답을 확인하십시오.

Word Box					
_X_	hatcHet	___	home	_X_	Healthy
___	Harlem	_X_	Hills	___	houses
___	hint	___	Haiti	_X_	hawaii
_X_	History	___	heart	_X_	Hotel

Directions: Read each unedited sentence and underline the word that is written incorrectly. Write each sentence correctly on the line.

지도: 편집되지 않은 각 문장을 읽고 잘못 쓰여진 단어에 밑줄을 긋습 니다. 각 문장을 줄에 올바르게 쓰십시오.

Model
Mr. Hitt has a big house on <u>hope</u> Avenue.
<u>Mr. Hitt has a big house on Hope Avenue.</u>

1. Mrs. Harley was honored in <u>hollywood</u>.
<u>Mrs. Harley was honored in Hollywood.</u>

2. I am <u>Hiking</u> up the hill to the Halifax Hotel.
<u>I am hiking up the hill to the Halifax Hotel.</u>

3. Harriet's class went to <u>hartway</u> Horse Stable.
<u>Harriet's class went to Hartway Horse Stable.</u>

4. I am learning interesting facts about <u>hispanic</u> history.
<u>I am learning interesting facts about Hispanic history.</u>

Answer Key

 Name: _____ Date: ___/___/_____ Score: _____

Lesson 9.1

Reading Words with the Letter I/i

✓ Lesson Check Point

 Directions: Read each target word. Find the letter "i" and put a check (✓) in the column that identifies its position: beginning, within or end.
지도: 각 대상 단어를 읽으십시오. 문자"i"를 찾아 체크 표시(✓)위치 를 식별하는 열에서 시작, 내부 또는 끝.

Target Words	Beginning (First Letter)	Within	End (Last Letter)
1. deli			✓
2. bite		✓	
3. circle		✓	
4. impress	✓		
5. important	✓		

 Directions: Read each target word. Read the words in the row and circle the word that has a different vowel "i" sound.
지도: 각 대상 단어를 읽으십시오. 행에 있는 단어를 읽고 모음"i" 소리가 다른 단어에 동그라미를 치십시오.

Target Words				
6. list	brink	(dime)	crick	dill
7. chip	kick	limp	disk	(like)
8. bill	(mild)	him	bring	dig
9. clip	drip	blink	grip	(pint)
10. miss	cling	(fine)	his	bin

Assessment

 Name: _____ Date: ___/___/_____ Score: _____

Lesson 9.2

Reading Words with the Short Vowel "i" Sound

✓ **Lesson Check Point**

 Directions: Read the words in the four boxes. Circle two words with the short vowel /ĭ/ sound. The anchor word for the short vowel /ĭ/ sound is insect.
지도: 네 개의 상자에 있는 단어를 읽으십시오. 짧은 모음/ĭ/ 소리로 두 단어에 동그라미를 치십시오. 단모음/ĭ/ 소리의 기준어는 insect입니다.

side	(kick)		mine	(lit)		(wig)	(tin)
lice	(fish)		(mix)	rise		item	price

(rim)	wise		smile	lime		(rip)	time
idea	(tip)		(pig)	(kid)		drive	(his)

 Directions: Read the words in the four boxes. Circle two words that rhyme. Rhyming words have the same ending sound, such as hip and dip.
지도: 네 개의 상자에 있는 단어를 읽으십시오. 운이 맞는 두 단어에 동그라미를 치십시오. 운율이 있는 단어는 hip와dip과 같이 끝 소리가같습니다.

slice	(milk)		(hint)	spite		(disk)	fine
(silk)	vine		(mint)	pride		(risk)	white

tile	site		(sink)	Mike		(bill)	(hill)
(sick)	(pick)		wide	(pink)		nine	five

Answer Key

Name: _____ Date: ___/___/_____ Score: _____

Lesson 9.2

Reading & Writing Words with the Short Vowel "i" Sound

✓ **Lesson Check Point**

Directions: Read each sentence and underline three words with the short vowel /ĭ/ sound. Then, write the underlined words on the lines below. The anchor word for the short vowel /ĭ/ sound is <u>insect</u>.

지도: 각 문장을 읽고 세 단어에 짧은 모음/ĭ/ 소리에 밑줄을 긋습니다. 그런 다음 밑줄 친 단어를 아래 줄에 쓰십시오. 단모음/ĭ/ 소리의 기준어는 insect입니다.

Model

<u>Jim</u> placed a <u>big</u> cup of ice on the <u>windowsill</u>.

    Jim   big   windowsill

1. The baby <u>in</u> the <u>crib</u> has white <u>milk</u>.

    in   crib   milk

2. The <u>wind</u> <u>lifted</u> Mike's kite <u>into</u> the sky.

    wind   lifted   into

3. At night, the <u>twins</u> are <u>in</u> their <u>cribs</u>.

    twins   in   cribs

4. James <u>will</u> <u>win</u> the grand prize for <u>swimming</u>.

    will   win   swimming

5. Dad said, "Be careful not to <u>slip</u> <u>into</u> the wide <u>pit</u>."

    slip   into   pit

Assessment

 Name: _____ Date: ___/___/_____ Score: _____

Lesson 9.3

Reading Words with the Long Vowel "i" Sound

✓ **Lesson Check Point**

 Directions: Read the words in the four boxes. Circle two words with the long vowel /ī/ sound. The anchor word for the long vowel /ī/ sound is ice.
지도: 네 개의 상자에 있는 단어를 읽으십시오. 장모음/ī/ 소리로두단어에 동그라미를 치십시오. 장모음/ī/ 소리의 기준어는 ice입니다.

| ring | (dive) | vain | (like) | pill | (jive) |
| size | drip | wink | (idea) | grain | (slice) |

| ring | (dive) | vain | (like) | pill | (jive) |
| (size) | drip | wink | (idea) | grain | (slice) |

| (crime) | (rice) | pinch | tint | (hike) | (lime) |
| fish | plain | (wipe) | (smile) | dish | silk |

 Directions: Read the words in the four boxes. Circle two words that rhyme. Rhyming words have the same ending sound, such as rice and nice.
지도: 네 개의 상자에 있는 단어를 읽으십시오. 운이 맞는 두 단어에동그라미를 치십시오. 운율이 있는 단어는 rice와 nice와 같은 끝 소리가같습니다.

| (fire) | will | gift | (rise) | (five) | hill |
| (tire) | mint | (wise) | wick | (dive) | fist |

| hint | tilt | limp | (wire) | list | risk |
| (wipe) | (pipe) | mink | (hire) | (ride) | (side) |

Answer Key

L Name: _____ Date: ___/___/_____ Score: _____

Lesson 9.3

Reading & Writing Words with the Long Vowel "i" Sound

✓ **Lesson Check Point**

Directions: Read each sentence and underline three words with the long vowel /ī/ sound. Then, write the underlined words on the lines below. The anchor word for the long vowel /ī/ sound is ice.
지도: 각 문장을 읽고 장모음/ī/ 소리로 세 단어에 밑줄을 긋습니다. 그런 다음 밑줄 친 단어를 아래 줄에 쓰십시오. 장모음/ī/ 소리의 기준어는 ice 입니다.

Model

David and <u>I</u> flew our big, <u>white</u> <u>kite</u> along the riverbank.

| I | white | kite |

1. At <u>night</u>, the big <u>island</u> comes <u>alive</u>.

| night | island | alive |

2. Timothy <u>likes</u> to <u>drive</u> his car on the <u>highway</u>.

| likes | drive | highway |

3. Our friend will win a <u>prize</u> for <u>biking</u> six <u>miles</u>.

| prize | biking | miles |

4. The <u>bride</u> will <u>smile</u> as she walks down the <u>aisle</u>.

| bride | smile | aisle |

5. The <u>divers</u> were instructed not to <u>dive</u> into the pool at <u>night</u>.

| divers | dive | night |

Assessment

Name: _____ Date: ___/___/_____ Score: _____

Review Lessons 9.2 & 9.3

Reading Short Vowel and Long Vowel Words

✓ **Lesson Check Point**

Directions: Read the target words in the word box. In the first column, write the words that have the short vowel /ĭ/ sound, as in the word <u>insect</u>. In the second column, write the words that have the long vowel /ī/ sound, as in the word <u>ice</u>.

지도: 단어 상자에 있는 대상 단어를 읽습니다. 첫 번째 열에는 insect라는 단어와 같이 단모음/ĭ/ 소리가 나는 단어를 씁니다. 두 번째 열에는 ice 라는 단어에서처럼 장모음/ī/ 소리가 나는 단어를 씁니다.

Target Word Box				
dime	hill	lift	drip	hid
bib	tie	silent	fin	wild
clip	dip	find	pick	bite
spider	light	this	pint	like

Letter "i" has the /ĭ/ sound as in the word <u>insect</u>

- hill
- lift
- drip
- hid
- bib
- fin
- clip
- dip
- pick
- this

Letter "i" has the /ī/ sound as in the word <u>ice</u>

- dime
- tie
- silent
- wild
- find
- bite
- spider
- light
- pint
- like

Answer Key

 Name: _____ Date: ___/___/_____ Score: _____

Lesson 9.4

Reading Words with Letter "i" Vowel Pairs

✓ **Lesson Check Point**

 Directions: Read each target word. Circle the word in the column that has the same vowel "ia," "ie," "io" or "iu" sound(s) as the target word.
지도: 각 대상 단어를 읽으십시오. 대상 단어와 같은 모음 "ia," "ie," "io" 또는 "iu" 소리가 있는 열의 단어에 동그라미를 치십시오.

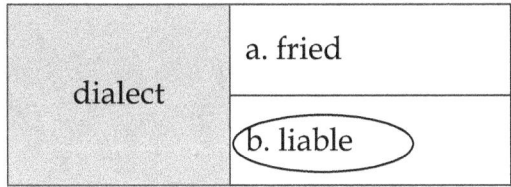

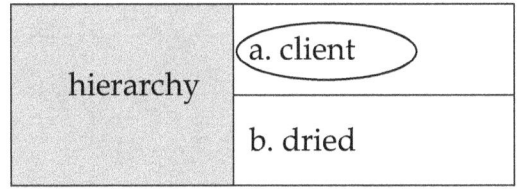

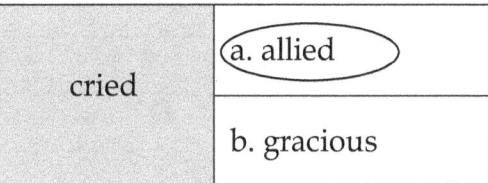

 Directions: Read each target word. Put a check (✓) under the correct column heading.
지도: 각 대상 단어를 읽으십시오. 올바른 열 제목 아래에 체크(✓)를 하십시오.

Target Words	Words have the long "i" sound as in the word <u>dial</u>	Words do not have the long "i" sound
1. dialect	✓	
2. spacious		✓
3. hierarchy	✓	
4. cried	✓	

Assessment

 Name: _____ Date: ___/___/_____ Score: _____

Lesson 9.5

Reading Words with the Final Letter "i"

✓ Lesson Check Point

 Directions: Read each target word. Find the letter "i" and put a check (✓) in the column that identifies its position within the syllable.
지도: 각 대상 단어를 읽으십시오. 문자"i"를 찾아 체크 표시(✓)음절내에서 위치를 식별하는 열에서.

Target Words	"i" is at the end of a one syllable word	"i" is at the end of the first syllable	"i" is at the end of a multi-syllable word
1. hi	✓		
2. anti			✓
3. bias		✓	
4. direct		✓	
5. Bengali			✓

 Directions: Read each target word. Put a check (✓) under the correct column heading.
지도: 각 대상 단어를 읽으십시오. 올바른 열 제목 아래에 체크(✓)를하십시오.

Target Words	"i" has the /ĭ/ sound as in the word <u>insect</u>	"i" has the /ī/ sound as in the word <u>bike</u>	"i" has the /ə/ sound as in the word <u>pencil</u>	"i" is silent as in the word <u>maid</u>
6. limit	✓			
7. right		✓		
8. mortify			✓	
9. Jamaica				✓
10. utensil			✓	

Answer Key

 Name: _____ Date: ___/___/_____ Score: _____

Lesson 9.6

Reading Letter "i" Words with the Schwa Vowel Sound

✓ Lesson Check Point

 Directions: Read each target word. Circle the word in the column that has the same "i" sound as the target word.
지도: 각 대상 단어를 읽으십시오. 목표 단어와 동일한"i" 소리가 나는 열의 단어에 동그라미를 치십시오.

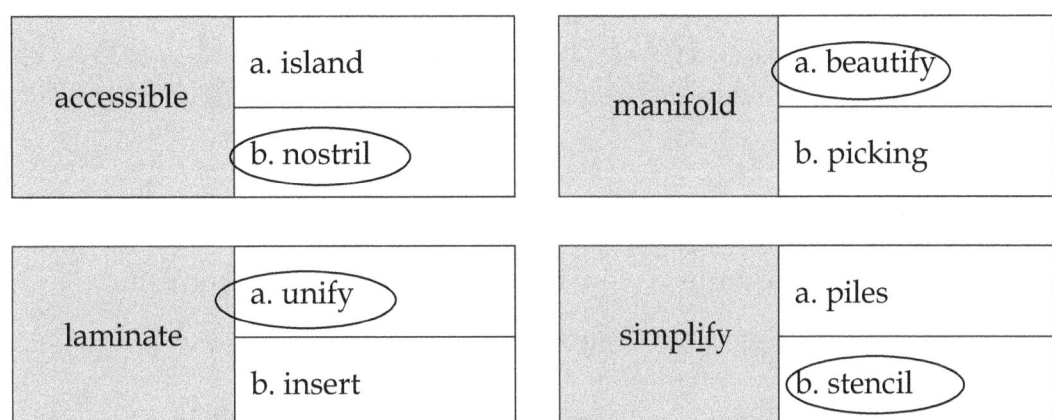

 Directions: Read each sentence and underline the letter "i" word that has the schwa vowel /ə/ sound. The anchor word for the letter "i" schwa vowel sound is pencil.
지도: 각 문장을 읽고 슈와 모음 /ə/ 소리가 있는 문자"i" 단어에 밑줄을 긋습니다. 문자"i" 슈와 모음 소리의 앵커 단어는 pencil입니다.

1. My family enjoys ice skating and skiing.

2. The hotels have similar cancellation policies.

3. The five nominees have interesting points of view.

4. The warm bottle of milk will pacify the crying baby.

5. The doctor will notify the interns about the procedures.

6. The president of Mexico delivered an incredible inauguration speech.

Assessment

Name: _____ Date: ___/___/_____ Score: _____

Lesson 9.7

Reading Words with the "ir" Letter Combination

Dictionary Skills/ Vocabulary

✓ **Lesson Check Point**

Directions: Read each target word and its definition. Write the letter of the definition on the line of each target word. Use a dictionary or the Internet to check your answers.

지도: 각 대상 단어와 그 정의를 읽으십시오. 각 대상 단어의 행에 정의의 문자를 씁니다. 사전이나 인터넷을 사용하여 답을 확인하십시오.

Target Words	Definitions
1. _d_ squirms	a. having a desire to drink something
2. _b_ girls	b. young females
3. _e_ stirs	c. something hard to the touch
4. _c_ firm	d. to slowly move in response to something
5. _a_ thirsty	e. the use of circular motions to mix or blend

Directions: Read each sentence and write the target word that completes the sentence.

지도: 각 문장을읽고 다음과 같은 목표 단어를 쓰십시오. 장을올바르게 완성합니다.

6. She _____squirms_____ at the sight of blood.

7. The _____thirsty_____ girl drank a glass of water.

8. The apples on the kitchen counter are _____firm_____.

9. All the _____girls_____ in my class are wearing pretty dresses.

10. Jane _____stirs_____ thirteen chocolate chips into the ice cream.

Answer Key

 Name: _____ Date: ___/___/_____ Score: _____

Lesson 9.8

Reading Letter "i" Words with the Long Vowel "e" Sound

✓ **Lesson Check Point**

 Directions: Read each target word. Circle the word in the column that has the same "i" sound as the target word.
지도: 각 대상 단어를 읽으십시오. 목표 단어와 동일한 "i" 소리가 나는 열의 단어에 동그라미를 치십시오.

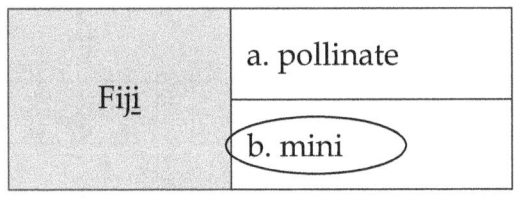
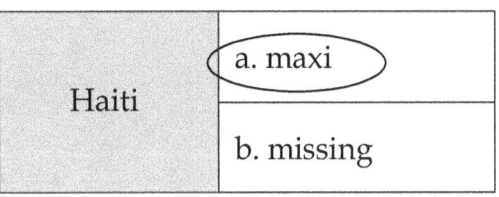
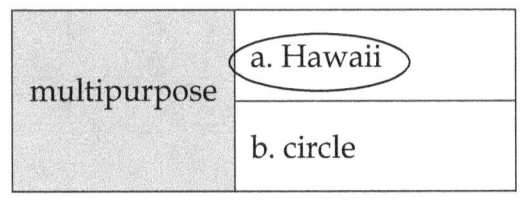
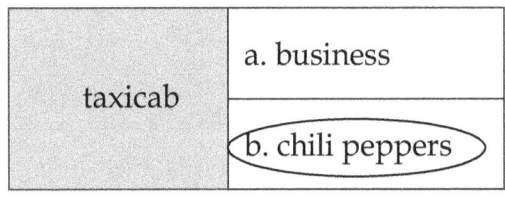

 Directions: Read each sentence and underline the letter "i" word that has the long vowel /ē/ sound. Then, write the word on the line. The anchor word, taxi has a letter "i" that has the long vowel /ē/ sound.
지도: 각 문장을 읽고 장모음 /ē/ 소리가 나는 "i" 단어에 밑줄을 긋습니다. 그런 다음 줄에 단어를 쓰십시오. 앵커 단어인 taxi에는 장모음 /ē/ 소리를 나타내는 문자 "i"가 있습니다.

1. I am planning a fun-filled trip to <u>Malawi</u>.   <u>Malawi</u>

2. The children like to eat <u>broccoli</u> with cheese.   <u>broccoli</u>

3. This summer, Keith is going to <u>Mississippi</u>.   <u>Mississippi</u>

4. Since I am on a diet, I will only eat five <u>mini</u> muffins.   <u>mini</u>

5. Levi will join our school's <u>intermediate</u> diving team.   <u>intermediate</u>

6. On Saturdays, I enjoy looking at <u>Punjabi</u> music videos. <u>Punjabi</u>

Learn To Read English With Directions In Korean

Assessment

Name: _____ Date: ___/___/_____ Score: _____

Lesson 9.9

Reading Words with a Silent Letter "i"

✓ **Lesson Check Point**

Directions: Read the target words in the word box. Write the words that have a silent letter "i" in the first column. Write the words that do not have a silent letter "i" in the second column.

지도: 단어 상자에 있는 대상 단어를 읽습니다. 첫 번째 열에 묵음문자 "i"가 있는 단어를 쓰십시오. 두 번째 열에 묵음 문자"i"가 없는 단어를 쓰십시오.

Target Word Box				
middle	digits	Jamaica	nail	obtaining
stains	bait	print	insisting	aimed
suitable	conflict	nice	suits	bills
inside	bike	details	five	business

Letter "i" is silent	Letter "i" has a letter "i" sound
suits	bills
stains	five
bait	digits
nail	nice
aimed	bike
details	print
business	conflict
suitable	inside
Jamaica	middle
obtaining	insisting

Answer Key

 Name: _____ Date: ___/___/_____ Score: _____

Unit Review - I/i

Reading Words with Vowel "i" Sounds: /ĭ/, /ī/, /ə/ & Silent

✓ Lesson Check Point

 Directions: Read each target word. Circle the word in the column that has the same "i" sound as the target word.
지도: 각 대상 단어를 읽으십시오. 목표 단어와 동일한"i" 소리가 나는 열의 단어에 동그라미를 치십시오.

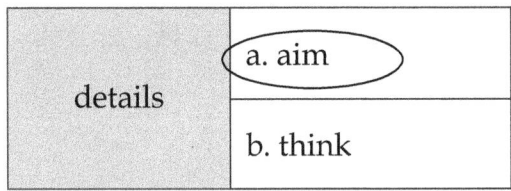
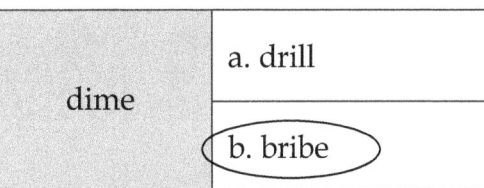
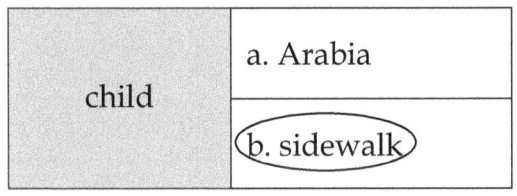
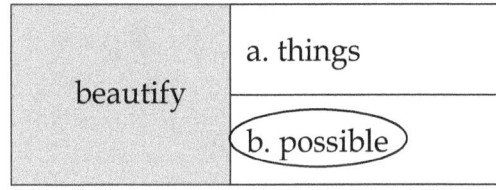

 Directions: Read each target word. Put a check (✓) under the correct column heading.
지도: 각 대상 단어를 읽으십시오. 올바른 열 제목 아래에 체크(✓)를 하십시오.

Target Words	"i" has the /ĭ/ sound as in the word <u>insect</u>	"i" has the /ī/ sound as in the word <u>bike</u>	"i" has the /ə/ sound as in the word <u>pencil</u>	"i" is silent as in the word <u>maid</u>
1. details				✓
2. dime		✓		
3. child		✓		
4. beautify			✓	

Assessment

Name: _____ Date: ___/___/_____ Score: _____

The Reading Challenge

Lesson 9.10

Reading Multisyllable Words

✓ Lesson Check Point

Directions: Read and divide each target word into syllables. Write each word and place a hyphen (-) between the syllables in the second column. Write the number of syllables in the third column. Use a dictionary or the Internet to check your answers.

지도: 각 대상 단어를 읽고 음절로 나눕니다. 각 단어를 쓰고 두 번째 열의 음절 사이에 하이픈(-)을 넣습니다. 세 번째 열에 음절 수를 쓰십시오. 사전이나 인터넷을 사용하여 답을 확인하십시오.

Target Words	Words Divided into Syllables	Number of Syllables
1. align	a-lign	2
2. miner	min-er	2
3. notion	no-tion	2
4. highly	high-ly	2
5. lighting	light-ing	2
6. itemized	i-tem-ized	3
7. diverting	di-vert-ing	3
8. optional	op-tion-al	3
9. anxiously	anx-ious-ly	3
10. midnight	mid-night	2

Answer Key

 Name: _____   Date: ___/___/_____   Score: _____

The Reading Challenge

Lesson 9.10

Reading Multisyllable Words

✓ Lesson Check Point

 Directions: Read each target word. Circle the word in the row that is divided correctly into syllables. Use a dictionary or the Internet to check your answers.
지도: 각 대상 단어를 읽으십시오. 음절로 올바르게 나누어진 행에 있는 단어에 동그라미를 치십시오. 사전이나 인터넷을 사용하여 답을 확인하십시오.

Model

| interesting | a. (in-ter-est-ing) | b. int-er-est-ing | c. inte-rest-ing |

1. interview	a. int-e-rview	b. (in-ter-view)	c. int-er-view
2. crazier	a. (cra-zi-er)	b. craz-i-er	c. cr-a-zier
3. opinion	a. (o-pin-ion)	b. op-i-nion	c. o-pi-nion
4. vacation	a. vac-at-ion	b. va-cat-ion	c. (va-ca-tion)
5. radiate	a. rad-i-ate	b. (ra-di-ate)	c. ra-dia-te
6. regional	a. reg-ion-al	b. (re-gion-al)	c. re-gio-nal
7. interact	a. int-er-act	b. int-e-ract	c. (in-ter-act)
8. tradition	a. (tra-di-tion)	b. tra-dit-ion	c. trad-iti-on

Assessment

Name: _____ Date:___/___/_____ Score: _____

Lesson 9.11

Reading and Writing

Proper and Common Nouns and Adjectives

✓ **Lesson Check Point**

Directions: Read the words in the word box. Put an (X) on the line next to each word that is written incorrectly. Remember that all proper nouns and proper adjectives are capitalized. Use a dictionary or the Internet to check your answers.

지도: 단어 상자에 있는 단어를 읽으십시오. 잘못 쓰여진 각 단어 옆의 줄에 (X)를 표시하십시오. 모든 고유 명사와 고유 형용사는 대문자임을 기억하십시오. 사전이나 인터넷을 사용하여 답을 확인하십시오.

Word Box					
__	impression	X	Inoperative	X	Independent
X	Intestines	__	Iron Age	__	indulgence
X	italian	X	isle of France	__	Indian
__	idealistic	__	irresponsible	X	italy

Directions: Read each unedited sentence and underline the word that is written incorrectly. Write each sentence correctly on the line.

지도: 편집되지 않은 각 문장을 읽고 잘못 쓰여진 단어에 밑줄을 긋습니다. 각 문장을 줄에 올바르게 쓰십시오.

Model
New Delhi and Indore are beautiful cities in <u>india</u>.
<u>New Delhi and Indore are beautiful cities in India.</u>

1. In the afternoon, Irene <u>Introduced</u> me to Ian.
<u>In the afternoon, Irene introduced me to Ian.</u>

2. Mr. <u>iston</u> drove along Interstate 65 to Indiana.
<u>Mr. Iston drove along Interstate 65 to Indiana.</u>

3. Did you know that <u>Iron</u> was developed during the Iron Age?
<u>Did you know that iron was developed during the Iron Age?</u>

4. Idama is studying the <u>industrial</u> Revolution at the institute.
<u>Idama is studying the Industrial Revolution at the institute.</u>

Answer Key

Name: _____ Date: ___/___/_____ Score: _____

Lesson 10.1

Reading Words with the Letter J/j

✓ Lesson Check Point

Directions: Read each target word. Find the letter "j" and put a check (✓) in the column that identifies its position: beginning, within or end.
지도: 각 대상 단어를 읽으십시오. 문자"j"를 찾아 체크 표시(✓)위치를 식별하는 열에서 시작, 내부 또는 끝.

Target Words	Beginning (First Letter)	Within	End (Last Letter)
1. eject		✓	
2. jeans	✓		
3. join	✓		
4. judge	✓		
5. conjure		✓	

Directions: Read each sentence and underline the words that begin with the letter "j." Write all the underlined words in alphabetical order on the lines below.
지도: 각 문장을 읽고"j"로 시작하는 단어에 밑줄을 긋습니다. 밑줄 친 모든 단어를 아래 줄에 알파벳 순서로 쓰십시오.

6. Last Friday, <u>Jordan</u> ate too much <u>junk</u> food.

7. I bought a <u>jeweled</u> chain at the <u>jewelry</u> store.

8. Ms. <u>Jasmine</u> always eats <u>jerk</u> chicken for dinner.

9. Everyone in the <u>jazz</u> band wore sky blue <u>jackets</u>.

10. Bobby is reading a book about <u>jackals</u> and <u>jaguars</u>.

jackals   jackets   jaguars
Jasmine   jazz   jerk
jeweled   jewelry   Jordon
                 junk

Assessment

 Name: _____ Date: ___/___/_____ Score: _____

The Reading Challenge

Lesson 10.2

Reading Multisyllable Words

✓ Lesson Check Point

 Directions: Read and divide each target word into syllables. Write each word and place a hyphen (-) between the syllables in the second column. Write the number of syllables in the third column. Use a dictionary or the Internet to check your answers.

지도: 각 대상 단어를 읽고 음절로 나눕니다. 각 단어를 쓰고 두 번째 열의 음절 사이에 하이픈(-)을 넣습니다. 세 번째 열에 음절 수를 쓰십시오. 사전이나 인터넷을 사용하여 답을 확인하십시오.

Target Words	Words Divided into Syllables	Number of Syllables
1. java	ja-va	2
2. jury	jur-y	2
3. jostle	jos-tle	2
4. jangle	jan-gle	2
5. jumble	jum-ble	2
6. jargon	jar-gon	2
7. jacket	jack-et	2
8. jester	jest-er	2
9. justly	just-ly	2
10. jockey	jock-ey	2

Answer Key

Name: _____ Date: ___/___/_____ Score: _____

The Reading Challenge

Lesson 10.2

Reading Multisyllable Words

✓ Lesson Check Point

Directions: Read each target word. Circle the word in the row that is divided correctly into syllables. Use a dictionary or the Internet to check your answers.
지도: 각 대상 단어를 읽으십시오. 음절로 올바르게 나누어진 행에 있는 단어에 동그라미를 치십시오. 사전이나 인터넷을 사용하여 답을 확인하십시오.

Model

| janitor | a. ja-ni-tor | b. jan-it-or | c. jan-i-tor ⭕ |

1. jocular	a. jo-cu-lar	b. joc-u-lar ⭕	c. joc-ul-ar
2. juxtapose	a. juxt-a-pose	b. jux-ta-pose ⭕	c. jux-tap-ose
3. jeopardize	a. jeo-pard-ize	b. je-opar-dize	c. jeop-ard-ize ⭕
4. jewelry	a. jew-el-ry ⭕	b. je-wel-r-y	c. jewel-ry
5. jealousy	a. jea-lou-sy	b. jeal-ous-y ⭕	c. jeal-ou-sy
6. Jupiter	a. Jup-i-ter	b. Ju-pi-ter ⭕	c. Ju-pit-er
7. jointly	a. joint-ly ⭕	b. joi-ntly	c. jo-intly
8. jokingly	a. jo-kingl-y	b. jok-ing-ly ⭕	c. jok-in-gly

Assessment

Name: _____ Date: ___/___/_____ Score: _____

Lesson 10.3

Reading and Writing

Proper and Common Nouns and Adjectives

✓ Lesson Check Point

Directions: Read the words in the word box. Put an (X) on the line next to each word that is written incorrectly. Remember that all proper nouns and proper adjectives are capitalized. Use a dictionary or the Internet to check your answers.

지도: 단어 상자에 있는 단어를 읽으십시오. 잘못 쓰여진 각 단어 옆의 줄에 (X)를 표시하십시오. 모든 고유 명사와 고유 형용사는 대문자임을 기억하십시오. 사전이나 인터넷을 사용하여 답을 확인하십시오.

Word Box		
X Jump	__ New Jersey	X jamaica
X Joints	__ jumbo	X julia
__ Johnson	X Janitor	__ Jordan
X july	__ Joseph	__ juggle

Directions: Read each unedited sentence and underline the word that is written incorrectly. Write each sentence correctly on the line.

지도: 편집되지 않은 각 문장을 읽고 잘못 쓰여진 단어에 밑줄을 긋습니다. 각 문장을 줄에 올바르게 쓰십시오.

Model
Junior has a book about <u>jupiter</u> and Earth.
Junior has a book about Jupiter and Earth.

1. John will join the <u>Jazz</u> band.
John will join the jazz band.

2. Joy and <u>jasmine</u> saw a jellyfish.
Joy and Jasmine saw a jellyfish.

3. Joey likes to juggle his <u>Jellybeans</u>.
Joey likes to juggle his jellybeans.

4. <u>june</u> said, "It is not healthy to eat junk food."
June said, "It is not healthy to eat junk food."

Answer Key

Name: _____   Date: ___/___/_____   Score: _____

Lesson 11.1

Reading Words with the Letter K/k

✓ Lesson Check Point

Directions: Read each target word. Find the letter "k" and put a check (✓) in the column that identifies its position: beginning, within or end.
지도: 각 대상 단어를 읽으십시오. 문자"k"를 찾아 체크 표시(✓)위치를 식별하는 열에서 시작, 내부 또는 끝.

Target Words	Beginning (First Letter)	Within	End (Last Letter)
1. joker		✓	
2. mask			✓
3. keep	✓		
4. kennel	✓		
5. parking		✓	

Directions: Read each sentence and underline the words that begin with the letter "k." Write all the underlined words in alphabetical order on the lines below.
지도: 각 문장을 읽고 문자"k"로 시작하는 단어에 밑줄을 긋습니다. 밑줄 친 모든 단어를 아래 줄에 알파벳 순서로 쓰십시오.

6. Carolyn puts <u>ketchup</u> on her <u>knish</u>.

7. <u>Karen</u> said, "<u>Kiwi</u> is a delicious fruit."

8. The excited campers went <u>kayaking</u> in <u>Key</u> Largo.

9. Mr. <u>Keys</u> said to <u>knock</u> on the door before entering.

10. Children are not allowed to play with <u>kitchen</u> <u>knives</u>.

<u>Karen</u>   <u>kayaking</u>   <u>ketchup</u>
<u>Key</u>   <u>Keys</u>   <u>kitchen</u>
<u>Kiwi</u>   <u>knish</u>   <u>knives</u>
               <u>knock</u>

Assessment

 Name: _____ Date: ___/___/_____ Score: _____

Lesson 11.2

Reading Words with the Letter "k" and "ck" Letter Combination

✓ Lesson Check Point

 Directions: Read each target word. Put a check (✓) in the second column if the target word has one vowel. Put a check (✓) in the third column if the target word has two vowels.

지도: 각 대상 단어를 읽으십시오. 대상 단어에 모음이 하나 있는 경우 두 번째 열에 체크(✓)를 합니다. 대상 단어에 두 개의 모음이 있는경우제삼 열에 체크(✓)를 합니다.

Target Words	Words with 1 Vowel	Words with 2 Vowels
1. cheek		✓
2. joke		✓
3. rock	✓	
4. rake		✓
5. stock	✓	

 Directions: Read each target word in the first column and write the number of vowels within the word in the second column. Read each target word in the third column and write the number of vowels within the word in the fourth column.

지도: 첫 번째 열의 각 대상 단어를 읽고 두 번째 열의 단어 내 모음 수를 쓰십시오. 세 번째 열의 각 대상 단어를 읽고 네 번째 열의 단어에 포함된 모음의 수를 쓰십시오.

Target Words	Number of Vowels	Target Words	Number of Vowels
6. stoke	2	stock	1
7. snake	2	snack	1
8. Luke	2	luck	1
9. rack	1	rake	2
10. lack	1	lake	2

Answer Key

 Name: _____ Date:___/___/_____ Score:_____

Lesson 11.3

Reading Words with the "kle" Letter Combination

✓ Lesson Check Point

 Directions: Read each target word. Find the "kle" letter combination and put a check (✓) in the column that identifies its position: beginning, within or end.

지도: 각 대상 단어를 읽으십시오. "kle" 문자 조합을 찾아 해당 위치를 식별하는 열에 체크(✓)를 하십시오: 시작, 내부 또는 끝.

Target Words	Beginning (First 3 Letters)	Within	End (Last 3 Letters)
1. suckle			✓
2. crinkle			✓
3. trickled		✓	
4. speckle			✓
5. kleptomaniacs	✓		

 Directions: Read each target word. Put a check (✓) in the "yes" column if the "kle" letter combination has the /k/ + /ə/ + /l/ sounds. Put a check (✓) in the "no" column if the "kle" letter combination does not have the /k/ + /ə/ + /l/ sounds.

지도: 각 대상 단어를 읽으십시오. "kle" 문자 조합에/k/ + /ə/ + /l/ 소리가있으 면"yes" 열에 체크(✓)를 하십시오. "kle" 문자 조합에/k/ + /ə/ + /l/ 소리가없으 면"no" 열에 체크(✓)를 하십시오.

Target Words	Yes	No
6. suckle	✓	
7. crinkle	✓	
8. trickled	✓	
9. speckle	✓	
10. kleptomaniacs		✓

Assessment

Name: _____ Date:___/___/_____ Score:_____

Lesson 11.4

Reading Words with a Silent Letter "k"

✓ Lesson Check Point

Directions: Read the target words in the word box. Write the words that have a silent letter "k" in the first column. Write the words that do not have a silent letter "k" in the second column.

지도: 단어 상자에 있는 대상 단어를 읽으십시오. 첫 번째 열에 묵음문자 "k"가 있는 단어를 쓰십시오. 두 번째 열에 묵음 문자"k"가 없는 단어를 쓰십시오.

Target Word Box				
silky	knack	knowledge	kitten	knife
knowingly	shirk	making	kneeling	shrink
koala	milk	knish	kicking	knot
knitting	knead	knights	knock	kebab

Letter "k" is silent

- knot
- knitting
- knack
- knead
- knights
- knife
- knock
- kneeling
- knowingly
- knowledge

Letter "k" has the /k/ sound

- silky
- koala
- shirk
- milk
- knish
- shrink
- kebab
- kitten
- making
- kicking

Answer Key

 Name: _____ Date: ___/___/_____ Score: _____

The Reading Challenge

Lesson 11.5

Reading Multisyllable Words

✓ Lesson Check Point

 Directions: Read and divide each target word into syllables. Write each word and place a hyphen (-) between the syllables in the second column. Write the number of syllables in the third column. Use a dictionary or the Internet to check your answers.

지도: 각 대상 단어를 읽고 음절로 나눕니다. 각 단어를 쓰고 두 번째 열의 음절 사이에 하이픈(-)을 넣습니다. 세 번째 열에 음절 수를 쓰십시오. 사전이나 인터넷을 사용하여 답을 확인하십시오.

Target Words	Words Divided into Syllables	Number of Syllables
1. khaki	khak-i	2
2. kebab	ke-bab	2
3. kidney	kid-ney	2
4. keynote	key-note	2
5. kayaking	kay-ak-ing	3
6. knuckle	knuck-le	2
7. keepsake	keep-sake	2
8. knapsack	knap-sack	2
9. kaleidoscope	ka-lei-do-scope	4
10. kindergarten	kin-der-gar-ten	4

Assessment

Name: _____ Date: ___/___/_____ Score: _____

The Reading Challenge

Lesson 11.5

Reading Multisyllable Words

✓ Lesson Check Point

Directions: Read each target word. Circle the word in the row that is divided correctly into syllables. Use a dictionary or the Internet to check your answers.

지도: 각 대상 단어를 읽으십시오. 음절로 올바르게 나누어진 행에 있는 단어에 동그라미를 치십시오. 사전이나 인터넷을 사용하여 답을확인하십시오.

Model

kangaroo	a. kang-a-roo	b. kan-ga-roo ⭕	c. kan-gar-oo
1. knowingly	a. know-ing-ly ⭕	b. kno-wing-ly	c. know-in-gly
2. kindle	a. ki-ndle	b. kin-dle ⭕	c. kind-le
3. kickback	a. kick-back ⭕	b. ki-ckba-ck	c. ki-ck-back
4. kitchenette	a. ki-tchen-ette	b. kit-chen-ette	c. kitch-en-ette ⭕
5. kingdom	a. kingd-om	b. kin-gdom	c. king-dom ⭕
6. Kentucky	a. Ken-tuc-ky	b. Kent-uck-y	c. Ken-tuck-y ⭕
7. kindness	a. ki-ndness	b. ki-nd-ness	c. kind-ness ⭕
8. kerosene	a. ker-o-sene ⭕	b. ke-ros-ene	c. ker-os-ene

Answer Key

Name: _____ Date: ___/___/_____ Score: _____

Lesson 11.6

Reading and Writing

Proper and Common Nouns and Adjectives

 Lesson Check Point

 Directions: Read the words in the word box. Put an (X) on the line next to each word that is written incorrectly. Remember that all proper nouns and proper adjectives are capitalized. Use a dictionary or the Internet to check your answers.

지도: 단어 상자에 있는 단어를 읽으십시오. 잘못 쓰여진 각 단어 옆의 줄에 (X)를 표시하십시오. 모든 고유 명사와 고유 형용사는 대문자임을 기억하십시오. 사전이나 인터넷을 사용하여 답을 확인하십시오.

Word Box					
_	Kentucky	_	kingdom	X	kingston
X	kuwait	_	kisses	X	Keypad
_	Helen Keller	_	kilometers	_	Key West
X	Ketchup	X	Keepers	X	Mr. king

 Directions: Read each unedited sentence and underline the word that is written incorrectly. Write each sentence correctly on the line.

지도: 편집되지 않은 각 문장을 읽고 잘못 쓰여진 단어에 밑줄을긋습 니다. 각 문장을 줄에 올바르게 쓰십시오.

Model
Helen <u>keller</u> was a kind person.
<u>Helen Keller was a kind person.</u>

1. The new karate class is being held in <u>kingston</u>, Kansas.
<u>The new karate class is being held in Kingston, Kansas.</u>

2. Katie said, "The <u>kenyan</u> culture is rooted in history."
<u>Katie said, "The Kenyan culture is rooted in history."</u>

3. My friend, Kelly, likes to fly her kite in <u>key</u> Largo.
<u>My friend, Kelly, likes to fly her kite in Key Largo.</u>

4. Karen and Karim always put ketchup on their <u>Knishes</u>.
<u>Karen and Karim always put ketchup on their knishes.</u>

Assessment

Name: _____ **Date:** ___/___/_____ **Score:** _____

Lesson 12.1

Reading Words with the Letter L/l

✓ Lesson Check Point

Directions: Read each target word. Find the letter "l" and put a check (✓) in the column that identifies its position: beginning, within or end.
지도: 각 대상 단어를 읽으십시오. 문자"l"을 찾아 체크 표시(✓)위치를 식별하는 열에서 시작, 내부 또는 끝.

Target Words	Beginning (First Letter)	Within	End (Last Letter)
1. lift	✓		
2. garlic		✓	
3. lounge	✓		
4. graceful			✓
5. happily		✓	

Directions: Read each sentence and underline the words that begin with the letter "l." Write all the underlined words in alphabetical order on the lines below.
지도: 각 문장을 읽고 문자"l"로 시작하는 단어에 밑줄을 긋습니다. 밑줄 친 모든 단어를 아래 줄에 알파벳 순서로 쓰십시오.

6. I am <u>late</u> for my <u>literature</u> class.

7. The <u>laundry</u> has a <u>lavender</u> scent.

8. Danny drank a <u>large</u> glass of <u>lemonade</u>.

9. Today's <u>lecture</u> will be held in the <u>library</u>.

10. My <u>lilies</u> and <u>lilacs</u> are growing in the garden.

late	large	laundry
lavender	lecture	lemonade
library	lilacs	lilies
	literature	

Answer Key

Name: _____ Date: ___/___/_____ Score: _____

Lesson 12.2

Reading Words with the Letter "l" Combinations: "bl," "pl" & "sl"

Dictionary Skills/ Vocabulary

✓ Lesson Check Point

Directions: Read each target word and its definition. Write the target word on the line in front of its meaning. Use a dictionary or the Internet to check your answers.

지도: 각 대상 단어와 그 정의를 읽으십시오. 의미 앞 줄에 대상단어를 쓰십시오. 사전이나 인터넷을 사용하여 답을 확인하십시오.

Target Word Box				
blender	plane	sled	sliced	slowly

1. <u>sliced</u>   to have cut something with a knife
2. <u>blender</u>   a machine that mixes things together
3. <u>slowly</u>   not moving quickly
4. <u>plane</u>   a winged vehicle that can fly
5. <u>sled</u>   to glide on packed snow or ice

Directions: Read each sentence. Underline the word in the parentheses that correctly completes each sentence. Then, write the underlined word on the line.

지도: 각 문장을 읽으십시오. 각 문장을 올바르게 완성하는 괄호 안에 있는 단어에 밑줄을 긋습니다. 그런 다음 밑줄 친 단어를 줄에 쓰십시오.

6. On snowy days, the kids ___sled___ down the hills. (<u>sled</u>, sliced)

7. Mrs. Blake ___sliced___ the loaf of bread in half. (<u>sliced</u>, slowly)

8. Mr. Cloud took a ___plane___ from Poland to America. (sled, <u>plane</u>)

9. Paul was walking ___slowly___ in the crowded hallway. (<u>slowly</u>, blender)

10. I placed two strawberries in the ___blender___. (plane, <u>blender</u>)

Assessment

Name: _____ Date: ___/___/_____ Score: _____

Lesson 12.3

Reading Words with a Silent Letter "l"

✓ Lesson Check Point

Directions: Read the target words in the word box. Write the words that have a silent letter "l" in the first column. Write the words that do not have a silent letter "l" in the second column.

지도: 단어 상자에 있는 대상 단어를 읽으십시오. 첫 번째 열에 묵음문자 "l"이 있는 단어를 쓰십시오. 두 번째 열에 묵음 문자"l"이 없는 단어를 쓰십 시오.

Target Word Box				
little	balm	calves	wheel	like
could	salmon	below	dollar	listen
valley	believe	pool	half	ball
lilies	Hellenic	balloon	library	late

Letter "l" is silent	Letter "l" has the /l/ sound
balm	like
ball	pool
half	late
could	lilies
calves	below
dollar	listen
valley	wheel
salmon	little
balloon	believe
Hellenic	library

Learn To Read English With Directions In Korean

Answer Key

 Name: _____ Date: ___/___/_____ Score: _____

The Reading Challenge

Lesson 12.4

Reading Multisyllable Words

✓ Lesson Check Point

 Directions: Read and divide each target word into syllables. Write each word and place a hyphen (-) between the syllables in the second column. Write the number of syllables in the third column. Use a dictionary or the Internet to check your answers.

지도: 각 대상 단어를 읽고 음절로 나눕니다. 각 단어를 쓰고 두 번째 열의 음절 사이에 하이픈(-)을 넣습니다. 세 번째 열에 음절 수를 쓰십시오. 사전이나 인터넷을 사용하여 답을 확인하십시오.

Target Words	Words Divided into Syllables	Number of Syllables
1. latex	la-tex	2
2. logical	log-i-cal	3
3. leopard	leop-ard	2
4. lingers	lin-gers	2
5. lawyer	law-yer	2
6. lonely	lone-ly	2
7. linkage	link-age	2
8. leisurely	lei-sure-ly	3
9. language	lan-guage	2
10. lemonade	lem-on-ade	3

Assessment

Name: _____ Date: ___/___/_____ Score: _____

The Reading Challenge

Lesson 12.4

Reading Multisyllable Words

✓ Lesson Check Point

Directions: Read each target word. Circle the word in the row that is divided correctly into syllables. Use a dictionary or the Internet to check your answers.
지도: 각 대상 단어를 읽으십시오. 음절로 올바르게 나누어진 행에 있는 단어에 동그라미를 치십시오. 사전이나 인터넷을 사용하여 답을 확인하십시오.

Model

| liberty | a. li-ber-ty | (b. lib-er-ty) | c. lib-ert-y |

1. liable	(a. li-a-ble)	b. li-able	c. li-ab-le
2. lieutenant	a. lieut-en-ant	(b. lieu-ten-ant)	c. lie-uten-ant
3. lineage	a. li-ne-age	b. lin-ea-ge	(c. lin-e-age)
4. laminate	a. la-mi-nate	(b. lam-i-nate)	c. la-min-ate
5. literate	a. li-ter-ate	b. lite-ra-te	(c. lit-er-ate)
6. location	a. loc-a-tion	b. lo-cat-ion	(c. lo-ca-tion)
7. logical	a. lo-gi-cal	(b. log-i-cal)	c. lo-gic-al
8. levitate	(a. lev-i-tate)	b. le-vit-ate	c. lev-it-ate

Answer Key

Name: _____ Date: ___/___/_____ Score: _____

Lesson 12.5

Reading and Writing

Proper and Common Nouns and Adjectives

✓ Lesson Check Point

Directions: Read the words in the word box. Put an (X) on the line next to each word that is written incorrectly. Remember that all proper nouns and proper adjectives are capitalized. Use a dictionary or the Internet to check your answers.

지도: 단어 상자에 있는 단어를 읽으십시오. 잘못 쓰여진 각 단어 옆의 줄에 (X)를 표시하십시오. 모든 고유 명사와 고유 형용사는 대문자임을 기억하십시오. 사전이나 인터넷을 사용하여 답을 확인하십시오.

Word					
__	Lima, Peru	X	Lecturer	X	lithuania
__	laboratory	X	Language	__	leather
X	Lawsuit	__	literature	__	Lexington
X	london	__	Louisiana	X	League

Directions: Read each unedited sentence and underline the word that is written incorrectly. Write each sentence correctly on the line.

지도: 편집되지 않은 각 문장을 읽고 잘못 쓰여진 단어에 밑줄을 긋습 니 다. 각 문장을 줄에 올바르게 쓰십시오.

Model
<u>last</u> night, I read a long article about tourism in London.
Last night, I read a long article about tourism in London.

1. I drank the best lemonade on <u>long</u> Island.
   I drank the best lemonade on Long Island.

2. Lucy was lost in Las Vegas for two <u>Long</u> days.
   Lucy was lost in Las Vegas for two long days.

3. The Arabic language is spoken in <u>libya</u> and Lebanon.
   The Arabic language is spoken in Libya and Lebanon.

4. Lydia said, "South America is also called <u>latin</u> America."
   Lydia said, "South America is also called Latin America."

Assessment

Name: _____ Date:__/_____/_____ Score: _____

Lesson 13.1

Reading Words with the Letter M/m

✓ Lesson Check Point

Directions: Read each target word. Find the letter "m" and put a check (✓) in the column that identifies its position: beginning, within or end.
지도: 각 대상 단어를 읽으십시오. 문자"m"을 찾아 체크 표시(✓)위치 를 식별하는 열에서 시작, 내부 또는 끝.

Target Words	Beginning (First Letter)	Within	End (Last Letter)
1. limit		✓	
2. model	✓		
3. helmet		✓	
4. removal		✓	
5. bedroom			✓

Directions: Read each sentence and underline the words that begin with the letter "m." Write all the underlined words in alphabetical order on the lines below.
지도: 각 문장을 읽고 문자"m"으로 시작하는 단어에 밑줄을 긋습니다. 밑줄 친 모든 단어를 아래 줄에 알파벳 순서로 쓰십시오.

6. Old <u>MacDonald</u> has a <u>mule</u> on his farm.

7. Every <u>Monday</u>, Peg drinks <u>mineral</u> water.

8. In <u>March</u>, I received a toy <u>mouse</u> as a gift.

9. Amber and her family <u>moved</u> to <u>Missouri</u>.

10. Did you receive the <u>memo</u> from Dr. <u>Maxwell</u>?

<u>MacDonald</u>   <u>March</u>   <u>Maxwell</u>
memo   mineral   Missouri
<u>Monday</u>   mouse   moved
                     mule

Answer Key

Name: _____ Date: ___/___/_____ Score: _____

Lesson 13.2
Reading Words with a Silent Letter "m"

 Lesson Check Point

 Directions: Read each target word. Find the letter "m" and put a check (✓) in the column that identifies its position: beginning, within or end.
지도: 각 대상 단어를 읽으십시오. 문자"m"을 찾아 체크 표시(✓)위치 를 식별하는 열에서 시작, 내부 또는 끝.

Target Words	Beginning (First Letter)	Within	End (Last Letter)
1. hammer		✓	
2. summer		✓	
3. mnemonic	✓		
4. bedroom			✓
5. compromise		✓	

 Directions: Read each target word. Put a check (✓) in the "yes" column if the target word has a silent letter "m." Put a check (✓) in the "no" column if the target word does not have a silent letter "m."
지도: 각 대상 단어를 읽으십시오. 대상 단어에 묵음"m"이 있는 경우"yes" 열에 체크(✓) 표시 대상 단어에 묵음"m"이 없는 경우"no" 열에체크 (✓) 표시.

Target Words	Yes	No
6. hammer	✓	
7. summer	✓	
8. mnemonic	✓	
9. bedroom		✓
10. compromise		✓

Learn To Read English With Directions In Korean

Assessment

 Name: _____ Date: ___/___/_____ Score: _____

The Reading Challenge

Lesson 13.3

Reading Multisyllable Words

✓ Lesson Check Point

 Directions: Read and divide each target word into syllables. Write each word and place a hyphen (-) between the syllables in the second column. Write the number of syllables in the third column. Use a dictionary or the Internet to check your answers.

지도: 각 대상 단어를 읽고 음절로 나눕니다. 각 단어를 쓰고 두 번째 열의 음절 사이에 하이픈(-)을 넣습니다. 세 번째 열에 음절 수를 쓰십시오. 사전이나 인터넷을 사용하여 답을 확인하십시오.

Target Words	Words Divided into Syllables	Number of Syllables
1. movies	mov-ies	2
2. mighty	might-y	2
3. mandate	man-date	2
4. mariner	mar-i-ner	3
5. moisture	mois-ture	2
6. molding	mold-ing	2
7. mutual	mu-tu-al	3
8. medical	med-i-cal	3
9. microfilm	mi-cro-film	3
10. maintaining	main-tain-ing	3

Answer Key

Name: _____ Date: ___/___/_____ Score: _____

The Reading Challenge

Lesson 13.3

Reading Multisyllable Words

✓ Lesson Check Point

Directions: Read each target word. Circle the word in the row that is divided correctly into syllables. Use a dictionary or the Internet to check your answers.
지도: 각 대상 단어를 읽으십시오. 음절로 올바르게 나누어진 행에 있는 단어에 동그라미를 치십시오. 사전이나 인터넷을 사용하여 답을 확인하십시오.

Model

| magazine | **a. mag-a-zine** (circled) | b. ma-ga-zine | c. mag-az-ine |

| 1. Montana | **a. Mon-tan-a** (circled) | b. Mon-ta-na | c. Mont-an-a |

| 2. memory | a. me-mo-ry | b. mem-or-y | **c. mem-o-ry** (circled) |

| 3. manifold | **a. man-i-fold** (circled) | b. ma-ni-fold | c. man-if-old |

| 4. meander | a. mea-n-der | b. mean-der | **c. me-an-der** (circled) |

| 5. manicure | **a. man-i-cure** (circled) | b. ma-ni-cure | c. ma-nic-ure |

| 6. modify | a. mo-di-fy | **b. mod-i-fy** (circled) | c. modif-y |

| 7. manatee | a. ma-na-tee | b. ma-nat-ee | **c. man-a-tee** (circled) |

| 8. menial | a. men-i-al | **b. me-ni-al** (circled) | c. men-ia-l |

Learn To Read English With Directions In Korean   135   Copyrighted Material

Assessment

Name: _____ Date: ___/___/_____ Score: _____

Lesson 13.4

Reading and Writing

Proper and Common Nouns and Adjectives

Directions: Read the words in the word box. Put an (X) on the line next to each word that is written incorrectly. Remember that all proper nouns and proper adjectives are capitalized. Use a dictionary or the Internet to check your answers.

지도: 단어 상자에 있는 단어를 읽으십시오. 잘못 쓰여진 각 단어 옆의 줄에 (X)를 표시하십시오. 모든 고유 명사와 고유 형용사는 대문자임을 기억하십시오. 사전이나 인터넷을 사용하여 답을 확인하십시오.

Word Box					
__	Myanmar	X	Mechanic	__	medicine
X	Marble	__	Memphis	X	marshall Island
X	manhattan	__	Madagascar	__	meadow
__	Maldives	X	milky Way	X	Mammals

Directions: Read each unedited sentence and underline the word that is written incorrectly. Write each sentence correctly on the line.

지도: 편집되지 않은 각 문장을 읽고 잘못 쓰여진 단어에 밑줄을 긋습니다. 각 문장을 줄에 올바르게 쓰십시오.

Model
My son, Mark, is going to attend MIT in <u>massachusetts</u>.
<u>My son, Mark, is going to attend MIT in Massachusetts.</u>

1. Does a <u>Millipede</u> have a million legs?
<u>Does a millipede have a million legs?</u>

2. Mom had a marvelous time in <u>manchester</u>.
<u>Mom had a marvelous time in Manchester.</u>

3. The town's mayor must <u>Make</u> an important decision.
<u>The town's mayor must make an important decision.</u>

4. Max and Molly are getting married in <u>martha's</u> Vineyard.
<u>Max and Molly are getting married in Martha's Vineyard.</u>

Answer Key

 Name: _____ Date:____/____/_____ Score:_____

Lesson 14.1

Reading Words with the Letter N/n

✓ Lesson Check Point

 Directions: Read each target word. Find the letter "n" and put a check (✓) in the column that identifies its position: beginning, within or end.
지도: 각 대상 단어를 읽으십시오. 문자"n"을 찾아 체크 표시(✓)위치를 식별하는 열에서 시작, 내부 또는 끝.

Target Words	Beginning (First Letter)	Within	End (Last Letter)
1. muffin			✓
2. friend		✓	
3. needle	✓		
4. modern			✓
5. dancing		✓	

 Directions: Read each sentence and underline the words that begin with the letter "n." Write all the underlined words in alphabetical order on the lines below.
지도: 각 문장을 읽고"n"으로 시작하는 단어에 밑줄을 긋습니다. 밑줄 친 모든 단어를 아래 줄에 알파벳 순서로 쓰십시오.

6. Margaret said, "The <u>nighthawks</u> hunt at <u>night</u>."

7. The <u>nature</u> trails along the <u>Niagara</u> River are very clean.

8. My best friend, <u>Nathan</u>, was invited to <u>Northern</u> Africa.

9. <u>Newton</u> and the kids are eating chicken <u>nuggets</u> and fries.

10. The award-winning <u>North</u> Dakota <u>newspaper</u> is informative.

<u>Nathan</u>	<u>nature</u>	<u>newspaper</u>
<u>Newton</u>	<u>Niagara</u>	<u>night</u>
<u>nighthawks</u>	<u>North</u>	<u>Northern</u>
	<u>nuggets</u>	

Assessment

 Name: _____ Date:____/____/_____ Score: _____

Lesson 14.2

Reading Words with the "ng" Letter Combination

✓ Lesson Check Point

 Directions: Read each target word. Circle the word in the column that has the same "ng" sound(s) as the target word.
지도: 각 대상 단어를 읽으십시오. 대상 단어와 같은 "ng" 소리가 나는 열의 단어에 동그라미를 치십시오.

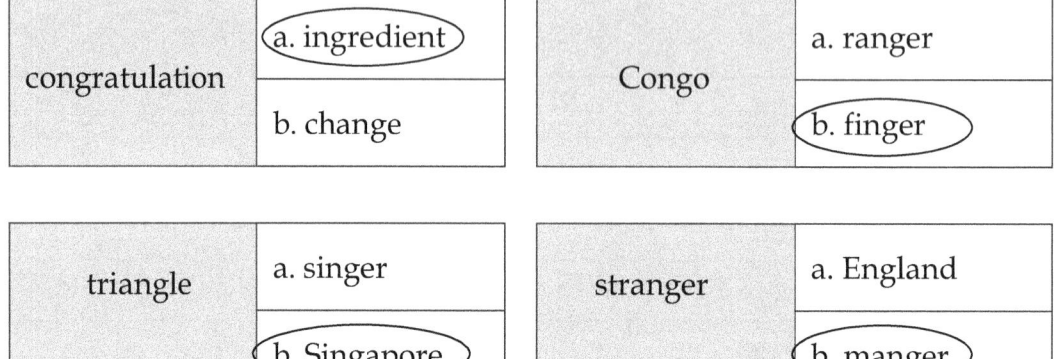

 Directions: Read each target word. Put a check (✓) under the correct column heading.
지도: 각 대상 단어를 읽으십시오. 올바른 열 제목 아래에 체크(✓)를 하십시오.

Target Words	"ng" has the /n/ + /g/ sounds as in the word <u>ingrain</u>	"ng" has the /n/ + /j/ sounds as in the word <u>ginger</u>	"ng" has the /ng/ sound as in the word <u>bang</u>	"ng" has the /ng/ + /g/ sounds as in the word <u>congress</u>
1. Congo				✓
2. triangle				✓
3. stranger		✓		
4. congratulation	✓			

Answer Key

 Name: _____ Date: ___/___/_____ Score: _____

Lesson 14.3

Reading Words with a Silent Letter "n"

✓ Lesson Check Point

 Directions: Read the target words in the word box. Write the words that have a silent letter "n" in the first column. Write the words that do not have a silent letter "n" in the second column.

지도: 단어 상자에 있는 대상 단어를 읽으십시오. 첫 번째 열에 묵음문자 "n"이 있는 단어를 쓰십시오. 두 번째 열에 묵음 문자"n"이 없는 단어를 쓰십시오.

Target Word Box				
partners	chimney	expand	channel	ringing
column	machine	autumn	annex	manners
ribbons	hornet	hymn	romantic	columns
network	penny	solemn	condemn	nonsense

Letter "n" is silent

- annex
- hymn
- penny
- solemn
- condemn
- autumn
- channel
- column
- manners
- columns

Letter "n" has the /n/ sound

- hornet
- nonsense
- ribbons
- network
- romantic
- machine
- ringing
- partners
- expand
- chimney

Assessment

 Name: _____ Date: ___/___/_____ Score: _____

The Reading Challenge

Lesson 14.4

Reading Multisyllable Words

✓ **Lesson Check Point**

 Directions: Read and divide each target word into syllables. Write each word and place a hyphen (-) between the syllables in the second column. Write the number of syllables in the third column. Use a dictionary or the Internet to check your answers.

지도: 각 대상 단어를 읽고 음절로 나눕니다. 각 단어를 쓰고 두 번째 열의 음절 사이에 하이픈(-)을 넣습니다. 세 번째 열에 음절 수를 쓰십시오. 사전이나 인터넷을 사용하여 답을 확인하십시오.

Target Words	Words Divided into Syllables	Number of Syllables
1. neon	ne-on	2
2. needle	nee-dle	2
3. necktie	neck-tie	2
4. natural	nat-u-ral	3
5. naughty	naugh-ty	2
6. nautilus	nau-ti-lus	3
7. November	No-vem-ber	3
8. nourishing	nour-ish-ing	3
9. Netherlands	Neth-er-lands	3
10. networking	net-work-ing	3

Answer Key

Name: _____ Date: ___/___/_____ Score: _____

The Reading Challenge

Lesson 14.4

Reading Multisyllable Words

 Lesson Check Point

 Directions: Read each target word. Circle the word in the row that is divided correctly into syllables. Use a dictionary or the Internet to check your answers.
지도: 각 대상 단어를 읽으십시오. 음절로 올바르게 나누어진 행에 있는 단어에 동그라미를 치십시오. 사전이나 인터넷을 사용하여 답을 확인하십시오.

Model

| napkin | a. na-pkin | b. napk-in | **c. nap-kin** ⭕ |

1. numeral	a. num-er-al	**b. nu-mer-al** ⭕	c. nu-me-ral
2. nominal	**a. nom-i-nal** ⭕	b. no-mi-nal	c. no-min-al
3. navigate	**a. nav-i-gate** ⭕	b. na-vi-gate	c. na-vig-ate
4. nectarine	a. nect-ar-ine	b. nec-ta-rine	**c. nec-tar-ine** ⭕
5. negotiate	**a. ne-go-ti-ate** ⭕	b. ne-got-iate	c. neg-o-ti-ate
6. national	a. nat-ion-al	**b. na-tion-al** ⭕	c. na-tio-nal
7. numerate	**a. nu-mer-ate** ⭕	b. num-er-ate	c. nu-me-rate
8. nursery	a. nur-ser-y	b. nurs-e-ry	**c. nurs-er-y** ⭕

Assessment

Name: _____ Date: ___/___/_____ Score: _____

Lesson 14.5

Reading and Writing

Proper and Common Nouns and Adjectives

✓ **Lesson Check Point**

Directions: Read the words in the word box. Put an (X) on the line next to each word that is written incorrectly. Remember that all proper nouns and proper adjectives are capitalized. Use a dictionary or the Internet to check your answers.

지도: 단어 상자에 있는 단어를 읽으십시오. 잘못 쓰여진 각 단어 옆의 줄에 (X)를 표시하십시오. 모든 고유 명사와 고유 형용사는 대문자임을 기억하십시오. 사전이나 인터넷을 사용하여 답을 확인하십시오.

Word Box		
__ Nevada	__ network	X november
X nile River	__ Nebraska	__ nurse
X Newspaper	X Neckbone	X Name
__ Nantucket	X new Orleans	__ North Dakota

Directions: Read each unedited sentence and underline the word that is written incorrectly. Write each sentence correctly on the line.

지도: 편집되지 않은 각 문장을 읽고 잘못 쓰여진 단어에 밑줄을 긋습니다. 각 문장을 줄에 올바르게 쓰십시오.

Model
In <u>november</u>, Newton would like to visit Nantucket.
In November, Newton would like to visit Nantucket.

1. My <u>Neighbor's</u> name is Nathan.
My neighbor's name is Nathan.

2. <u>nancy's</u> new nanny is from Nepal.
Nancy's new nanny is from Nepal.

3. The <u>Newscasters</u> reported from the Netherlands.
The newscasters reported from the Netherlands.

4. Nathalie said, "Newark is the capital of <u>new</u> Jersey."
Nathalie said, "Newark is the capital of New Jersey."

Answer Key

 Name: _____   Date: ___/___/_____   Score: _____

Lesson 15.1

Reading Words with the Letter O/o

✓ Lesson Check Point

 Directions: Read each target word. Find the letter "o" and put a check (✓) in the column that identifies its position: beginning, within or end.
지도: 각 대상 단어를 읽으십시오. 문자"o"를 찾아 체크 표시(✓)위치 를 식별하는 열에서 시작, 내부 또는 끝.

Target Words	Beginning (First Letter)	Within	End (Last Letter)
1. once	✓		
2. zero			✓
3. ghetto			✓
4. mostly		✓	
5. loving		✓	

 Directions: Read each target word. Read the words in the row and circle the word that has a different vowel "o" sound.
지도: 각 대상 단어를 읽으십시오. 행에 있는 단어를 읽고 모음"o" 소리가 다른 단어에 동그라미를 치십시오.

Target Words				
6. poster	goats	rope	(work)	foam
7. plotting	spots	hop	not	(tote)
8. mommy	(do)	rob	blot	pot
9. enrolled	pony	yo-yo	(crop)	hotel
10. hoping	both	(born)	road	loan

Learn To Read English With Directions In Korean   143   Copyrighted Material

Assessment

 Name: _____ Date: ___/___/_____ Score: _____

Lesson 15.2

Reading Words with the Short Vowel "o" Sound

✓ Lesson Check Point

 Directions: Read the words in the four boxes. Circle two words with the short vowel /ŏ/ or /ô/ sound. The anchor word for the short vowel /ŏ/ and /ô/ sounds is <u>frog</u>.

지도: 네 개의 상자에 있는 단어를 읽으십시오. 짧은 모음 /ŏ/ 또는 /ô/ 소리로 두 단어에 동그라미를 치십시오. 단모음 /ŏ/ 및 /ô/ 소리의 앵커 단어는 frog입니다.

jolt	(Bob)		post	both		do	(jog)
(rod)	info		(cop)	(mob)		cove	(got)
(hop)	over		most	droll		(stock)	bold
to	(ox)		(cod)	(not)		ghost	(rob)

 Directions: Read the words in the four boxes. Circle two words that rhyme. Rhyming words have the same ending sound, such as <u>hot</u> and <u>not</u>.

지도: 네 개의 상자에 있는 단어를 읽으십시오. 운이 맞는 두 단어에 동그라미를 치십시오. 운율이 있는 단어는 hot 및 not과 같이 끝 소리가 같습니다.

code	(sock)		(cross)	(dross)		go	(mom)
hole	(rock)		dole	bone		oval	(Tom)
(top)	home		(job)	lone		(Ron)	(con)
hose	(mop)		hope	(rob)		coat	coast

Answer Key

Name: _____ Date: ___/___/_____ Score: _____

Lesson 15.2

Reading & Writing Words with the Short Vowel "o" Sound

✓ Lesson Check Point

Directions: Read each sentence and underline three words with the short vowel /ŏ/ or /ô/ sound. Then, write the underlined words on the lines below. The anchor word for the short vowel /ŏ/ and /ô/ sounds is frog.
지도: 각 문장을 읽고 짧은 모음/ŏ/ 또는 /ô/ 소리로 세 단어에 밑줄을 긋습니다. 그런 다음 밑줄 친 단어를 아래 줄에 쓰십시오. 단모음/ŏ/ 및 /ô/ 소리의 앵커 단어는 frog입니다.

Model
Everyone saw the frog hop close to the rock.

frog	hop	rock

1. Mommy lost my doll in the house.

Mommy	lost	doll

2. Today, Bob's socks were floating in the pond.

Bob's	socks	pond

3. Owen tossed the cod back into the cold pond.

tossed	cod	pond

4. My mom and Todd cooked spicy octopus soup.

mom	Todd	octopus

5. When I was outside, I saw frogs with lots of spots.

frogs	lots	spots

Assessment

Name: _____ Date: ___/___/_____ Score: _____

Lesson 15.3

Reading Words with the Long Vowel "o" Sound

✓ Lesson Check Point

Directions: Read the words in the four boxes. Circle two words with the long vowel /ō/ sound. The anchor word for the long vowel /ō/ sound is <u>open</u>.

지도: 네 개의 상자에 있는 단어를 읽으십시오. 장모음 /ō/ 소리로 두 단어에 동그라미를 치십시오. 장모음 /ō/ 소리의 기준어는 open입니다.

loft	(boast)	(rose)	stomp	(goat)	fond
knock	(vote)	cloth	(coal)	(pose)	stock

smock	(robe)	frog	(most)	knob	prom
(loan)	font	snob	(stroll)	(hope)	(coast)

Directions: Read the words in the four boxes. Circle two words that rhyme. Rhyming words have the same ending sound, such as <u>hope</u> and <u>soap</u>.

지도: 네 개의 상자에 있는 단어를 읽으십시오. 운이 맞는 두 단어에 동그라미를 치십시오. 운율이 있는 단어는 hope 및 soap과 같이 끝 소리가 같습니다.

(zone)	(cone)	knot	(tone)	(yoke)	(woke)
shot	mole	(bone)	ago	over	smog

(no)	doze	(gold)	(fold)	open	crop
(go)	shop	coach	flock	(rode)	(toad)

Answer Key

Name: _____ Date:___/___/_____ Score:_____

Lesson 15.3

Reading & Writing Words with the Long Vowel "o" Sound

✓ Lesson Check Point

Directions: Read each sentence and underline three words with the long vowel /ō/ sound. Then, write the underlined words on the lines below. The anchor word for the long vowel /ō/ sound is <u>open</u>.
지도: 각 문장을 읽고 장모음 /ō/소리로 세 단어에 밑줄을 긋습니다. 그런 다음 밑줄 친 단어를 아래 줄에 쓰십시오. 장모음 /ō/ 소리의 앵커 단어는 open입니다.

Model

We will <u>go</u> to the <u>rodeo</u> and <u>limbo</u> competitions for fun.

      go   rodeo   limbo

1. <u>Owen</u> said, "The <u>robots</u> operate with two <u>tokens</u>."

    Owen   robots   tokens

2. The group of students is <u>focused</u> on the <u>yodeler's</u> <u>show</u>.

   focused   yodeler's   show

3. <u>Leo</u> said, "The <u>motel</u> will serve <u>donuts</u> in the morning."

     Leo   motel   donuts

4. The <u>poet</u> will write a <u>poem</u> about sailing on the Atlantic <u>Ocean</u>.

     poet   poem   Ocean

5. The <u>yellow</u> <u>envelope</u> has information about the car's <u>turbocharger</u>.

    yellow   envelope   turbocharger

Assessment

Name: _____ Date: ___/___/_____ Score: _____

Review Lessons 15.2 & 15.3

Reading Short Vowel and Long Vowel Words

Directions: Read the target words in the word box. In the first column, write the words that have the short vowel /ŏ/ or /ô/ sound, as in the word <u>frog</u>. In the second column, write the words that have the long vowel /ō/ sound, as in the word <u>open</u>.

지도: 단어 상자에 있는 대상 단어를 읽으십시오. 첫 번째 열에는 frog라는 단어에서와 같이 단모음 /ŏ/ 또는 /ô/ 소리가 나는 단어를 씁니다. 두번째 열에는 open이라는 단어에서와 같이 장모음 /ō/ 소리가 나는 단어를 씁니다.

Target Word Box				
pony	chopping	hotel	poet	knock
lockers	mocking	blotch	flopping	ago
odd	stroller	piano	scotch	total
moment	utmost	octopus	boldest	softer

Letter "o" has the /ŏ/ or /ô/ sound as in the word <u>frog</u>

- odd
- softer
- knock
- scotch
- blotch
- octopus
- flopping
- lockers
- mocking
- chopping

Letter "o" has the /ō/ sound as in the word <u>open</u>

- ago
- pony
- hotel
- poet
- total
- piano
- utmost
- stroller
- boldest
- moment

Answer Key

Name: _____ Date: ___/___/_____ Score: _____

Lesson 15.4

Reading Words with Letter "o" Vowel Pairs

✓ Lesson Check Point

Directions: Read each target word. Circle the word in the column that has the same vowel "oa," "oe," "oo" or "ou" sound(s) as the target word.
지도: 각 대상 단어를 읽으십시오. 대상 단어와 동일한 모음"oa," "oe," "oo" 또는"ou" 소리가 있는 열의 단어에 동그라미를 치십시오.

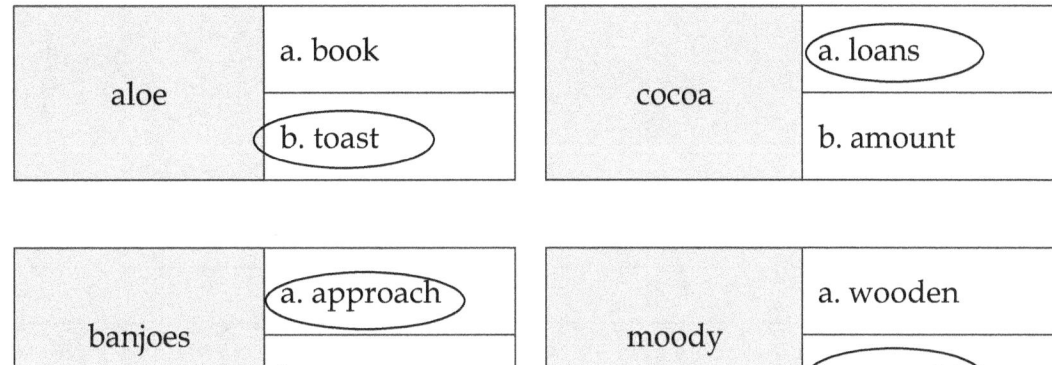

Directions: Read each target word. Put a check (✓) under the correct column heading.
지도: 각 대상 단어를 읽으십시오. 올바른 열 제목 아래에 체크(✓)를 하십시오.

Target Words	Words have the long "o" sound as in the word <u>coat</u>	Words do not have the long "o" sound
1. aloe	✓	
2. cocoa	✓	
3. banjoes	✓	
4. moody		✓

Assessment

 Name: _____ Date: ___/___/_____ Score: _____

Lesson 15.5

Reading Words with the Final Letter "o"

✓ Lesson Check Point

Directions: Read each target word. Find the letter "o" and put a check (✓) in the column that identifies its position within the syllable.
지도: 각 대상 단어를 읽으십시오. 문자"o"를 찾아 체크 표시(✓)음절 내에서 위치를 식별하는 열에서.

Target Words	"o" is at the end of a one syllable word	"o" is at the end of the first syllable	"o" is at the end of a multi-syllable word
1. motel		✓	
2. info			✓
3. go	✓		
4. also			✓
5. probate		✓	

Directions: Read each target word. Put a check (✓) under the correct column heading.
지도: 각 대상 단어를 읽으십시오. 올바른 열 제목 아래에 체크(✓)를 하십시오.

Target Words	"o" has the /ŏ/ sound as in the word <u>frog</u>	"o" has the /ō/ sound as in the word <u>go</u>	"o" has the /ə/ sound as in the word <u>carrot</u>	"o" is silent as in the word <u>people</u>
6. second			✓	
7. foxes	✓			
8. coach		✓		
9. poker		✓		
10. victory			✓	

Answer Key

 Name: _____ Date: ___/___/_____ Score: _____

Lesson 15.6

Reading Letter "o" Words with the Schwa Vowel Sound

✓ Lesson Check Point

  Directions: Read each target word. Circle the word in the column that has the same "o" sound as the target word.
지도: 각 대상 단어를 읽으십시오. 대상 단어와 동일한"o" 소리가 나는 열의 단어에 동그라미를 치십시오.

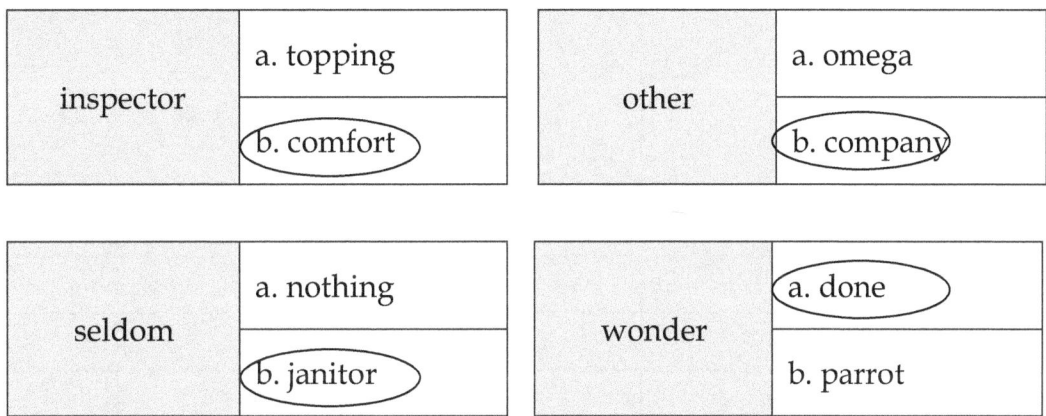

  Directions: Read each sentence and underline the letter "o" word that has the schwa vowel /ə/ sound or short vowel /ŭ/ sound. The anchor word for the letter "o" schwa vowel /ə/ sound is <u>carrot</u> and the letter "o" short vowel /ŭ/ sound is <u>dove</u>.
지도: 각 문장을 읽고 슈와 모음/ə/ 소리 또는 단모음/ŭ/ 소리가 있는 문자"o" 단어에 밑줄을 긋습니다. 문자"o" 슈와 모음/ə/ 소리의 앵커 단어는 carrot이고 문자"o" 단모음/ŭ/ 소리는 dove입니다.

1. The oldest <u>parrot</u> has great oral skills.

2. After the storm, Dad will <u>shovel</u> the snow.

3. On <u>Mother's</u> Day, I bought a flower bouquet.

4. Oscar's homemade <u>lemonade</u> costs one dollar.

5. The <u>janitor</u> opened the door and cleaned the room.

6. The <u>actors</u> and actresses are in an outstanding comedy.

Assessment

Name: _____ Date: ___/___/_____ Score: _____

Lesson 15.7

Reading Words with Vowel "o" Sounds: /ŏ/, /ō/ & /o͞o/

✓ Lesson Check Point

Directions: Read each target word. Put a check (✓) under the correct column heading.
지도: 각 대상 단어를 읽으십시오. 올바른 열 제목 아래에 체크(✓)를 하십시오.

Target Words	"o" has the /ŏ/ sound as in the word <u>frog</u>	"o" has the /ō/ sound as in the word <u>go</u>	"o" has the /o͞o/ sound as in the word <u>to</u>
1. spot	✓		
2. omit		✓	
3. proof			✓
4. profess		✓	
5. movies			✓

Directions: Read each sentence and underline the word that has a letter "o" that has the vowel /o͞o/ sound, as in the word <u>two</u>.
지도: 각 문장을 읽고 two라는 단어에서처럼 모음 /o͞o/ 소리가 있는 문자 "o"가 있는 단어에 밑줄을 긋습니다.

6. Can <u>you</u> tell me how yodelers yodel?

7. An explorer <u>proved</u> that Earth is round.

8. In October, I plan <u>to</u> visit Grandma's house.

9. <u>Who</u> placed the colorful rocks in the boxes?

10. The large <u>moving</u> van will arrive at one o'clock.

Answer Key

Name: _____ Date: ___/___/_____ Score: _____

Lesson 15.8

Reading Words with the "or" Letter Combination

✓ Lesson Check Point

Directions: Read each target word. Circle the word in the column that has the same "o" + "r" sounds as the target word.

지도: 각 대상 단어를 읽으십시오. 가 있는 열에 있는 단어에 동그라미를 치십시오. 동일한 "o" + "r"이 대상 단어로 들립니다.

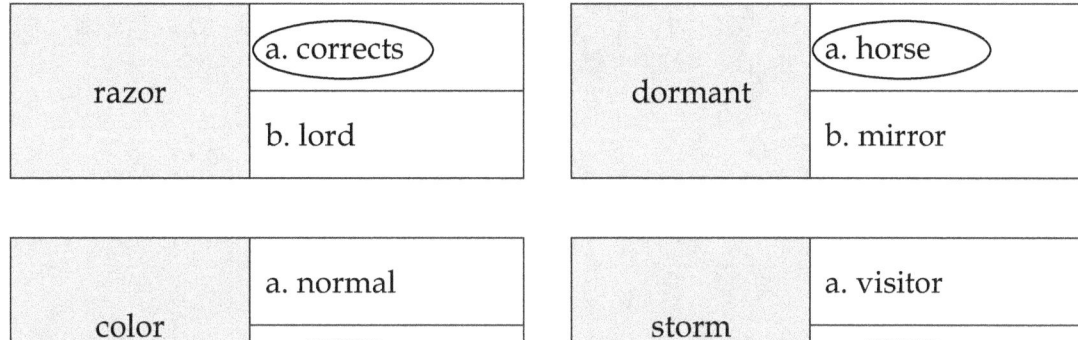

Directions: Read each target word. Put a check (✓) under the correct column heading.

지도: 각 대상 단어를 읽으십시오. 올바른 열 제목 아래에 체크(✓)를 하십시오.

Target Words	"or" has the /ô/ + /r/ sounds as in the word <u>door</u>	"or" has the /ə/ + /r/ sounds as in the word <u>doctor</u>
1. store	✓	
2. horse	✓	
3. correct		✓
4. formal	✓	

Assessment

Name: _____ Date: ___/___/_____ Score: _____

Lesson 15.8

Reading Words with the "or" Letter Combination

Dictionary Skills/ Vocabulary

✓ **Lesson Check Point**

Directions: Read each target word and its definition. Write the target word on the line in front of its meaning. Use a dictionary or the Internet to check your answers.
지도: 각 대상 단어와 그 정의를 읽으십시오. 의미 앞 줄에대상단어를 쓰십시오. 사전이나 인터넷을 사용하여 답을 확인하십시오.

Target Word Box				
dorm	cork	floor	cords	north

1. __north__ the upward direction
2. __floor__ the lowest surface in a room
3. __cork__   rope-like objects that are conduits of electricity
4. __cords__ a one-inch wide wooden cylinder used to seal a bottle
5. __dorm__   a living space for students at a college/university campus

Directions: Read each sentence and write the target word that correctly completes the sentence.
지도: 각 문장을읽고 다음과 같은 목표 단어를 쓰십시오. 장을올바르게 완성합니다.

6. The antique compass rose is pointing ____north____.

7. Ashley is going to mop the kitchen ____floor____.

8. It is difficult to remove the bottle's ____cork____.

9. Children are not allowed to plug in electric ____cords____.

10. The college students are living in small ____dorm____ rooms.

Answer Key

Name: _____ Date: ___/___/_____ Score: _____

Lesson 15.9

Reading Words with a Silent Letter "o"

✓ Lesson Check Point

Directions: Read the target words in the word box. Write the words that have a silent letter "o" in the first column. Write the words that do not have a silent letter "o" in the second column.

지도: 단어 상자에 있는 대상 단어를 읽으십시오. 첫 번째 열에 묵음 문자"o"가 있는 단어를 쓰십시오. 두 번째 열에 묵음 문자"o"가 없는 단어를 쓰십시오.

Target Word Box				
phoenix	holds	leopard	Phoenician	Leonard
jeopardy	people	tops	locker	costly
come	short	phone	grown	subpoena
long	colonel	subpoenas	jeopardize	town

Letter "o" is silent

- people
- phoenix
- colonel
- leopard
- Leonard
- jeopardy
- jeopardize
- subpoena
- subpoenas
- Phoenician

Letter "o" has a letter "o" sound

- tops
- holds
- come
- short
- long
- town
- phone
- grown
- costly
- locker

Assessment

Name: _____ Date: ___/___/_____ Score: _____

Unit Review - O/o

Reading Words with Vowel "o" Sounds: /ŏ/, /ō/, /ə/ & Silent

✓ Lesson Check Point

Directions: Read each target word. Circle the word in the column that has the same "o" sound as the target word.
지도: 각 대상 단어를 읽으십시오. 대상 단어와 동일한 "o" 소리가 나는 열의 단어에 동그라미를 치십시오.

| shopping | (a. document) |
| | b. phone |

| oldest | (a. poster) |
| | b. join |

| propel | a. rocking |
| | (b. produce) |

| leopard | (a. jeopardy) |
| | b. jockey |

Directions: Read each target word. Put a check (✓) under the correct column heading.
지도: 각 대상 단어를 읽으십시오. 올바른 열 제목 아래에 체크(✓)를 하십시오.

Target Words	"o" has the /ŏ/ sound as in the word <u>frog</u>	"o" has the /ō/ sound as in the word <u>go</u>	"o" has the /ə/ sound as in the word <u>carrot</u>	"o" is silent as in the word <u>people</u>
1. oldest		✓		
2. propel			✓	
3. leopard				✓
4. shopping	✓			

Learn To Read English With Directions In Korean

Answer Key

Name: _____ Date: ___/___/_____ Score: _____

The Reading Challenge

Lesson 15.10

Reading Multisyllable Words

✓ Lesson Check Point

Directions: Read and divide each target word into syllables. Write each word and place a hyphen (-) between the syllables in the second column. Write the number of syllables in the third column. Use a dictionary or the Internet to check your answers.

지도: 각 대상 단어를 읽고 음절로 나눕니다. 각 단어를 쓰고 두 번째 열의 음절 사이에 하이픈(-)을 넣습니다. 세 번째 열에 음절 수를 쓰십시오. 사전이나 인터넷을 사용하여 답을 확인하십시오.

Target Words	Words Divided into Syllables	Number of Syllables
1. aloe	al-oe	2
2. poetry	po-et-ry	3
3. cohort	co-hort	2
4. pointer	point-er	2
5. toiletry	toi-let-ry	3
6. border	bord-er	2
7. forestry	for-est-ry	3
8. normal	nor-mal	2
9. looking	look-ing	2
10. avoiding	a-void-ing	3

Learn To Read English With Directions In Korean

Assessment

Name: _____ Date: ___/___/_____ Score: _____

The Reading Challenge

Lesson 15.10

Reading Multisyllable Words

✓ Lesson Check Point

Directions: Read each target word. Circle the word in the row that is divided correctly into syllables. Use a dictionary or the Internet to check your answers.

지도: 각 대상 단어를 읽으십시오. 음절로 올바르게 나누어진 행에 있는 단어에 동그라미를 치십시오. 사전이나 인터넷을 사용하여 답을 확인하십시오.

Model

| proposal | a. prop-o-sal | b. pro-po-sal | c. pro-pos-al ⭕ |

1. conductor	a. cond-u-ctor	b. con-duc-tor ⭕	c. con-duct-or
2. emperor	a. em-pe-ror	b. em-per-or ⭕	c. e-mper-or
3. northerner	a. nor-ther-ner	b. north-e-rner	c. north-ern-er ⭕
4. counselor	a. cou-nsel-or	b. coun-sel-or ⭕	c. couns-e-lor
5. janitor	a. jan-i-tor ⭕	b. jan-it-or	c. ja-nit-or
6. discover	a. di-scov-er	b. dis-cov-er ⭕	c. dis-co-ver
7. royalty	a. roy-al-ty ⭕	b. roy-alt-y	c. ro-yal-ty
8. jeopardy	a. jeo-par-dy	b. je-opar-dy	c. jeop-ard-y ⭕

Answer Key

 Name: _____ Date: ___/___/_____ Score: _____

Lesson 15.11

Reading and Writing

Proper and Common Nouns and Adjectives

✓ Lesson Check Point

 Directions: Read the words in the word box. Put an (X) on the line next to each word that is written incorrectly. Remember that all proper nouns and proper adjectives are capitalized. Use a dictionary or the Internet to check your answers.
지도: 단어 상자에 있는 단어를 읽으십시오. 잘못 쓰여진 각 단어 옆의 줄에 (X)를 표시하십시오. 모든 고유 명사와 고유 형용사는 대문자임을 기억하십시오. 사전이나 인터넷을 사용하여 답을 확인하십시오.

Word Box					
X	oman	X	oregon Trail	__	Old French
__	Olympian	X	oceanside, NY	X	oort cloud
__	opening	__	occupant	__	otherwise
X	october	X	Omelet	__	observant

 Directions: Read each unedited sentence and underline the word that is written incorrectly. Write each sentence correctly on the line.
지도: 편집되지 않은 각 문장을 읽고 잘못 쓰여진 단어에 밑줄을긋습 니다. 각 문장을 줄에 올바르게 쓰십시오.

Model
At <u>One</u> o'clock, the Owens family went to Onega Bay.
<u>At one o'clock, the Owens family went to Onega Bay.</u>

1. My friend, Odessa, is reading an <u>Outstanding</u> book.
<u>My friend, Odessa, is reading an outstanding book.</u>

2. Dr. Orin's objective is to strengthen Olivia's <u>Optic</u> nerves.
<u>Dr. Orin's objective is to strengthen Olivia's optic nerves.</u>

3. The governor of <u>oregon</u> had a meeting at the Oval Office.
<u>The governor of Oregon had a meeting at the Oval Office.</u>

4. In October, Mr. O'Keeffe's class will read about the Indian <u>ocean</u>.
<u>In October, Mr. O'Keeffe's class will read about the Indian Ocean.</u>

Assessment

Name: _____ Date: ___/___/_____ Score: _____

Lesson 16.1

Reading Words with the Letter P/p

✓ Lesson Check Point

Directions: Read each target word. Find the letter "p" and put a check (✓) in the column that identifies its position: beginning, within or end.
지도: 각 대상 단어를 읽으십시오. 문자"p"를 찾아 체크 표시(✓)위치를 식별하는 열에서 시작, 내부 또는 끝.

Target Words	Beginning (First Letter)	Within	End (Last Letter)
1. tap			✓
2. stop			✓
3. parrots	✓		
4. captain		✓	
5. napkin		✓	

Directions: Read each sentence and underline the words that begin with the letter "p." Write all the underlined words in alphabetical order on the lines below.
지도: 각 문장을 읽고"p"로 시작하는 단어에 밑줄을 긋습니다. 아래 줄에 밑줄 친 단어를 알파벳 순서로 모두 쓰십시오.

6. Grandma is <u>packing</u> her <u>purple</u> suitcase.

7. The young girls have <u>pretty</u> <u>pink</u> dresses.

8. My report is in a clear <u>plastic</u> folder for <u>protection</u>.

9. Janice is buying <u>peppers</u> at <u>Pathmark</u> Supermarket.

10. The <u>people</u> are eating chicken and corn at the <u>picnic</u>.

packing   Pathmark   people
peppers   picnic   pink
plastic   pretty   protection
                 purple

Answer Key

 Name: _____ Date: ___/ ___/ _____ Score: _____

Lesson 16.2

Reading Words with the "ph" Letter Combination

✓ Lesson Check Point

 Directions: Read each target word. Circle the word in the column that has the same "ph" sound(s) as the target word.
지도: 각 대상 단어를 읽으십시오. 대상 단어와 동일한 "ph" 소리를 가진 열의 단어에 동그라미를 치십시오.

pamphlet	(a. phrases)
	b. upheaval

phonics	a. shepherd
	(b. phobia)

biographical	a. upholstery
	(b. phony)

haphazard	(a. uphold)
	b. physicist

 Directions: Read each target word. Put a check (✓) under the correct column heading.
지도: 각 대상 단어를 읽으십시오. 올바른 열 제목 아래에 체크(✓)를 하십시오.

Target Words	"ph" has the /f/ sound as in the word <u>phone</u>	"ph" has the /p/ + /h/ sounds as in the word <u>uphill</u>
1. pamphlet	✓	
2. phonics	✓	
3. biographical	✓	
4. haphazard		✓

Assessment

Name: _____ Date: ___/___/_____ Score: _____

Lesson 16.3

Reading Words with the "pr" Letter Combination

Dictionary Skills/ Vocabulary

✓ Lesson Check Point

Directions: Read each target word and its definition. Write the letter of the definition on the line of each target word. Use a dictionary or the Internet to check your answers.
지도: 각 대상 단어와 그 정의를 읽으십시오. 각 대상 단어의 행에 정의의 문자를 씁니다. 사전이나 인터넷을 사용하여 답을 확인하십시오.

Target Words	Definitions
1. _e_ predict	a. a school for students from the age of 3 to 5
2. _a_ preschool	b. a difficult situation or conflict
3. _d_ prepare	c. the amount of money something costs
4. _c_ price	d. to get ready
5. _b_ problem	e. to say or guess that something will happen

Directions: Read each sentence and write the target word that correctly completes the sentence.
지도: 각 문장을 읽고 다음과 같은 목표 단어를 쓰십시오. 장을 올바르게 완성합니다.

6. After ten absences, Pat developed an attendance __problem__.

7. Good readers ____predict____ the events of a story.

8. During the sale, Pat bought the car for half ____price____.

9. The ____preschool____ students are on a class trip.

10. Peter has to ____prepare____ dinner for the presidential ball.

Answer Key

Name: _____ Date: ___/___/_____ Score: _____

Lesson 16.4

Reading Words with the "pl" Letter Combination

Dictionary Skills/ Vocabulary

 Lesson Check Point

 Directions: Read each target word and its definition. Write the target word on the line in front of its meaning. Use a dictionary or the Internet to check your answers.
지도: 각 대상 단어와 그 정의를 읽으십시오. 의미 앞 줄에 대상단어를 쓰십시오. 사전이나 인터넷을 사용하여 답을 확인하십시오.

Target Word Box				
players	platinum	plentiful	pluck	plywood

1. platinum   a valuable silvery-white transition metal
2. plentiful   a large amount of something
3. pluck   to pull and release strings on an instrument
4. players   individuals involved in a game or sport
5. plywood   pressed wood that forms a solid piece of wood

 Directions: Read each sentence. Underline the word in the parentheses that correctly completes each sentence. Then, write the underlined word on the line.
지도: 각 문장을 읽으십시오. 각 문장을 올바르게 완성하는 괄호 안에 있는 단어에 밑줄을 긋습니다. 그런 다음 밑줄 친 단어를 줄에 쓰십시오.

6. The house was built with ____plywood____. (platinum, plywood)
7. I will buy a ___platinum___ chain as a gift for Peter. (pluck, platinum)
8. The plums are ____plentiful____ at harvest time. (players, plentiful)
9. My school's baseball team has six strong ___players___. (players, pluck)
10. The violinists will __pluck__ their strings in harmony. (pluck, platinum)

Learn To Read English With Directions In Korean

Assessment

 Name: _____ Date: ___/___/_____ Score: _____

Lesson 16.4

Reading Words with the "ple" Letter Combination

✓ Lesson Check Point

 Directions: Read each target word. Find the "ple" letter combination and put a check (✓) in the column that identifies its position: beginning, within or end.
지도: 각 대상 단어를 읽으십시오. "ple"문자 조합을 찾고위치를 식별하는 열에 체크(✓)를 하십시오: 시작, 내또는 끝.

Target Words	Beginning (First 3 Letters)	Within	End (Last 3 Letters)
1. people			✓
2. ripple			✓
3. pledge	✓		
4. deplete		✓	
5. temple			✓

 Directions: Read each target word. Put a check (✓) in the "yes" column if the "ple" letter combination has the /p/ + /ə/ + /l/ sounds. Put a check (✓) in the "no" column if the "ple" letter combination does not have the /p/ + /ə/ + /l/ sounds.
지도: 각 대상 단어를 읽으십시오. "ple" 문자 조합에/p/ + /ə/ + /l/ 소리가 있는 경우"yes" 열에 체크(✓)를 하십시오. "ple" 문자 조합에/p/ + /ə/ + /l/소리가 없으면"no" 열에 체크(✓)를 하십시오.

Target Words	Yes	No
6. people	✓	
7. ripple	✓	
8. pledge		✓
9. deplete		✓
10. temple	✓	

Answer Key

 Name: _____ Date: ___/___/_____ Score: _____

Lesson 16.5

Reading Words with a Silent Letter "p"

✓ Lesson Check Point

 Directions: Read the target words in the word box. Write the words that have a silent letter "p" in the first column. Write the words that do not have a silent letter "p" in the second column.
지도: 단어 상자에 있는 대상 단어를 읽으십시오. 첫 번째 열에 묵음문자 "p"가 있는 단어를 쓰십시오. 두 번째 열에 묵음 문자 "p"가 없는 단어를 쓰십시오.

Target Word Box				
maps	receipt	period	raspberry	depot
psychology	adapt	camping	flips	rapid
happy	cupboard	psycho	comprised	coup
psychotic	places	approach	pneumonia	repeat

Letter "p" is silent	Letter "p" has the /p/ sound
coup	maps
happy	adapt
receipt	depot
psycho	flips
psychotic	period
cupboard	rapid
raspberry	places
approach	repeat
psychology	camping
pneumonia	comprised

Assessment

 Name: _____ Date: ___/___/_____ Score: _____

The Reading Challenge

Lesson 16.6

Reading Multisyllable Words

✓ Lesson Check Point

 Directions: Read and divide each target word into syllables. Write each word and place a hyphen (-) between the syllables in the second column. Write the number of syllables in the third column. Use a dictionary or the Internet to check your answers.

지도: 각 대상 단어를 읽고 음절로 나눕니다. 각 단어를 쓰고 두 번째 열의 음절 사이에 하이픈(-)을 넣습니다. 세 번째 열에 음절 수를 쓰십시오. 사전이나 인터넷을 사용하여 답을 확인하십시오.

Target Words	Words Divided into Syllables	Number of Syllables
1. plaza	pla-za	2
2. partner	part-ner	2
3. printer	print-er	2
4. plentiful	plen-ti-ful	3
5. permit	per-mit	2
6. poem	po-em	2
7. procedure	pro-ce-dure	3
8. perfection	per-fec-tion	3
9. program	pro-gram	2
10. prodigy	prod-i-gy	3

Answer Key

Name: _____ Date: ___/___/_____ Score: _____

The Reading Challenge

Lesson 16.6

Reading Multisyllable Words

✓ Lesson Check Point

Directions: Read each target word. Circle the word in the row that is divided correctly into syllables. Use a dictionary or the Internet to check your answers.
지도: 각 대상 단어를 읽으십시오. 음절로 올바르게 나누어진 행에 있는 단어에 동그라미를 치십시오. 사전이나 인터넷을 사용하여 답을 확인하십시오.

Model

| paragraph | **a. par-a-graph** (circled) | b. pa-ra-graph | c. par-ag-raph |

1. potato	a. po-tat-o	b. pot-a-to	**c. po-ta-to** (circled)
2. papaya	**a. pa-pa-ya** (circled)	b. pa-pay-a	c. pap-a-ya
3. parachute	a. pa-ra-chute	**b. par-a-chute** (circled)	c. par-ach-ute
4. principal	a. princ-i-pal	b. prin-cip-al	**c. prin-ci-pal** (circled)
5. politics	**a. pol-i-tics** (circled)	b. po-li-ti-cs	c. pol-it-ics
6. pendulum	a. pend-u-lum	**b. pen-du-lum** (circled)	c. pen-dul-um
7. percentage	a. per-cen-tage	b. perc-ent-age	**c. per-cent-age** (circled)
8. pesticide	**a. pes-ti-cide** (circled)	b. pest-i-cide	c. pes-tic-ide

Assessment

Name: _____ Date: ___/___/_____ Score: _____

Lesson 16.7

Reading and Writing

Proper and Common Nouns and Adjectives

✓ Lesson Check Point

Directions: Read the words in the word box. Put an (X) on the line next to each word that is written incorrectly. Remember that all proper nouns and proper adjectives are capitalized. Use a dictionary or the Internet to check your answers.

지도: 단어 상자에 있는 단어를 읽으십시오. 잘못 쓰여진 각 단어 옆의 줄에 (X)를 표시하십시오. 모든 고유 명사와 고유 형용사는 대문자임을 기억하십시오. 사전이나 인터넷을 사용하여 답을 확인하십시오.

Word Box		
X Principal	__ Port of Spain	__ plumber
__ Poland	X Plaintiff	X princess Grace
X Pilot	__ pitcher	__ pedestrian
X puerto Rico	X President	__ Paris

Directions: Read each unedited sentence and underline the word that is written incorrectly. Write each sentence correctly on the line.

지도: 편집되지 않은 각 문장을 읽고 잘못 쓰여진 단어에 밑줄을 긋습니다. 각 문장을 줄에 올바르게 쓰십시오.

Model
The poem, "<u>puddles</u>," was written by Patrick Parker.
<u>The poem, "Puddles," was written by Patrick Parker.</u>

1. Pat has a <u>panamanian</u> passport in her handbag.
<u>Pat has a Panamanian passport in her handbag.</u>

2. <u>peter</u> will bring plums and peaches to the picnic.
<u>Peter will bring plums and peaches to the picnic.</u>

3. Mr. Paul is the <u>President</u> of the perfume company.
<u>Mr. Paul is the president of the perfume company.</u>

4. The Palmer family is having a picnic in Prospect <u>park</u>.
<u>The Palmer family is having a picnic in Prospect Park.</u>

Answer Key

Name: _____ Date: ___/___/_____ Score: _____

Lesson 17.1

Reading Words with the Letter Q/q

 Lesson Check Point

 Directions: Read each target word. Find the letter "q" and put a check (✓) in the column that identifies its position: beginning, within or end.
지도: 각 대상 단어를 읽으십시오. 문자"q"를 찾아 체크 표시(✓)위치를 식별하는 열에서 시작, 내부 또는 끝.

Target Words	Beginning (First Letter)	Within	End (Last Letter)
1. Iraq			✓
2. tranquil		✓	
3. requested		✓	
4. conquest		✓	
5. quicksand	✓		

 Directions: Read each sentence and underline the words that begin with the letter "q." Write all the underlined words in alphabetical order on the lines below.
지도: 각 문장을 읽고"q"로 시작하는 단어에 밑줄을 긋습니다. 아래 줄에 밑줄 친 단어를 알파벳 순서로 모두 쓰십시오.

6. <u>Quincy</u> ran <u>quickly</u> across the finish line.

7. It is <u>quicker</u> to travel to <u>Qatar</u> by plane than by boat.

8. The coaches <u>quarreled</u> about the <u>quarterback's</u> penalty.

9. We completed a <u>questionnaire</u> about the joy of <u>quilting</u>.

10. The supervisor asked <u>Quinn</u> about his <u>qualifications</u> for the job.

Qatar	qualifications	quarreled
quarterback's	questionnaire	quicker
quickly	quilting	Quincy
	Quinn	

Learn To Read English With Directions In Korean

Assessment

Name: _____ Date: ___/___/_____ Score: _____

Lesson 17.2

Reading Words with the Letter "q" and "qu" Letter Combination

✓ Lesson Check Point

Directions: Read each target word. Circle the word in the column that has the same "q" or "qu" sound(s) as the target word.
지도: 각 대상 단어를 읽으십시오. 대상 단어와 동일한 "q" 또는 "qu" 소리가 있는 열의 단어에 동그라미를 치십시오.

| antique | a. quit |
| | b. opaque ⭕ |

| aquatic | a. equator ⭕ |
| | b. Qatar |

| opaque | a. boutique ⭕ |
| | b. quicken |

| question | a. Iraq |
| | b. quarterly ⭕ |

Directions: Read each target word. Put a check (✓) under the correct column heading.
지도: 각 대상 단어를 읽으십시오. 올바른 열 제목 아래에 체크(✓)를 하십시오.

Target Words	"qu" has the /k/ sound as in the word <u>plaque</u>	"qu" has the /k/ + /w/ sounds as in the word <u>queen</u>
1. antique	✓	
2. aquatic		✓
3. opaque	✓	
4. question		✓

Answer Key

 Name: _____ Date: ___/___/_____ Score: _____

Lesson 17.2

Reading Words with the "qu" Letter Combination

✓ Lesson Check Point

 Directions: Read each target word. Circle the word in the column that has the same "qu" sound(s) as the target word.
지도: 각 대상 단어를 읽으십시오. 대상 단어와 동일한 "qu" 소리가 있는 열의 단어에 동그라미를 치십시오.

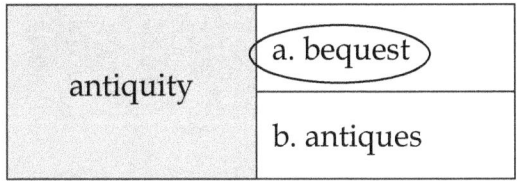
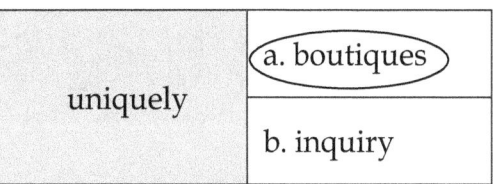

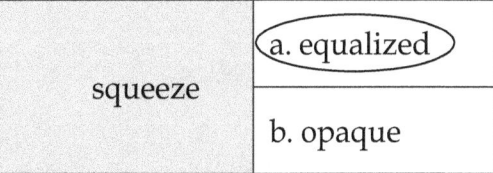

 Directions: Read each target word. Put a check (✓) under the correct column heading.
지도: 각 대상 단어를 읽으십시오. 올바른 열 제목 아래에 체크(✓)를 하십시오.

Target Words	"qu" has the /k/ + /w/ sounds as in the word <u>queen</u>	"qu" has the /k/ sound as in the word <u>plaque</u>	"qu" is silent as in the word <u>racquet</u>
1. antiquity	✓		
2. uniquely		✓	
3. lacquer			✓
4. squeeze	✓		

Assessment

 Name: _____ Date: ___/___/_____ Score: _____

The Reading Challenge

Lesson 17.3

Reading Multisyllable Words

✓ Lesson Check Point

Directions: Read and divide each target word into syllables. Write each word and place a hyphen (-) between the syllables in the second column. Write the number of syllables in the third column. Use a dictionary or the Internet to check your answers.

지도: 각 대상 단어를 읽고 음절로 나눕니다. 각 단어를 쓰고 두 번째 열의 음절 사이에 하이픈(-)을 넣습니다. 세 번째 열에 음절 수를 쓰십시오. 사전이나 인터넷을 사용하여 답을 확인하십시오.

Target Words	Words Divided into Syllables	Number of Syllables
1. quoting	quot-ing	2
2. quietly	qui-et-ly	3
3. qualifies	qual-i-fies	3
4. quandary	quan-da-ry	3
5. quarterly	quar-ter-ly	3
6. questioned	ques-tioned	2
7. quenching	quench-ing	2
8. quarterback	quar-ter-back	3
9. qualifying	qual-i-fy-ing	4
10. quadriplegic	quad-ri-ple-gic	4

Answer Key

 Name: _____ Date: ___/___/_____ Score: _____

The Reading Challenge

Lesson 17.3

Reading Multisyllable Words

✓ Lesson Check Point

 Directions: Read each target word. Circle the word in the row that is divided correctly into syllables. Use a dictionary or the Internet to check your answers.

지도: 각 대상 단어를 읽으십시오. 음절로 올바르게 나누어진 행에 있는 단어에 동그라미를 치십시오. 사전이나 인터넷을 사용하여 답을 확인하십시오.

Model

| quarter | a. quart-er | **b. quar-ter** (circled) | c. qu-arter |

1. qualify	a. qua-li-fy	**b. qual-i-fy** (circled)	c. qua-lif-y
2. quartet	**a. quar-tet** (circled)	b. qu-ar-tet	c. quar-t-et
3. quantity	a. qua-nti-ty	**b. quan-ti-ty** (circled)	c. quan-tit-y
4. quickly	**a. quick-ly** (circled)	b. qui-ck-ly	c. qu-ick-ly
5. quandary	**a. quan-da-ry** (circled)	b. quan-dar-y	c. quand-a-ry
6. queasy	a. qu-ea-sy	b. que-a-sy	**c. quea-sy** (circled)
7. quintet	**a. quin-tet** (circled)	b. quint-et	c. qu-intet
8. quintuple	**a. quin-tu-ple** (circled)	b. quin-tup-le	c. quint-u-ple

Learn To Read English With Directions In Korean

Assessment

Name: _____ Date: ___/___/_____ Score: _____

Lesson 17.4

Reading and Writing

Proper and Common Nouns and Adjectives

✓ Lesson Check Point

Directions: Read the words in the word box. Put an (X) on the line next to each word that is written incorrectly. Remember that all proper nouns and proper adjectives are capitalized. Use a dictionary or the Internet to check your answers.

지도: 단어 상자에 있는 단어를 읽으십시오. 잘못 쓰여진 각 단어 옆의 줄에 (X)를 표시하십시오. 모든 고유 명사와 고유 형용사는 대문자임을 기억하십시오. 사전이나 인터넷을 사용하여 답을 확인하십시오.

Word Box					
__	quintet	X	Quizzed	__	Qatar
__	Quebec	X	Queen	X	queen Anne
X	Quilted	__	quesadilla	__	quickened
X	queens, NY	X	Quarterly	__	quirky

Directions: Read each unedited sentence and underline the word that is written incorrectly. Write each sentence correctly on the line.

지도: 편집되지 않은 각 문장을 읽고 잘못 쓰여진 단어에 밑줄을 긋습니다. 각 문장을 줄에 올바르게 쓰십시오.

Model
Today's quiz is about the <u>queen</u> of England and her monarchy.
Today's quiz is about the Queen of England and her monarchy.

1. The quarterly payments were made by <u>quincy</u>.
The quarterly payments were made by Quincy.

2. I heard the ducks quack loudly at the <u>queens</u> Zoo.
I heard the ducks quack loudly at the Queens Zoo.

3. <u>queenie</u> puts a question mark at the end of her sentence.
Queenie puts a question mark at the end of her sentence.

4. Mr. and Mrs. <u>quill</u> are eating quiche and quail for dinner.
Mr. and Mrs. Quill are eating quiche and quail for dinner.

Answer Key

 Name: _____ Date: ___/___/_____ Score: _____

Lesson 18.1

Reading Words with the Letter R/r

✓ Lesson Check Point

 Directions: Read each target word. Find the letter "r" and put a check (✓) in the column that identifies its position: beginning, within or end.
지도: 각 대상 단어를 읽으십시오. 문자"r"을 찾아 체크 표시(✓)위치를 식별하는 열에서 시작, 내부 또는 끝.

Target Words	Beginning (First Letter)	Within	End (Last Letter)
1. rabbit	✓		
2. lawyer			✓
3. hammer			✓
4. converse		✓	
5. deodorant		✓	

 Directions: Read each sentence and underline the words that begin with the letter "r." Write all the underlined words in alphabetical order on the lines below.
지도: 각 문장을 읽고 문자"r"로 시작하는 단어에 밑줄을 긋습니다. 아래 줄에 밑줄 친 단어를 알파벳 순서로 모두 쓰십시오.

6. The long <u>rope</u> is in George's <u>rowboat</u>.

7. The park <u>rangers</u> are listening to the <u>radio</u>.

8. At the <u>restaurant</u>, I ate pasta and <u>roast</u> beef.

9. Josiah and his friends <u>ran</u> up the <u>ramp</u> quickly.

10. The <u>residents</u> of Georgetown <u>recycle</u> their plastic bottles.

radio   ramp   ran
rangers   recycle   residents
restaurant   roast   rope
                 rowboat

Assessment

Name: _____ Date: ___/___/_____ Score: _____

Lesson 18.2

Reading Words with the Letter "r" Combinations:
"br," "cr," "dr," "fr," "gr," "pr" and "tr"

✓ Lesson Check Point

Directions: Read the target words in the word box. Identify the words with the following letter combinations: "br," "cr," "dr," "fr," "gr," "pr" and "tr." Write the target word on the line that correctly completes each sentence.

지도: 단어 상자에 있는 대상 단어를 읽으십시오. "br," "cr," "dr," "fr," "gr," "pr" 및 "tr" 문자 조합으로 단어를 식별합니다. 각 문장을 올바르게 완성하는 행에 목표 단어를 쓰십시오.

Target Word Box			
traded	group	project	fries
trace	fragrance		grocery
breakfast	crossing		drive

1. Mary brushes her teeth after eating ____breakfast____.

2. Troy and Brandon ____traded____ their baseball cards.

3. This month, Trevor is learning to ____drive____ a car.

4. Brenda and Francis are ____crossing____ the street safely.

5. Brad's science ____project____ received the first place prize.

6. Brenda smells the ____fragrance____ of the expensive perfume.

7. Trisha can ____trace____ her ancestry back two hundred years.

8. Grace's food truck serves hamburgers and French ____fries____.

9. The ____group____ of students went on an exciting school trip.

10. Last night, Gloria and Fred had bread and grapes in their ____grocery____ cart.

Answer Key

Name: _____ Date: ___/___/_____ Score: _____

The Reading Challenge

Lesson 18.3

Reading Multisyllable Words

✓ Lesson Check Point

Directions: Read and divide each target word into syllables. Write each word and place a hyphen (-) between the syllables in the second column. Write the number of syllables in the third column. Use a dictionary or the Internet to check your answers.

지도: 각 대상 단어를 읽고 음절로 나눕니다. 각 단어를 쓰고 두 번째 열의 음절 사이에 하이픈(-)을 넣습니다. 세 번째 열에 음절 수를 쓰십시오. 사전이나 인터넷을 사용하여 답을 확인하십시오.

Target Words	Words Divided into Syllables	Number of Syllables
1. rebel	re-bel	2
2. recess	re-cess	2
3. razors	ra-zors	2
4. radar	ra-dar	2
5. rocker	rock-er	2
6. revision	re-vi-sion	3
7. reason	rea-son	2
8. rainfall	rain-fall	2
9. recently	re-cent-ly	3
10. righteously	right-eous-ly	3

Learn To Read English With Directions In Korean

Assessment

Name: _____ Date: ___/___/_____ Score: _____

The Reading Challenge

Lesson 18.3

Reading Multisyllable Words

✓ Lesson Check Point

Directions: Read each target word. Circle the word in the row that is divided correctly into syllables. Use a dictionary or the Internet to check your answers.

지도: 각 대상 단어를 읽으십시오. 음절로 올바르게 나누어진 행에 있는 단어에 동그라미를 치십시오. 사전이나 인터넷을 사용하여 답을 확인하십시오.

Model

runaway	a. ru-na-way	b. run-a-way ✓	c. run-aw-ay

1. retainer	a. re-tain-er ✓	b. ret-ain-er	c. re-tai-ner

2. revolting	a. re-volt-ing ✓	b. rev-olt-ing	c. rev-ol-ting
3. radio	a. ra-di-o ✓	b. rad-i-o	c. ra-dio

4. royalty	a. roya-lt-y	b. roy-al-ty ✓	c. ro-ya-lty

5. rewarding	a. rew-ard-ing	b. re-war-ding	c. re-ward-ing ✓

6. routinely	a. rou-tine-ly ✓	b. rout-ine-ly	c. rout-in-ely

7. radiate	a. rad-i-ate	b. ra-dia-te	c. ra-di-ate ✓

8. refugee	a. ref-ug-ee	b. re-fug-ee	c. ref-u-gee ✓

Answer Key

Name: _____ Date: ___/___/_____ Score: _____

Lesson 18.4

Reading and Writing

Proper and Common Nouns and Adjectives

✓ Lesson Check Point

Directions: Read the words in the word box. Put an (X) on the line next to each word that is written incorrectly. Remember that all proper nouns and proper adjectives are capitalized. Use a dictionary or the Internet to check your answers.

지도: 단어 상자에 있는 단어를 읽으십시오. 잘못 쓰여진 각 단어 옆의 줄에 (X)를 표시하십시오. 모든 고유 명사와 고유 형용사는 대문자임을 기억하십시오. 사전이나 인터넷을 사용하여 답을 확인하십시오.

Word Box					
__	Rapid City	X	King ramses	X	Racetrack
X	romania	X	Road	__	Rembrandt
X	romeo and Juliet	__	redemption	__	receptionist
__	river	__	Rome	X	Rectangle

Directions: Read each unedited sentence and underline the word that is written incorrectly. Write each sentence correctly on the line.

지도: 편집되지 않은 각 문장을 읽고 잘못 쓰여진 단어에 밑줄을긋습 니다. 각 문장을 줄에 올바르게 쓰십시오.

Model
We saw two <u>Retired</u> racehorses at Richardson Ranch.
<u>We saw two retired racehorses at Richardson Ranch.</u>

1. I met <u>rosalind</u> at Rutherford's Roller Rink.
<u>I met Rosalind at Rutherford's Roller Rink.</u>

2. Mr. and Mrs. <u>remfort</u> bought a new Rolls Royce.
<u>Mr. and Mrs. Remfort bought a new Rolls Royce.</u>

3. <u>raymond</u> is the chief radiologist at Rock Hospital.
<u>Raymond is the chief radiologist at Rock Hospital.</u>

4. Did you know <u>ronald</u> Reagan was an American president?
<u>Did you know Ronald Reagan was an American president?</u>

Assessment

Name: _____ Date: ___/___/_____ Score: _____

Lesson 19.1

Reading Words with the Letter S/s

✓ **Lesson Check Point**

Directions: Read each target word. Find the letter "s" and put a check (✓) in the column that identifies its position: beginning, within or end.
지도: 각 대상 단어를 읽으십시오. 문자"s"를 찾아 체크 표시(✓)위치를 식별하는 열에서 시작, 내부 또는 끝.

Target Words	Beginning (First Letter)	Within	End (Last Letter)
1. seven	✓		
2. astonish		✓	
3. pockets			✓
4. consider		✓	
5. signify	✓		

Directions: Read each sentence and underline the words that begin with the letter "s." Write all the underlined words in alphabetical order on the lines below.
지도: 각 문장을 읽고"s"로 시작하는 단어에 밑줄을 긋습니다. 아래 줄에 밑줄 친 단어를 알파벳 순서로 모두 쓰십시오.

6. I am shopping for a silk dress.

7. Randy is singing at the seaport.

8. Jim and Samuel are eating sandwiches.

9. The students stood in the long line for lunch.

10. The senators are working in the state office building.

Samuel	sandwiches	seaport
senators	shopping	silk
singing	state	stood
	students	

Answer Key

Name: _____ Date: ___/___/_____ Score: _____

Lesson 19.1

Reading Words with the Letter S/s

✓ **Lesson Check Point**

Directions: Read each target word. Circle the word in the column that has the same "s" sound as the target word.
지도: 각 대상 단어를 읽으십시오. 대상 단어와 동일한 "s" 소리가 나는 열의 단어에 동그라미를 치십시오.

| boys | a. delicious |
| | (b. busy) |

| television | a. story |
| | (b. pleasure) |

| issued | a. computers |
| | (b. assuring) |

| increase | a. resident |
| | (b. impulse) |

Directions: Read each target word. Put a check (✓) under the correct column heading.
지도: 각 대상 단어를 읽으십시오. 올바른 열 제목 아래에 체크(✓)를 하십시오.

Target Words	"s" has the /s/ sound as in the word <u>sun</u>	"s" has the /sh/ sound as in the word <u>sugar</u>	"s" has the /z/ sound as in the word <u>his</u>	"s" has the /zh/ sound as in the word <u>vision</u>
1. boys			✓	
2. television				✓
3. issued		✓		
4. increase	✓			

Learn To Read English With Directions In Korean

Assessment

 Name: _____ Date: ___/___/_____ Score: _____

Lesson 19.2

Reading Words with the "sion," "sial" & "scious" Suffixes

✓ **Lesson Check Point**

 Directions: Read each target word. Circle the word in the column that has the same "sion," "sial" or "scious" sound as the target word.
지도: 각 대상 단어를 읽으십시오. 대상 단어와 동일한"sion," "sial" 또는"scious" 소리가 나는 열의 단어에 동그라미를 치십시오.

| profession | a. (extension) |
| | b. division |

| admission | a. television |
| | b. (impression) |

| luscious | a. controversial |
| | b. (conscious) |

| inclusion | a. mansion |
| | b. (decision) |

 Directions: Read each target word. Put a check (✓) under the correct column heading.
지도: 각 대상 단어를 읽으십시오. 올바른 열 제목 아래에 체크(✓)를 하십시오.

Target Words	"sion" has the /sh/ +/ə/+/n/ sounds as in the word <u>passion</u>	"sion" has the /zh/ +/ə/+/n/ sounds as in the word <u>vision</u>	"scious" has the /sh/ +/ə/+/s/ sounds as in the word <u>conscious</u>
1. profession	✓		
2. admission	✓		
3. luscious			✓
4. inclusion		✓	

Answer Key

 Name: _____ Date: ___/___/_____ Score: _____

Lesson 19.3

Reading Words with the "sch" Letter Combination

✓ **Lesson Check Point**

 Directions: Read each target word. Circle the word in the column that has the same "sch" sound(s) as the target word.
지도: 각 대상 단어를 읽으십시오. 대상 단어와 같은 "sch" 소리가 나는 열의 단어에 동그라미를 치십시오.

| schmooze | a. schematic |
| | **b. schillings** (circled) |

| scholarly | **a. schooner** (circled) |
| | b. schmuck |

| schematic | **a. school** (circled) |
| | b. schilling |

| schwa | a. scholar |
| | **b. schmear** (circled) |

 Directions: Read each target word. Put a check (✓) under the correct column heading.
지도: 각 대상 단어를 읽으십시오. 올바른 열 제목 아래에 체크(✓)를 하십시오.

Target Words	"sch" has the /s/ + /k/ sounds as in the word school	"sch" has the /sh/ sound as in the word schilling
1. schmooze		✓
2. scholarly	✓	
3. schematic	✓	
4. schwa		✓

Learn To Read English With Directions In Korean   183   Copyrighted Material

Assessment

Name: _____ Date: ___/___/_____ Score: _____

Lesson 19.4

Reading Words with the "scr," "shr," "spr" & "str" Letter Combinations

Dictionary Skills/ Vocabulary

✓ **Lesson Check Point**

Directions: Read each target word and its definition. Write the letter of the definition on the line of each target word. Use a dictionary or the Internet to check your answers.
지도: 각 대상 단어와 그 정의를 읽으십시오. 각 대상 단어의 행에 정의의 문자를 씁니다. 사전이나 인터넷을 사용하여 답을 확인하십시오.

Target Words	Definitions
1. _d_ sprout	a. the process of becoming smaller
2. _e_ screamed	b. the physical ability to carry or lift heavy objects
3. _a_ shrink	c. a tiny, shelled sea animal
4. _b_ strong	d. the early stage of a plant
5. _c_ shrimp	e. to have made a loud piercing sound

Directions: Read each sentence. Underline the word in the parentheses that correctly completes each sentence. Then, write the underlined word on the line.
지도: 각 문장을 읽으십시오. 각 문장을 올바르게 완성하는 괄호 안에 있는 단어에 밑줄을 긋습니다. 그런 다음 밑줄 친 단어를 줄에 쓰십시오.

6. In the spring, my seeds will start to ___sprout___. (<u>sprout</u>, strong)

7. The excess heat caused my sweater to ___shrink___. (sprout, <u>shrink</u>)

8. Sam's seafood platter has ___shrimp___ and lobster. (strong, <u>shrimp</u>)

9. She ___screamed___ when the patient fell off the bed. (<u>screamed</u>, shrink)

10. The ___strong___ girl lifted a sixty-pound weight. (screamed, <u>strong</u>)

Answer Key

Name: _____ Date: ___/___/_____ Score: _____

Lesson 19.5

Reading Words with the "sl" & "sle" Letter Combinations

Dictionary Skills/ Vocabulary

✓ Lesson Check Point

 Directions: Read each target word and its definition. Write the target word on the line in front of its meaning. Use a dictionary or the Internet to check your answers.
지도: 각 대상 단어와 그 정의를 읽으십시오. 의미 앞 줄에 대상단어를 쓰십시오. 사전이나 인터넷을 사용하여 답을 확인하십시오.

Target Word Box				
slapped	slash	slender	slipped	slur

1. <u>slur</u>   to speak unclearly
2. <u>slipped</u>   the past tense of the verb, to slip
3. <u>slender</u>   small, thin or slim
4. <u>slapped</u>   to have put something down quickly with force
5. <u>slash</u>   to make a major reduction; to make prices lower

 Directions: Read each sentence. Underline the word in the parentheses that correctly completes each sentence. Then, write the underlined word on the line.
지도: 각 문장을 읽으십시오. 각 문장을 올바르게 완성하는 괄호 안에 있는 단어에 밑줄을 긋습니다. 그런 다음 밑줄 친 단어를 줄에 쓰십시오.

6. Sue started to __slur__ her words before falling asleep. (slender, <u>slur</u>)

7. During the holidays, prices are __slashed__ in half. (slapped, <u>slashed</u>)

8. She won the election by a __slender__ margin. (slipped, <u>slender</u>)

9. Yesterday, a student __slipped__ on the wet floor. (<u>slipped</u>, slashed)

10. Stan __slapped__ the slip of paper on the table. (<u>slapped</u>, slur)

Assessment

 Name: _____ Date: ___/___/_____ Score: _____

Lesson 19.5

Reading Words with the "sle" Letter Combination

✓ **Lesson Check Point**

 Directions: Read each target word. Find the "sle" letter combination and put a check (✓) in the column that identifies its position: beginning, within or end.
지도: 각 대상 단어를 읽으십시오. "sle" 문자 조합을 찾고 위치를 식별하는 열에 체크(✓)를 하십시오: 시작, 내 또는 끝.

Target Words	Beginning (First 3 Letters)	Within	End (Last 3 Letters)
1. aisle			✓
2. asleep		✓	
3. sleet	✓		
4. hassle			✓
5. tussle			✓

 Directions: Read each target word. Put a check (✓) in the "yes" column if the "sle" letter combination has the /s/ + /ə/ + /l/ or /z/ + /ə/ + /l/ sounds. Put a check (✓) in the "no" column if the "sle" letter combination does not have the /s/ + /ə/ + /l/ or /z/ + /ə/ + /l/ sounds.
지도: 각 대상 단어를 읽으십시오. "sle" 문자 조합에 /s/ + /ə/ + /l/ 또는 /z/ + /ə/ + /l/ 소리 가 있으면 "yes" 열에 체크(✓)를 하십시오. "sle" 문자 조합에 /s/ + /ə/ + /l/ 또는 /z/ + /ə/ + /l/ 소리가 없으면 "no" 열에 체크(✓)를 하십시오.

Target Words	Yes	No
6. aisle		✓
7. asleep		✓
8. sleet		✓
9. hassle	✓	
10. tussle	✓	

Answer Key

Name: _____ Date: ___/___/_____ Score: _____

Lesson 19.6

Reading Words with the "sm" Letter Combination

✓ Lesson Check Point

Directions: Read each target word. Circle the word in the column that has the same "sm" sounds as the target word.
지도: 각 대상 단어를 읽으십시오. 대상 단어와 동일한"sm" 소리가 나는 열의 단어에 동그라미를 치십시오.

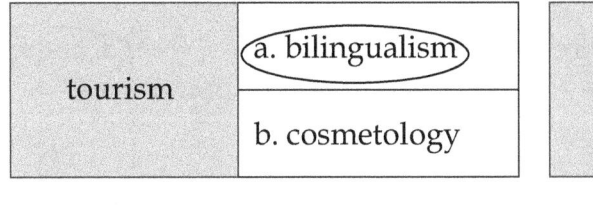

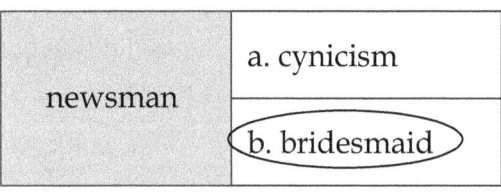

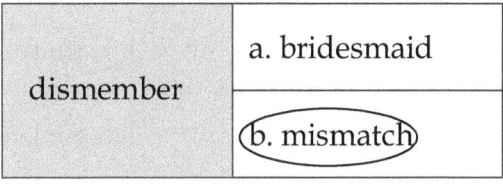

Directions: Read each target word. Put a check (✓) under the correct column heading.
지도: 각 대상 단어를 읽으십시오. 올바른 열 제목 아래에 체크(✓)를 하십시오.

Target Words	"sm" has the /s/ + /m/ sounds as in the word smell	"sm" has the /z/ + /m/ sounds as in the word cosmic	"sm" has the /z/ + /ə/ + /m/ sounds as in the word autism
1. tourism			✓
2. newsman		✓	
3. capitalism			✓
4. dismember	✓		

Learn To Read English With Directions In Korean

Assessment

Name: _____ Date: ___/___/_____ Score: _____

Lesson 19.7

Reading Words with the "ss" Letter Combination

✓ **Lesson Check Point**

Directions: Read each target word. Circle the word in the column that has the same "ss" sound(s) as the target word.
지도: 각 대상 단어를 읽으십시오. 대상 단어와 동일한 "ss" 소리가 나는 열의 단어에 동그라미를 치십시오.

concussion	a. expressing
	(b. expression)

compassion	**(a. aggression)**
	b. aggressive

misstated	**(a. dissatisfaction)**
	b. massive

Missouri	**(a. dissolve)**
	b. concession

Directions: Read each target word. Put a check (✓) under the correct column heading.
지도: 각 대상 단어를 읽으십시오. 올바른 열 제목 아래에 체크(✓)를 하십시오.

Target Words	"ss" has the /sh/ sound as in the word <u>tissue</u>	"ss" has the /s/ + /s/ sounds as in the word <u>misspell</u>	"ss" has the /z/ sound as in the word <u>dissolve</u>
1. concussion	✓		
2. compassion	✓		
3. misstated		✓	
4. Missouri			✓

Answer Key

 Name: _____   Date: ___/___/_____   Score: _____

Lesson 19.8

Reading Words with a Silent Letter "s"

✓ Lesson Check Point

Directions: Read the target words in the word box. Write the words that have a silent letter "s" in the first column. Write the words that do not have a silent letter "s" in the second column.

지도: 단어 상자에 있는 대상 단어를 읽으십시오. 첫 번째 열에 묵음문자 "s"가 있는 단어를 씁니다. 두 번째 열에 묵음 문자"s"가 없는 단어를쓰십시오.

Target Word Box				
bless	apropos	bunches	fossil	debris
extends	islet	houses	actress	shower
ears	smooth	likes	graders	wipes
isle	comprise	aisle	assert	islands

Letter "s" is silent

- isle
- islet
- bless
- aisle
- assert
- debris
- fossil
- islands
- actress
- apropos

Letter "s" has the /s/, /z/ or /sh/ sound

- ears
- likes
- wipes
- graders
- smooth
- shower
- houses
- extends
- bunches
- comprise

Assessment

 Name: _____ Date:___/___/_____ Score:_____

The Reading Challenge

Lesson 19.9

Reading Multisyllable Words

✓ Lesson Check Point

 Directions: Read and divide each target word into syllables. Write each word and place a hyphen (-) between the syllables in the second column. Write the number of syllables in the third column. Use a dictionary or the Internet to check your answers.

지도: 각 대상 단어를 읽고 음절로 나눕니다. 각 단어를 쓰고 두 번째 열의 음절 사이에 하이픈(-)을 넣습니다. 세 번째 열에 음절 수를 쓰십시오. 사전이나 인터넷을 사용하여 답을 확인하십시오.

Target Words	Words Divided into Syllables	Number of Syllables
1. single	sin-gle	2
2. setup	set-up	2
3. secretly	se-cret-ly	3
4. Scotland	Scot-land	2
5. servicing	ser-vic-ing	3
6. secondary	sec-ond-ar-y	4
7. sculpture	sculp-ture	2
8. sectional	sec-tion-al	3
9. saturated	sat-u-rat-ed	4
10. slenderized	slen-der-ized	3

Answer Key

Name: _____ Date: ___/___/_____ Score: _____

The Reading Challenge

Lesson 19.9

Reading Multisyllable Words

✓ Lesson Check Point

Directions: Read each target word. Circle the word in the row that is divided correctly into syllables. Use a dictionary or the Internet to check your answers.
지도: 각 대상 단어를 읽으십시오. 음절로 올바르게 나누어진 행에 있는 단어에 동그라미를 치십시오. 사전이나 인터넷을 사용하여 답을 확인하십시오.

Model

| Saturday | a. Sa-tur-day | **b. Sat-ur-day** ⭕ | c. Sa-turd-ay |

1. signify	a. sig-nif-y	**b. sig-ni-fy** ⭕	c. sign-i-fy
2. solution	a. sol-u-tion	b. so-lut-ion	**c. so-lu-tion** ⭕
3. secular	a. se-cul-ar	**b. sec-u-lar** ⭕	c. se-cu-lar
4. simulate	a. si-mu-late	**b. sim-u-late** ⭕	c. si-mul-ate
5. solitude	**a. sol-i-tude** ⭕	b. so-li-tude	c. so-lit-ude
6. saliva	a. sa-liv-a	b. sa-l-iva	**c. sa-li-va** ⭕
7. selection	a. se-lect-ion	b. sel-ect-ion	**c. se-lec-tion** ⭕
8. satiate	**a. sa-ti-ate** ⭕	b. sat-i-ate	c. sa-tia-te

Learn To Read English With Directions In Korean   Copyrighted Material

Assessment

Name: _____ Date: ___/___/_____ Score: _____

Lesson 19.10

Reading and Writing

Proper and Common Nouns and Adjectives

✓ Lesson Check Point

Directions: Read the words in the word box. Put an (X) on the line next to each word that is written incorrectly. Remember that all proper nouns and proper adjectives are capitalized. Use a dictionary or the Internet to check your answers.

지도: 단어 상자에 있는 단어를 읽으십시오. 잘못 쓰여진 각 단어 옆의 줄에 (X)를 표시하십시오. 모든 고유 명사와 고유 형용사는 대문자임을 기억하십시오. 사전이나 인터넷을 사용하여 답을 확인하십시오.

Word Box					
X	september	X	Sergeant sam	X	san Francisco
X	siamese cat	X	sunday	__	sextuplet
__	semester	__	senator	__	Saturn
__	Senegal	X	scotland	__	San Jose

Directions: Read each unedited sentence and underline the word that is written incorrectly. Write each sentence correctly on the line.

지도: 편집되지 않은 각 문장을 읽고 잘못 쓰여진 단어에 밑줄을 긋습니다. 각 문장을 줄에 올바르게 쓰십시오.

Model
The <u>Seafood</u> is sensational at Salton Restaurant!
The seafood is sensational at Salton Restaurant!

1. <u>silverfish</u> is a staple in the Senegalese diet.
   Silverfish is a staple in the Senegalese diet.

2. In science class, I am studying the planet <u>saturn</u>.
   In science class, I am studying the planet Saturn.

3. The local silversmith, Sam, is moving to <u>san</u> Juan.
   The local silversmith, Sam, is moving to San Juan.

4. My sister, Cindy, is the newly elected <u>State</u> senator.
   My sister, Cindy, is the newly elected state senator.

Answer Key

Name: _____ Date: ___/___/_____ Score: _____

Lesson 20.1

Reading Words with the Letter T/t

Directions: Read each target word. Find the letter "t" and put a check (✓) in the column that identifies its position: beginning, within or end.
지도: 각 대상 단어를 읽으십시오. 문자 "t"를 찾아 체크 표시(✓)위치를 식별하는 열에서 시작, 내부 또는 끝.

Target Words	Beginning (First Letter)	Within	End (Last Letter)
1. today	✓		
2. drift			✓
3. jacket			✓
4. partner		✓	
5. telephone	✓		

Directions: Read each sentence and underline the words that begin with the letter "t." Write all the underlined words in alphabetical order on the lines below.
지도: 각 문장을 읽고 문자 "t"로 시작하는 단어에 밑줄을 긋습니다. 아래 줄에 밑줄 친 단어를 알파벳 순서로 모두 쓰십시오.

6. <u>Tonight</u>, Susan has a very painful <u>toothache</u>.

7. My art <u>teacher</u> drew baby <u>turtles</u> on canvas.

8. My <u>teammate</u>, Fred, received an athletic <u>trophy</u>.

9. Stacey is brushing her <u>teeth</u> with a new <u>toothbrush</u>.

10. In Santo Domingo, a major <u>thunderstorm</u> is scheduled for <u>Tuesday</u>.

teacher	teammate	teeth
thunderstorm	Tonight	toothache
toothbrush	trophy	Tuesday
	turtles	

Assessment

 Name: _____ Date: ___/___/_____ Score: _____

Lesson 20.2

Reading Words with the "thm" Letter Combination

✓ Lesson Check Point

 Directions: Read each target word. Circle the word in the column that has the same "thm" sound(s) as the target word.
지도: 각 대상 단어를 읽으십시오. 대상 단어와 동일한 "thm" 소리가 있는 열의 단어에 동그라미를 치십시오.

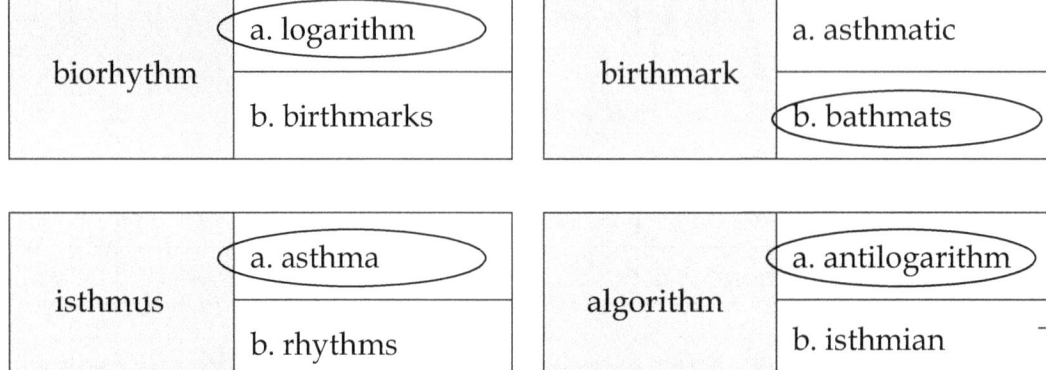

 Directions: Read each target word. Put a check (✓) under the correct column heading.
지도: 각 대상 단어를 읽으십시오. 올바른 열 제목 아래에 체크(✓)를 하십시오.

Target Words	"thm" has the /th/ + /ə/ + /m/ sounds as in the word <u>rhythm</u>	"thm" has the /th/ + /m/ sounds as in the word <u>bathmat</u>	"thm" silent "th" + /m/ sound as in the word <u>asthma</u>
1. biorhythm	✓		
2. birthmark		✓	
3. isthmus			✓
4. algorithm	✓		

Answer Key

 Name: _____ Date:___/___/_____ Score: _____

Lesson 20.3

Reading Words with the "tion," "tial" & "tious" Suffixes

✓ Lesson Check Point

 Directions: Read each target word. Circle the word in the column that has the same "tion," "tial" or "tious" sound as the target word.
지도: 각 대상 단어를 읽으십시오. 대상 단어와 같은"tion," "tial" 또는 "tious" 소리가 나는 열의 단어에 동그라미를 치십시오.

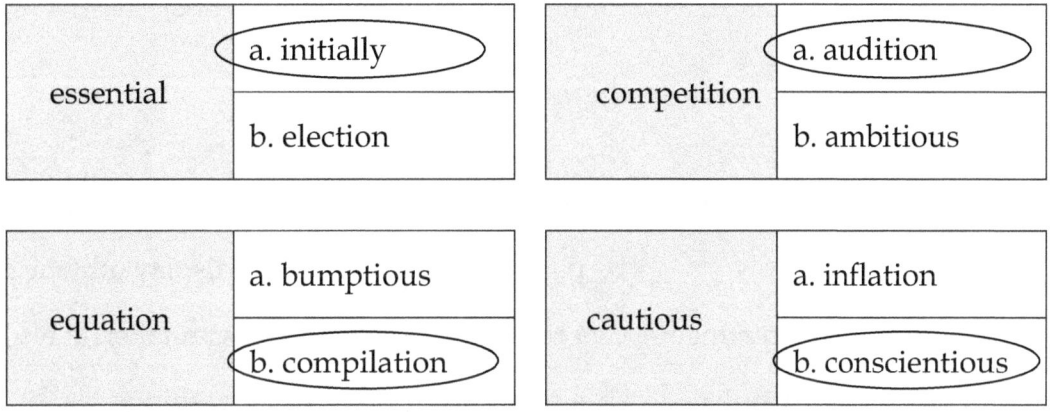

 Directions: Read each target word. Put a check (✓) under the correct column heading.
지도: 각 대상 단어를 읽으십시오. 올바른 열 제목 아래에 체크(✓)를 하십시오.

Target Words	"tion" has the /sh/ +/ə/+/n/ sounds as in the word <u>education</u>	"tial" has the /sh/ +/ə/+/l/ sounds as in the word <u>partial</u>	"tious" has the /sh/ +/ə/+/s/ sounds as in the word <u>ambitious</u>
1. essential		✓	
2. competition	✓		
3. equation	✓		
4. cautious			✓

Assessment

Name: _____ Date: ___/___/_____ Score: _____

Lesson 20.4

Reading Words with the "tr" Letter Combination

Dictionary Skills/ Vocabulary

✓ Lesson Check Point

Directions: Read each target word and its definition. Write the letter of the definition on the line of each target word. Use a dictionary or the Internet to check your answers.
지도: 각 대상 단어와 그 정의를 읽으십시오. 각 대상 단어의 행에 정의의 문자를 씁니다. 사전이나 인터넷을 사용하여 답을 확인하십시오.

Target Words		Definitions
1. <u>c</u>	transcript	a. doctor's care designed to relieve or cure a disease
2. <u>d</u>	tray	b. performance designed to display athletic skills
3. <u>a</u>	treatment	c. a record of grades and classes taken at a school
4. <u>e</u>	trouble	d. a firm surface used to carry things
5. <u>b</u>	tryouts	e. to go out of one's way, to do a little extra

Directions: Read each sentence. Underline the word in the parentheses that correctly completes each sentence. Then, write the underlined word on the line.
지도: 각 문장을 읽으십시오. 각 문장을 올바르게 완성하는 괄호 안에 있는 단어에 밑줄을 긋습니다. 그런 다음 밑줄 친 단어를 줄에 쓰십시오.

6. I requested my college ____transcript____. (treatment, <u>transcript</u>)

7. Trent placed his food on a clean _____tray_____. (<u>tray</u>, tryouts)

8. She is scheduled to have a medical ____treatment____. (<u>treatment</u>, tray)

9. The team is having ___tryouts___ for new players. (<u>tryouts</u>, trouble)

10. I took the __trouble__ to write the names on tags. (transcript, <u>trouble</u>)

Answer Key

 Name: _____ Date:___/___/_____ Score: _____

Lesson 20.5

Reading Words with the "tle" Letter Combination

✓ Lesson Check Point

 Directions: Read each target word. Find the "tle" letter combination and put a check (✓) in the column that identifies its position: beginning, within or end.
지도: 각 대상 단어를 읽으십시오. "tle" 문자 조합을 찾고 위치를 식별하는 열에 체크(✓)를 하십시오: 시작, 내 또는 끝.

Target Words	Beginning (First 3 Letters)	Within	End (Last 3 Letters)
1. turtle			✓
2. little			✓
3. cutlet		✓	
4. bustle			✓
5. heartless		✓	

 Directions: Read each target word. Put a check (✓) in the "yes" column if the "tle" letter combination has the /t/ + /ə/ + /l/ sounds. Put a check (✓) in the "no" column if the "tle" letter combination does not have the /t/ + /ə/ + /l/ sounds.
지도: 각 대상 단어를 읽으십시오. "tle" 문자 조합에 /t/ + /ə/ + /l/ 소리가 있으면 "yes" 열에 체크(✓)를 하십시오. "tle" 문자 조합에 /t/ + /ə/ + /l/ 소리가 없으면 "no" 열에 체크(✓)를 하십시오.

Target Words	Yes	No
6. turtle	✓	
7. little	✓	
8. cutlet		✓
9. bustle		✓
10. heartless		✓

Assessment

Name: _____ Date: ___/___/_____ Score: _____

Lesson 20.6

Reading Words with the Letter "t" Sounds

✓ Lesson Check Point

Directions: Read each target word. Circle the word in the column that has the same "t" sound as the target word.
지도: 각 대상 단어를 읽으십시오. 대상 단어와 "t" 소리가 같은 열의 단어에 동그라미를 치십시오.

| agriculture | a. acting |
| | (b. immature) |

| adjunct | (a. connect) |
| | b. denture |

| expectancy | (a. factor) |
| | b. action |

| unrighteous | a. acting |
| | (b. actuality) |

Directions: Read each target word. Put a check (✓) under the correct column heading.
지도: 각 대상 단어를 읽으십시오. 올바른 열 제목 아래에 체크(✓)를 하십시오.

Target Words	"t" has the /t/ sound as in the word <u>multiply</u>	"t" has the /ch/ sound as in the word <u>picture</u>	"t" has the /sh/ sound as in the word <u>position</u>
1. agriculture		✓	
2. adjunct	✓		
3. expectancy	✓		
4. unrighteous		✓	

Answer Key

 Name: _____ Date: ___/___/_____ Score: _____

Lesson 20.7

Reading Words with a Silent Letter "t"

✓ Lesson Check Point

 Directions: Read the target words in the word box. Write the words that have a silent letter "t" in the first column. Write the words that do not have a silent letter "t" in the second column.

지도: 단어 상자에 있는 대상 단어를 읽으십시오. 첫 번째 열에 묵음문자 "t"가 있는 단어를 쓰십시오. 두 번째 열에 묵음 문자"t"가 없는 단어를 쓰십시오.

Target Word Box				
appointment	listeners	conflict	depot	cutting
debut	dependent	testing	empty	gourmet
mortgage	tactile	soften	different	street
decorate	castle	moisten	little	transform

Letter "t" is silent	Letter "t" has the /t/ sound
debut	street
depot	empty
castle	conflict
soften	tactile
cutting	testing
little	decorate
gourmet	different
listeners	transform
moisten	dependent
mortgage	appointment

Learn To Read English With Directions In Korean

Assessment

 Name: _____ Date: ___/___/_____ Score: _____

The Reading Challenge

Lesson 20.8

Reading Multisyllable Words

✓ Lesson Check Point

 Directions: Read and divide each target word into syllables. Write each word and place a hyphen (-) between the syllables in the second column. Write the number of syllables in the third column. Use a dictionary or the Internet to check your answers.

지도: 각 대상 단어를 읽고 음절로 나눕니다. 각 단어를 쓰고 두 번째 열의 음절 사이에 하이픈(-)을 넣습니다. 세 번째 열에 음절 수를 쓰십시오. 사전이나 인터넷을 사용하여 답을 확인하십시오.

Target Words	Words Divided into Syllables	Number of Syllables
1. ticket	tick-et	2
2. table	ta-ble	2
3. twinkle	twin-kle	2
4. textual	tex-tu-al	3
5. totality	to-tal-i-ty	4
6. takeover	take-o-ver	3
7. trumpeting	trum-pet-ing	3
8. teenagers	teen-ag-ers	3
9. Thursday	Thurs-day	2
10. throughout	through-out	2

Answer Key

 Name: _____ Date: ___/___/_____ Score: _____

The Reading Challenge

Lesson 20.8

Reading Multisyllable Words

✓ Lesson Check Point

Directions: Read each target word. Circle the word in the row that is divided correctly into syllables. Use a dictionary or the Internet to check your answers.

지도: 각 대상 단어를 읽으십시오. 음절로 올바르게 나누어진 행에 있는 단어에 동그라미를 치십시오. 사전이나 인터넷을 사용하여 답을 확인하십시오.

Model

| telephone | a. te-lep-hone | (b. tel-e-phone) | c. te-le-phone |

| 1. talkative | a. ta-lka-tive | b. talk-at-ive | (c. talk-a-tive) |

| 2. tolerance | a. to-ler-ance | (b. tol-er-ance) | c. tol-e-rance |

| 3. therapy | a. ther-ap-y | b. the-rap-y | (c. ther-a-py) |

| 4. tabletop | (a. ta-ble-top) | b. tab-le-top | c. ta-blet-op |

| 5. thermostat | (a. ther-mo-stat) | b. the-rmos-tat | c. ther-mos-tat |

| 6. trimester | (a. tri-mes-ter) | b. tri-mest-er | c. trim-es-ter |

| 7. telecast | a. te-le-cast | b. te-lec-ast | (c. tel-e-cast) |

| 8. trainable | a. trai-nab-le | (b. train-a-ble) | c. tra-ina-ble |

Learn To Read English With Directions In Korean

Assessment

Name: _____ Date: ___/___/_____ Score: _____

Lesson 20.9

Reading and Writing

Proper and Common Nouns and Adjectives

✓ Lesson Check Point

Directions: Read the words in the word box. Put an (X) on the line next to each word that is written incorrectly. Remember that all proper nouns and proper adjectives are capitalized. Use a dictionary or the Internet to check your answers.

지도: 단어 상자에 있는 단어를 읽으십시오. 잘못 쓰여진 각 단어 옆의 줄에 (X)를 표시하십시오. 모든 고유 명사와 고유 형용사는 대문자임을 기억하십시오. 사전이나 인터넷을 사용하여 답을 확인하십시오.

Word Box					
X	Trunk	X	trinidad	__	track
__	traffic	__	Texas	__	Thailand
__	truck	__	towel	X	Train
X	togo	X	Trick	X	thursday

Directions: Read each unedited sentence and underline the word that is written incorrectly. Write each sentence correctly on the line.

지도: 편집되지 않은 각 문장을 읽고 잘못 쓰여진 단어에 밑줄을 긋습니다. 각 문장을 줄에 올바르게 쓰십시오.

Model
Tracy named her beautiful <u>Twin</u> daughters Tia and Tina.
<u>Tracy named her beautiful twin daughters Tia and Tina.</u>

1. <u>this</u> year, thousands of tourists will visit Turkey.
<u>This year, thousands of tourists will visit Turkey.</u>

2. My favorite television show is "The <u>twilight</u> Zone."
<u>My favorite television show is "The Twilight Zone."</u>

3. The assigned <u>Textbook</u> is entitled "Today's Technology."
<u>The assigned textbook is entitled "Today's Technology."</u>

4. I ordered a <u>Tender</u> T-bone steak at the Turkish restaurant.
<u>I ordered a tender T-bone steak at the Turkish restaurant.</u>

Answer Key

 Name: _____ Date: ___/___/_____ Score: _____

Lesson 21.1

Reading Words with the Letter U/u

✓ Lesson Check Point

 Directions: Read each target word. Find the letter "u" and put a check (✓) in the column that identifies its position: beginning, within or end.
지도: 각 대상 단어를 읽으십시오. 문자"u"를 찾아 체크 표시(✓)위치를 식별하는 열에서 시작, 내부 또는 끝.

Target Words	Beginning (First Letter)	Within	End (Last Letter)
1. upper	✓		
2. Hindu			✓
3. subject		✓	
4. umpire	✓		
5. haiku			✓

 Directions: Read each target word. Read the words in the row and circle the word that has a different vowel "u" sound.
지도: 각 대상 단어를 읽으십시오. 줄에 있는 단어를 읽고 모음"u" 소리가 다른 단어에 동그라미를 치세요.다른 단어에 동그라미를 치세요.

Target Words					
6. plunk	yuck	lull	dung	(tune)	
7. snuff	hunk	(cute)	chug	hut	
8. slung	(used)	bunt	cud	tub	
9. husk	muck	snug	(prune)	bunk	
10. buses	under	jump	(quick)	unzip	

Learn To Read English With Directions In Korean

Assessment

Name: _____ Date: ___/___/_____ Score: _____

Lesson 21.2

Reading Words with the Short Vowel "u" Sound

✓ Lesson Check Point

Directions: Read the words in the four boxes. Circle two words with the short vowel /ŭ/ sound. The anchor word for the short vowel /ŭ/ sound is <u>up</u>.
지도: 네 개의 상자에 있는 단어를 읽으십시오. 짧은 모음 /ŭ/ 소리로 두 단어에 동그라미를 치십시오. 단모음 /ŭ/ 소리의 기준어는 up입니다.

lute	(club)		elude	(pulp)		dupe	nude
(shut)	flume		jute	(rump)		(drum)	(thus)

(mush)	dude		(club)	(fun)		plume	(plug)
spruce	(musk)		fume	Luke		(bus)	prude

Directions: Read the words in the four boxes. Circle two words that rhyme. Rhyming words have the same ending sound, such as <u>just</u> and <u>must</u>.
지도: 네 개의 상자에 있는 단어를 읽으십시오. 해당하는 두 단어에 동그라미 표시운. 운율이 있는 단어는 just 및 must와 같이 끝 소리가 같습니다.

tune	(gum)		(shun)	(stun)		(cup)	shush
Peru	(sum)		menu	pluck		ruler	(pup)

flung	(trunk)		struck	(lunch)		(truck)	guest
(sunk)	rust		bluff	(bunch)		(chuck)	clung

Answer Key

Name: _____ Date: ___/___/_____ Score: _____

Lesson 21.2

Reading & Writing Words with the Short Vowel "u" Sound

✓ **Lesson Check Point**

Directions: Read each sentence and underline three words with the short vowel /ŭ/ sound. Then, write the underlined words on the lines below. The anchor word for the short vowel /ŭ/ sound is <u>up</u>.

지도: 각 문장을 읽고 세 단어에 짧은 모음 /ŭ/ 소리에 밑줄을 긋습니다. 그런 다음 밑줄 친 단어를 아래 줄에 쓰십시오. 단모음 /ŭ/ 소리의 기준어는 up입니다.

Model

Ulysses, the <u>drummer</u>, <u>jumps</u> when he plays the <u>drums</u>.

    drummer   jumps   drums

1. Do not <u>run</u> with a <u>mug</u> or <u>cup</u> in your hands.

    run   mug   cup

2. In June, it is <u>fun</u> to take the <u>bus</u> to the reading <u>club</u>.

    fun   bus   club

3. Duke's <u>puppy</u> used to <u>run</u> <u>up</u> and down the ramp.

    puppy   run   up

4. I noticed that my student's <u>muffin</u> had <u>crushed</u> <u>nuts</u>.

    muffin   crushed   nuts

5. As Luke <u>rushed</u> for the <u>bus</u>, he started to <u>run</u> very fast.

    rushed   bus   run

Assessment

 Name: _____ Date: ___/___/_____ Score: _____

Lesson 21.3

Reading Words with the Long Vowel "u" Sound

✓ Lesson Check Point

 Directions: Read the words in the four boxes. Circle two words with the long vowel /yoo/ or /oo/ sound. The anchor word for the long vowel /yoo/ and /oo/ sounds is <u>tube</u>.
지도: 네 개의 상자에 있는 단어를 읽으십시오. 장모음/yoo/ 또는/oo/소리 로 두 단어에 동그라미를 치십시오. 장모음의 앵커 단어/yoo/ 및/oo/ 소리는 tube입니다.

trunk	(hue)		(argue)	circuit		hutch	(Luke)
(attitude)	jumper		such	(mule)		skull	(ritual)

(avenue)	(fuse)		plush	(costume)		(annual)	punch
flush	guess		flung	(perfume)		surely	(commute)

 Directions: Read the words in the four boxes. Circle two words that rhyme. Rhyming words have the same ending sound, such as <u>rule</u> and <u>mule</u>.
지도: 네 개의 상자에 있는 단어를 읽으십시오. 해당하는 두 단어에동그라미 표시운. 운율이 있는 단어는 rule 및 mule과 같이 끝 소리가같습니다.

(cube)	pluck		(spruce)	(truce)		chuck	(rescue)
chunk	(tube)		skunk	slung		crush	(avenue)

(consume)	shush		(usual)	(gradual)		(abuse)	strung
(presume)	bluff		pushing	struck		suckling	(amuse)

Answer Key

🕮 Name: _____ Date: ___/___/_____ Score: _____

Lesson 21.3

Reading & Writing Words with the Long Vowel "u" Sound

✓ Lesson Check Point

Directions: Read each sentence and underline three words with the long vowel /y$\overline{oo}$/ or /$\overline{oo}$/ sound. Then, write the underlined words on the lines below. The anchor word for the long vowel /y$\overline{oo}$/ and /$\overline{oo}$/ sounds is <u>tube</u>.

지도: 각 문장을 읽고 긴 단어로 세 단어에 밑줄을 긋습니다. 모음/y$\overline{oo}$/ 또는 / $\overline{oo}$/ 소리. 그런 다음 밑줄 친 단어를 아래 줄에 쓰십시오. 장모음 /y$\overline{oo}$/ 및 / $\overline{oo}$/ 소리의 앵커 워드는 tube입니다.

Model

<u>Bruce</u> is going to play the <u>tuba</u> and drums in <u>Uganda</u>.

   Bruce   tuba   Uganda

1. My trees <u>usually</u> <u>produce</u> an abundance of <u>fruits</u>.

   usually   produce   fruits

2. In <u>June</u>, <u>Eugene</u> and his family will have fun in <u>Yugoslavia</u>.

   June   Eugene   Yugoslavia

3. <u>Sue</u> was fortunate to ride the <u>cute</u> <u>mule</u> around the farm.

   Sue   cute   mule

4. It is unacceptable to have a <u>rude</u>, <u>crude</u> <u>attitude</u> with adults.

   rude   crude   attitude

5. Destiny told Ursula to <u>reduce</u> the amount of <u>perfume</u> she <u>uses</u>.

   reduce   perfume   uses

Assessment

Name: _____ Date: ___/___/_____ Score: _____

Review Lessons 21.2 & 21.3

Reading Short Vowel and Long Vowel Words

 Directions: Read the target words in the word box. In the first column, write the words that have the short vowel /ŭ/ sound, as in the word <u>up</u>. In the second column, write the words that have the long vowel /yōō/ or /ōō/ sound, as in the word <u>tube</u>.

지도: 단어 상자에 있는 대상 단어를 읽으십시오. 첫 번째 열에는 up 단어와 같이 단모음 /ŭ/ 소리가 나는 단어를 씁니다. 두 번째 칸에는 장모음 /yōō/ 또는 /ōō/ 소리, 단어 tube에서와 같이.

Target Word Box				
absolute	dispute	gradual	bluffing	hunch
crushing	produce	punch	bugle	duel
slushy	munch	exclude	sucking	include
consume	skunk	much	avenue	stump

Letter "u" has the /ŭ/ sound as in the word <u>up</u>

- much
- skunk
- stump
- munch
- slushy
- punch
- hunch
- bluffing
- sucking
- crushing

Letter "u" has the /yōō/ or /ōō/ sound as in the word <u>tube</u>

- duel
- bugle
- exclude
- include
- consume
- avenue
- dispute
- gradual
- produce
- absolute

Answer Key

 Name: _____ Date: ___/___/_____ Score: _____

Lesson 21.4

Reading Words with Letter "u" Vowel Pairs

✓ Lesson Check Point

 Directions: Read each target word. Circle the word in the column that has the same vowel "ua," "ue" or "ui" sound(s) as the target word.
지도: 각 대상 단어를 읽으십시오. 대상 단어와 동일한 모음 "ua," "ue" 또는 "ui" 소리를 갖는 열의 단어에 동그라미를 치십시오.

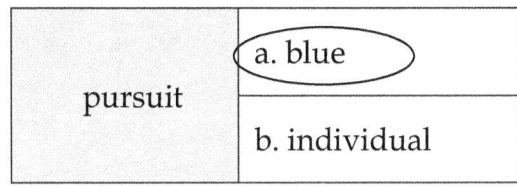
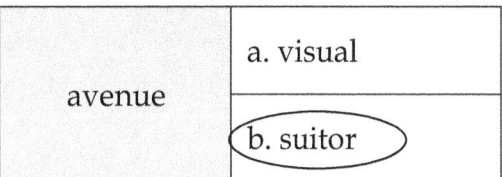
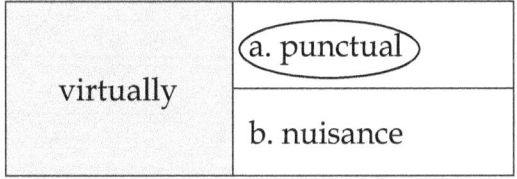
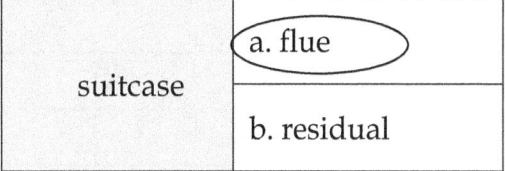

 Directions: Read each target word. Put a check (✓) under the correct column heading.
지도: 각 대상 단어를 읽으십시오. 올바른 열 제목 아래에 체크(✓)를 하십시오.

Target Words	Words have the long "u" sound as in the word <u>blue</u>	Words do not have the long "u" sound
1. dual	✓	
2. built		✓
3. suite		✓
4. influence	✓	

Learn To Read English With Directions In Korean

Assessment

 Name: _____ Date:___/___/_____ Score:_____

Lesson 21.5

Reading Words with the Final Letter "u"

✓ Lesson Check Point

 Directions: Read each target word. Find the letter "u" and put a check (✓) in the column that identifies its position within the syllable.
지도: 각 대상 단어를 읽으십시오. 문자 "u"를 찾아 체크 표시(✓)음절 내에서 위치를 식별하는 열에서.

Target Words	"u" is at the end of a one syllable word	"u" is at the end of the first syllable	"u" is at the end of a multi-syllable word
1. fl<u>u</u>	✓		
2. d<u>u</u>al		✓	
3. <u>u</u>nify		✓	
4. <u>u</u>sual		✓	
5. m<u>u</u>tual		✓	

 Directions: Read each target word. Put a check (✓) under the correct column heading.
지도: 각 대상 단어를 읽으십시오. 올바른 열 제목 아래에 체크(✓)를 하십시오.

Target Words	"u" has the /ŭ/ sound as in the word <u>tub</u>	"u" has the /yoo/ sound as in the word <u>tube</u>	"u" has the /ə/ sound as in the word <u>circus</u>	"u" is silent as in the word <u>build</u>
6. built				✓
7. mule		✓		
8. jump	✓			
9. until	✓			
10. surprise			✓	

Answer Key

 Name: _____ Date: ___/___/_____ Score: _____

Lesson 21.6

Reading Letter "u" Words with the Schwa Vowel Sound

✓ Lesson Check Point

 Directions: Read each target word. Circle the word in the column that has the same "u" sound as the target word.
지도: 각 대상 단어를 읽으십시오. 대상 단어와 "u" 소리가 같은 열의 단어에 동그라미를 치십시오.

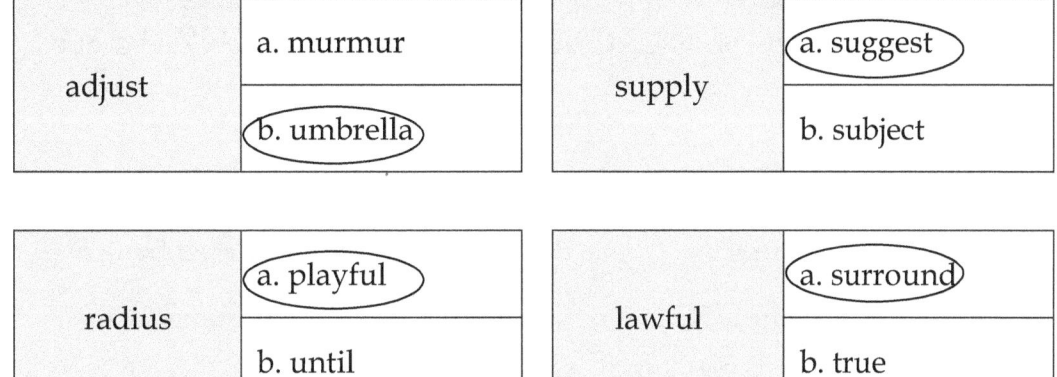

 Directions: Read each sentence and underline the letter "u" word that has the schwa vowel /ə/ sound. The anchor word for the letter "u" schwa vowel sound is <u>campus</u>.
지도: 각 문장을 읽고 슈와 모음 /ə/ 소리가 있는 문자 "u" 단어에 밑줄을 긋습니다. 문자 "u" 슈와 모음 소리의 앵커 단어는 campus입니다.

1. The <u>popular</u> students attend Utah University.

2. The <u>beautiful</u> flowers enhance the house's value.

3. Gus was unable to determine the <u>radius</u> of a circle.

4. My family and I used to visit the Yucatan <u>Peninsula</u>.

5. My university professor worked in the music <u>industry</u>.

6. The security guards monitor the cameras on a <u>regular</u> basis.

Assessment

Name: _____ Date: ___/___/_____ Score: _____

Lesson 21.7

Reading Words with the "ur" Letter Combination

Dictionary Skills/ Vocabulary

✓ Lesson Check Point

Directions: Read each target word and its definition. Write the letter of the definition on the line of each target word. Use a dictionary or the Internet to check your answers.
지도: 각 대상 단어와 그 정의를 읽으십시오. 각 대상 단어의 행에 정의의 문자를 씁니다. 사전이나 인터넷을 사용하여 답을 확인하십시오.

Target Words	Definitions
1. _d_ curls	a. destroyed and/or consumed by fire
2. _a_ burned	b. something of high importance
3. _e_ curse	c. the act of not succeeding
4. _b_ urgent	d. the act of twisting something into coils
5. _c_ failure	e. to say bad words or swear

Directions: Read each sentence and write the target word on the line that correctly completes the sentence.
지도: 각 문장을읽고 다음과 같은 목표 단어를 쓰십시오. 장을올바르게 완성합니다.

6. At two o'clock, I received an ____urgent____ phone call.

7. Successful people believe ____failure____ is not an option.

8. My hair ____curls____ up when the weather is humid.

9. It is not acceptable to ____curse____ in class.

10. We are going out for dinner because Dad ____burned____ the chicken.

Answer Key

Name: _____ Date: ___/___/_____ Score: _____

Lesson 21.8

Reading Words with a Silent Letter "u"

✓ Lesson Check Point

Directions: Read the target words in the word box. Write the words that have a silent letter "u" in the first column. Write the words that do not have a silent letter "u" in the second column.

지도: 단어 상자에 있는 대상 단어를 읽으십시오. 첫 번째 열에 묵음문자 "u"가 있는 단어를 쓰십시오. 두 번째 열에 묵음 문자"u"가 없는 단어를 쓰십시오.

Target Word Box				
intrigue	student	guest	individual	guardian
continual	guilty	antique	occupy	prologue
argument	brushing	dumpster	guard	drummers
guarded	confusion	technique	lunch	guide

Letter "u" is silent

- guest
- guard
- guide
- guilty
- antique
- guarded
- intrigue
- technique
- prologue
- guardian

Letter "u" has a letter "u" sound

- lunch
- occupy
- student
- brushing
- dumpster
- drummers
- argument
- continual
- confusion
- individual

Learn To Read English With Directions In Korean

Assessment

 Name: _____ Date:___/___/_____ Score:_____

Unit Review - U/u

Reading Words with Vowel "u" Sounds: /ŭ/, /oo/, /ə/ & Silent

✓ Lesson Check Point

 Directions: Read each target word. Circle the word in the column that has the same "u" sound as the target word.
지도: 각 대상 단어를 읽으십시오. 대상 단어와 "u" 소리가 같은 열의 단어에 동그라미를 치십시오.

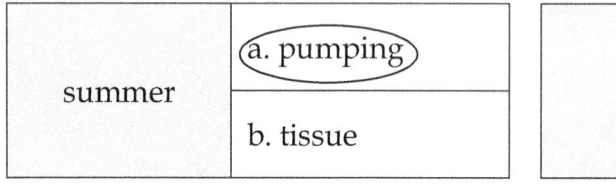
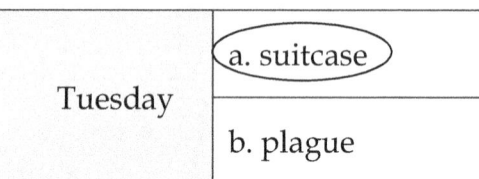
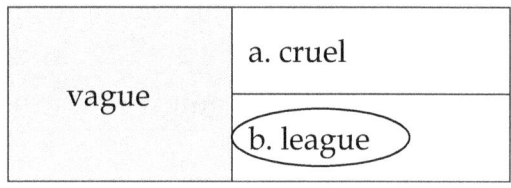
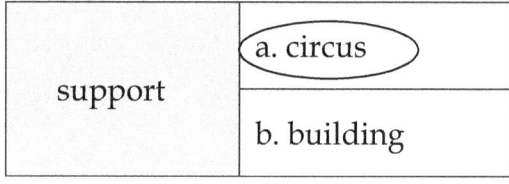

 Directions: Read each target word. Put a check (✓) under the correct column heading.
지도: 각 대상 단어를 읽으십시오. 올바른 열 제목 아래에 체크(✓)를 하십시오.

Target Words	"u" has the /ŭ/ sound as in the word <u>tub</u>	"u" has the /oo/ sound as in the word <u>tube</u>	"u" has the /ə/ sound as in the word <u>circus</u>	"u" is silent as in the word <u>build</u>
1. summer	✓			
2. Tuesday		✓		
3. vague				✓
4. support			✓	

Answer Key

 Name: _____ Date:___/___/_____ Score:_____

The Reading Challenge

Lesson 21.9

Reading Multisyllable Words

✓ Lesson Check Point

 Directions: Read and divide each target word into syllables. Write each word and place a hyphen (-) between the syllables in the second column. Write the number of syllables in the third column. Use a dictionary or the Internet to check your answers.

지도: 각 대상 단어를 읽고 음절로 나눕니다. 각 단어를 쓰고 두 번째 열의 음절 사이에 하이픈(-)을 넣습니다. 세 번째 열에 음절 수를 쓰십시오. 사전이나 인터넷을 사용하여 답을 확인하십시오.

Target Words	Words Divided into Syllables	Number of Syllables
1. juicy	juic-y	2
2. album	al-bum	2
3. bushes	bush-es	2
4. rushing	rush-ing	2
5. perfume	per-fume	2
6. shoulder	shou-lder	2
7. building	build-ing	2
8. tribunal	tri-bu-nal	3
9. disputing	dis-put-ing	3
10. dumpster	dump-ster	2

Assessment

Name: _____ Date: ___/___/_____ Score: _____

The Reading Challenge

Lesson 21.9

Reading Multisyllable Words

✓ Lesson Check Point

Directions: Read each target word. Circle the word in the row that is divided correctly into syllables. Use a dictionary or the Internet to check your answers.

지도: 각 대상 단어를 읽으십시오. 음절로 올바르게 나누어진 행에 있는 단어에 동그라미를 치십시오. 사전이나 인터넷을 사용하여 답을 확인하십시오.

Model

| visualize | a. vis-ua-lize | b. vi-su-al-ize ⭕ | c. vis-u-a-lize |

1. inclusion	a. in-clu-sion ⭕	b. in-clus-ion	c. incl-u-sion
2. excusing	a. ex-cus-ing ⭕	b. exc-u-sing	c. ex-cu-sing
3. producing	a. prod-u-cing	b. pro-duc-ing ⭕	c. prod-uc-ing
4. residual	a. res-id-ual	b. re-sid-u-al ⭕	c. re-sid-ual
5. publishing	a. publ-ish-ing	b. pu-blish-ing	c. pub-lish-ing ⭕
6. exclusive	a. e-xclu-sive	b. ex-clu-sive ⭕	c. ex-clus-ive
7. presuming	a. pre-sum-ing ⭕	b. pres-u-ming	c. pr-esum-ing
8. consonant	a. con-son-ant	b. cons-o-nant	c. con-so-nant ⭕

Answer Key

 Name: _____ Date: ___/___/_____ Score: _____

Lesson 21.10

Reading and Writing

Proper and Common Nouns and Adjectives

✓ Lesson Check Point

 Directions: Read the words in the word box. Put an (X) on the line next to each word that is written incorrectly. Remember that all proper nouns and proper adjectives are capitalized. Use a dictionary or the Internet to check your answers.

지도: 단어 상자에 있는 단어를 읽으십시오. 잘못 쓰여진 각 단어 옆의 줄에 (X)를 표시하십시오. 모든 고유 명사와 고유 형용사는 대문자임을 기억하십시오. 사전이나 인터넷을 사용하여 답을 확인하십시오.

Word Box					
__	Umbria	__	upbringing	X	Ace university
X	upper Canada	X	Ultimately	__	UFO
__	united	__	Uganda	X	Unblock
__	umbrella	X	universal Time	X	Umpire

 Directions: Read each unedited sentence and underline the word that is written incorrectly. Write each sentence correctly on the line.

지도: 편집되지 않은 각 문장을 읽고 잘못 쓰여진 단어에 밑줄을긋습 니다. 각 문장을 줄에 올바르게 쓰십시오.

Model
Mrs. Ubangi usually has union meetings at a local <u>University</u>.
<u>Mrs. Ubangi usually has union meetings at a local university.</u>

1. Oxford University is located in the <u>united</u> Kingdom.
<u>Oxford University is located in the United Kingdom.</u>

2. Last summer, Uncle moved from <u>uganda</u> to the USA.
<u>Last summer, Uncle moved from Uganda to the USA.</u>

3. Did you know that Uncle Udell speaks <u>urdu</u> and Hindi fluently?
<u>Did you know that Uncle Udell speaks Urdu and Hindi fluently?</u>

4. Ulric said, "The <u>united</u> States of America has excellent universities."
<u>Ulric said, "The United States of America has excellent universities."</u>

Assessment

Name: _____ Date:___/___/_____ Score:_____

Lesson 22.1

Reading Words with the Letter V/v

✓ Lesson Check Point

Directions: Read each target word. Find the letter "v" and put a check (✓) in the column that identifies its position: beginning, within or end.
지도: 각 대상 단어를 읽으십시오. 문자"v"를 찾아 체크 표시(✓)위치를 식별하는 열에서 시작, 내부 또는 끝.

Target Words	Beginning (First Letter)	Within	End (Last Letter)
1. vapor	✓		
2. server		✓	
3. violet	✓		
4. violins	✓		
5. provided		✓	

Directions: Read each sentence and underline the words that begin with the letter "v." Write all the underlined words in alphabetical order on the lines below.
지도: 각 문장을 읽고"v"로 시작하는 단어에 밑줄을 긋습니다. 아래 줄에 밑줄 친 단어를 알파벳 순서로 모두 쓰십시오.

6. Mr. Samuel was <u>voted</u> <u>volunteer</u> of the month.

7. Ryan placed all the <u>valuables</u> in his bank <u>vault</u>.

8. This fall, Teresa and Bobby plan to <u>visit</u> <u>Vienna</u>.

9. The antagonist in the story, "<u>Vampire's</u> Heart," is <u>vain</u>.

10. My challenging <u>vocabulary</u> words are <u>vertebrate</u> and invertebrate.

vain	valuables	Vampire's
vault	vertebrate	Vienna
visit	vocabulary	volunteer
	voted	

Answer Key

 Name: _____ Date: ___/___/_____ Score: _____

The Reading Challenge

Lesson 22.2

Reading Multisyllable Words

✓ Lesson Check Point

 Directions: Read and divide each target word into syllables. Write each word and place a hyphen (-) between the syllables in the second column. Write the number of syllables in the third column. Use a dictionary or the Internet to check your answers.

지도: 각 대상 단어를 읽고 음절로 나눕니다. 각 단어를 쓰고 두 번째 열의 음절 사이에 하이픈(-)을 넣습니다. 세 번째 열에 음절 수를 쓰십시오. 사전이나 인터넷을 사용하여 답을 확인하십시오.

Target Words	Words Divided into Syllables	Number of Syllables
1. very	ver-y	2
2. velvet	vel-vet	2
3. visible	vis-i-ble	3
4. Viking	Vi-king	2
5. vertical	ver-ti-cal	3
6. valuable	val-u-a-ble	4
7. vibrantly	vi-brant-ly	3
8. voltage	volt-age	2
9. visionary	vi-sion-ar-y	4
10. validation	val-i-da-tion	4

Assessment

Name: _____ Date: ___/___/_____ Score: _____

The Reading Challenge

Lesson 22.2

Reading Multisyllable Words

✓ Lesson Check Point

Directions: Read each target word. Circle the word in the row that is divided correctly into syllables. Use a dictionary or the Internet to check your answers.

지도: 각 대상 단어를 읽으십시오. 음절로 올바르게 나누어진 행에 있는 단어에 동그라미를 치십시오. 사전이나 인터넷을 사용하여 답을 확인하십시오.

Model

| volcano | a. vo-lcan-o | b. vol-can-o | c. vol-ca-no ⭕ |

| 1. vehicle | a. ve-hi-cle ⭕ | b. ve-hic-le | c. veh-i-cle |

| 2. various | a. va-rio-us | b. va-ri-ous | c. var-i-ous ⭕ |

| 3. vinegar | a. vi-neg-ar | b. vi-ne-gar | c. vin-e-gar ⭕ |

| 4. ventilate | a. vent-i-late | b. ven-ti-late ⭕ | c. ven-til-ate |

| 5. violence | a. vi-ol-ence | b. vio-le-nce | c. vi-o-lence ⭕ |

| 6. vindicate | a. vin-di-cate ⭕ | b. vin-dic-ate | c. vin-dica-te |

| 7. volition | a. vo-li-tion ⭕ | b. vol-i-tion | c. vol-it-ion |

| 8. vaporize | a. vap-o-rize | b. va-por-ize ⭕ | c. vap-or-ize |

Answer Key

Name: _____ Date: ___/___/_____ Score: _____

Lesson 22.3

Reading and Writing

Proper and Common Nouns and Adjectives

✓ Lesson Check Point

Directions: Read the words in the word box. Put an (X) on the line next to each word that is written incorrectly. Remember that all proper nouns and proper adjectives are capitalized. Use a dictionary or the Internet to check your answers.

지도: 단어 상자에 있는 단어를 읽으십시오. 잘못 쓰여진 각 단어 옆의 줄에 (X)를 표시하십시오. 모든 고유 명사와 고유 형용사는 대문자임을 기억하십시오. 사전이나 인터넷을 사용하여 답을 확인하십시오.

Word Box					
X	virgin Islands	X	Verse	__	Venice
__	vibrant	X	Volcano	X	valley Forge
X	Vintage	__	Vermont	__	Vienna
__	Vietnamese	__	villager	X	Visiting

Directions: Read each unedited sentence and underline the word that is written incorrectly. Write each sentence correctly on the line.

지도: 편집되지 않은 각 문장을 읽고 잘못 쓰여진 단어에 밑줄을긋습 니다. 각 문장을 줄에 올바르게 쓰십시오.

Model
The villagers in Vienna love to receive <u>Visitors</u>.
<u>The villagers in Vienna love to receive visitors.</u>

1. Valerie <u>Volunteers</u> at General Veterans Hospital.
<u>Valerie volunteers at General Veterans Hospital.</u>

2. On Tuesday, <u>vice</u> President Vernon voted on the bill.
<u>On Tuesday, Vice President Vernon voted on the bill.</u>

3. My music <u>Video</u> features Voldoff, the professional violinist.
<u>My music video features Voldoff, the professional violinist.</u>

4. Historians record that the Vikings made strong, seafaring <u>Vessels</u>.
<u>Historians record that the Vikings made strong, seafaring vessels.</u>

Assessment

Name: _____ Date: ___/___/_____ Score: _____

Lesson 23.1

Reading Words with the Letter W/w

✓ Lesson Check Point

Directions: Read each target word. Find the letter "w" and put a check (✓) in the column that identifies its position: beginning, within or end.
지도: 각 대상 단어를 읽으십시오. 문자"w"를 찾아 체크 표시(✓)위치를 식별하는 열에서 시작, 내부 또는 끝.

Target Words	Beginning (First Letter)	Within	End (Last Letter)
1. unwilling		✓	
2. overview			✓
3. wishbone	✓		
4. weather	✓		
5. trustworthy		✓	

Directions: Read each sentence and underline the words that begin with the letter "w." Write all the underlined words in alphabetical order on the lines below.
지도: 각 문장을 읽고"w"로 시작하는 단어에 밑줄을 긋습니다. 아래 줄에 밑줄 친 단어를 알파벳 순서로 모두 쓰십시오.

6. It is cold and <u>windy</u> in the <u>winter</u>.

7. On Tuesday, they ate <u>watermelon</u> and <u>waffles</u>.

8. The <u>wheelbarrow</u> has a pile of dirt and <u>worms</u>.

9. Samuel bought his <u>watch</u> from the local <u>wholesale</u> store.

10. The <u>weather</u> in Los Angeles, California is generally <u>warm</u>.

waffles   warm   watch
watermelon   weather   wheelbarrow
wholesale   windy   winter
               worms

Answer Key

 Name: _____ Date: ___/___/_____ Score: _____

Lesson 23.2

Reading Words with a Vowel before the Letter "w"

✓ Lesson Check Point

 Directions: Read each target word. Circle the word in the column that has the same "aw," "ew" or "ow" sound as the target word.
지도: 각 대상 단어를 읽으십시오. 대상 단어와 같은"aw," "ew" 또는"ow" 소리가 나는 열의 단어에 동그라미를 치십시오.

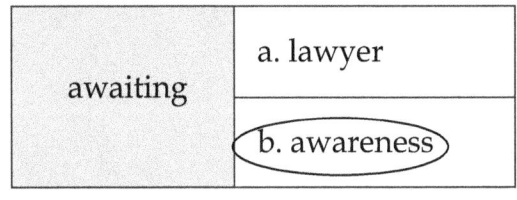
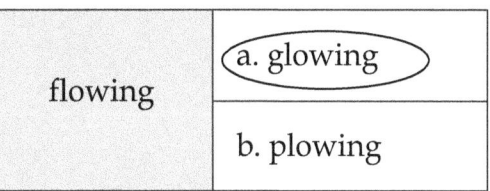
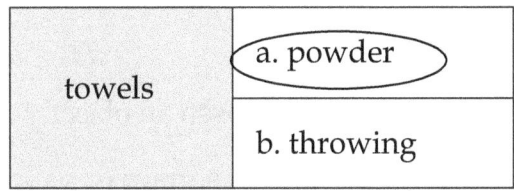
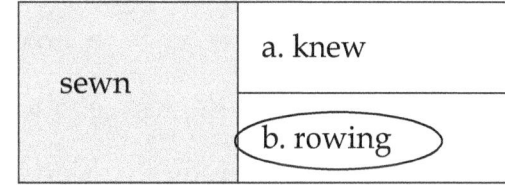

 Directions: Read each target word. Put a check (✓) under the correct column heading.
지도: 각 대상 단어를 읽으십시오. 올바른 열 제목 아래에 체크(✓)를 하십시오.

Target Words	Underlined letters have /o͞o/ sound as in the word <u>few</u>	Underlined letters have /ô/ sound as in the word <u>law</u>	Underlined letters have /ō/ sound as in the word <u>sew</u>	Underlined letters have /ou/ sound as in the word <u>cow</u>
1. f<u>aw</u>n		✓		
2. fl<u>ow</u>ing			✓	
3. t<u>ow</u>els				✓
4. s<u>ew</u>n			✓	

Assessment

Name: _____ Date:___/___/_____ Score: _____

Lesson 23.3

Reading Words with a Silent "w" and "wr" Letter Combination

Dictionary Skills/ Vocabulary

✓ Lesson Check Point

Directions: Read each target word and its definition. Write the letter of the definition on the line of each target word. Use a dictionary or the Internet to check your answers.
지도: 각 대상 단어와 그 정의를 읽으십시오. 각 대상 단어의 행에 정의의 문자를 씁니다. 사전이나 인터넷을 사용하여 답을 확인하십시오.

Target Words	Definitions
1. _e_ wrap	a. incorrect or erroneous
2. _c_ wrench	b. to move or squirm
3. _b_ wriggles	c. a tool used to tighten or loosen an object
4. _a_ wrong	d. to have printed words on a surface or paper
5. _d_ wrote	e. to fold in a tight covering

Directions: Read each sentence. Underline the word in the parentheses that correctly completes each sentence. Then, write the underlined word on the line.
지도: 각 문장을 읽으십시오. 각 문장을 올바르게 완성하는 괄호 안에 있는 단어에 밑줄을 긋습니다. 그런 다음 밑줄 친 단어를 줄에 쓰십시오.

6. Wendell has a _____wrench_____ in his toolbox. (wrench, wrote)

7. My favorite author _____wrote_____ five books. (wrapped, wrote)

8. I accidentally rang the _____wrong_____ doorbell. (wrong, wrench)

9. I will _____wrap_____ my sandwich in foil paper. (wriggles, wrap)

10. My baby __wriggles__ her fingers when she is happy. (wrong, wriggles)

Answer Key

 Name: _____ Date: ___/___/_____ Score: _____

Lesson 23.3

Reading Words with a Silent Letter "w"

✓ Lesson Check Point

 Directions: Read the target words in the word box. Write the words that have a silent letter "w" in the first column. Write the words that do not have a silent letter "w" in the second column.
지도: 단어 상자에 있는 대상 단어를 읽으십시오. 첫 번째 열에 묵음문자 "w"가 있는 단어를 쓰십시오. 두 번째 열에 묵음 문자"w"가 없는 단어를 쓰십시오.

Target Word Box				
two	crow	firewood	waiters	farewell
dwelling	writing	wrap	beware	answering
earwax	biweekly	wreck	window	freeway
tow	sword	driveway	backward	wrote

Letter "w" is silent

- two
- tow
- crow
- wrap
- wreck
- wrote
- sword
- window
- writing
- answering

Letter "w" has the /w/ sound

- earwax
- beware
- waiters
- farewell
- freeway
- biweekly
- firewood
- dwelling
- backward
- driveway

Assessment

 Name: _____ Date:___/___/_____ Score:_____

The Reading Challenge

Lesson 23.4

Reading Multisyllable Words

✓ Lesson Check Point

 Directions: Read and divide each target word into syllables. Write each word and place a hyphen (-) between the syllables in the second column. Write the number of syllables in the third column. Use a dictionary or the Internet to check your answers.

지도: 각 대상 단어를 읽고 음절로 나눕니다. 각 단어를 쓰고 두 번째 열의 음절 사이에 하이픈(-)을 넣습니다. 세 번째 열에 음절 수를 쓰십시오. 사전이나 인터넷을 사용하여 답을 확인하십시오.

Target Words	Words Divided into Syllables	Number of Syllables
1. walrus	wal-rus	2
2. working	work-ing	2
3. wisdom	wis-dom	2
4. wholesaling	whole-sal-ing	3
5. wastefulness	waste-ful-ness	3
6. Washington	Wash-ing-ton	3
7. wanderer	wan-der-er	3
8. watermelon	wa-ter-mel-on	4
9. wraparound	wrap-a-round	3
10. weatherize	weath-er-ize	3

Answer Key

 Name: _____ Date: ___/___/_____ Score: _____

The Reading Challenge

Lesson 23.4

Reading Multisyllable Words

✓ Lesson Check Point

 Directions: Read each target word. Circle the word in the row that is divided correctly into syllables. Use a dictionary or the Internet to check your answers.
지도: 각 대상 단어를 읽으십시오. 음절로 올바르게 나누어진 행에 있는 단어에 동그라미를 치십시오. 사전이나 인터넷을 사용하여 답을 확인하십시오.

Model

wonderful	a. wo-nder-ful	(b. won-der-ful)	c. won-derf-ul
1. winery	a. wi-ner-y	(b. win-er-y)	c. win-e-ry
2. Wisconsin	a. Wi-scon-sin	(b. Wis-con-sin)	c. Wis-cons-in
3. westerner	a. west-er-ner	b. wes-ter-ner	(c. west-ern-er)
4. whenever	a. whe-nev-er	(b. when-ev-er)	c. when-e-ver
5. whimsical	(a. whim-si-cal)	b. whi-msic-al	c. whim-sic-al
6. wilderness	(a. wil-der-ness)	b. wil-dern-ess	c. wild-er-ness
7. wonderful	a. wond-er-ful	b. won-derf-ul	(c. won-der-ful)
8. woefulness	a. woef-u-lness	(b. woe-ful-ness)	c. woe-fuln-ess

Learn To Read English With Directions In Korean

Assessment

 Name: _____ Date: ___/___/_____ Score: _____

Lesson 23.5

Reading and Writing

Proper and Common Nouns and Adjectives

✓ Lesson Check Point

 Directions: Read the words in the word box. Put an (X) on the line next to each word that is written incorrectly. Remember that all proper nouns and proper adjectives are capitalized. Use a dictionary or the Internet to check your answers.

지도: 단어 상자에 있는 단어를 읽으십시오. 잘못 쓰여진 각 단어 옆의 줄에 (X)를 표시하십시오. 모든 고유 명사와 고유 형용사는 대문자임을 기억하십시오. 사전이나 인터넷을 사용하여 답을 확인하십시오.

Word Box					
X	Window	__	wasteland	__	Walachia
__	West Indies	__	Washington	X	weddell Sea
X	wales	__	whatever	X	Wedding
__	Welsh	X	White rice	X	Webpage

 Directions: Read each unedited sentence and underline the word that is written incorrectly. Write each sentence correctly on the line.

지도: 편집되지 않은 각 문장을 읽고 잘못 쓰여진 단어에 밑줄을 긋습니다. 각 문장을 줄에 올바르게 쓰십시오.

Model

We walked along the winding path that led to the <u>Waterfalls</u>.
<u>We walked along the winding path that led to the waterfalls.</u>

1. We check the <u>Weather</u> forecast on the World Wide Web.
<u>We check the weather forecast on the World Wide Web.</u>

2. Warren is wearing a <u>Wool</u> sweater and a pair of gloves.
<u>Warren is wearing a wool sweater and a pair of gloves.</u>

3. We saw a walrus and two wildcats at the <u>west</u> Virginia Zoo.
<u>We saw a walrus and two wildcats at the West Virginia Zoo.</u>

4. On <u>wednesday</u>, Whitney and her family are going to the water park.
<u>On Wednesday, Whitney and her family are going to the water park.</u>

Answer Key

 Name: _____ Date: ___/___/_____ Score: _____

Lesson 24.1

Reading Words with the Letter X/x

✓ Lesson Check Point

 Directions: Read each target word. Find the letter "x" and put a check (✓) in the column that identifies its position: beginning, within or end.
지도: 각 대상 단어를 읽으십시오. 문자"x"를 찾아 체크 표시(✓)위치를 식별하는 열에서 시작, 내부 또는 끝.

Target Words	Beginning (First Letter)	Within	End (Last Letter)
1. x-ray	✓		
2. boxer		✓	
3. duplex			✓
4. examine		✓	
5. xylograph	✓		

 Directions: Read each sentence and underline the words that begin with the letter "x." Write all the underlined words in alphabetical order on the lines below.
지도: 각 문장을 읽고 문자"x"로 시작하는 단어에 밑줄을 긋습니다. 아래 줄에 밑줄 친 단어를 알파벳 순서로 모두 쓰십시오.

6. The <u>xylophonist</u> skillfully plays the <u>xylophone</u>.

7. <u>Xavier</u> said, "The <u>x-axis</u> is perpendicular to the y-axis."

8. I am reading historical details about <u>Xining</u> and <u>Xanthus</u>.

9. There are two brown bottles of <u>xanthine</u> and <u>xanthene</u> in the lab.

10. <u>Xenophilia</u> and <u>xenophily</u> refer to love for people from different cultures.

x-axis   xanthene   xanthine
Xanthus   Xavier   xenophilia
xenophily   Xining   xylophone
                  xylophonist

Assessment

 Name: _____ Date: _____/____/_____ Score: _____

Lesson 24.1

Reading Words with the Letter X/x

✓ **Lesson Check Point**

 Directions: Read each target word. Circle the word in the column that has the same "x" sound(s) as the target word.
지도: 각 대상 단어를 읽으십시오. 대상 단어와 동일한"x" 소리가 있는 열의 단어에 동그라미를 치십시오.

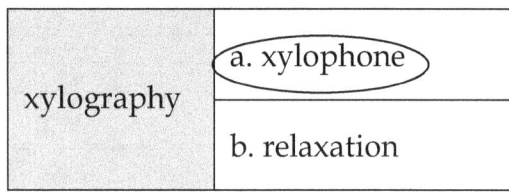

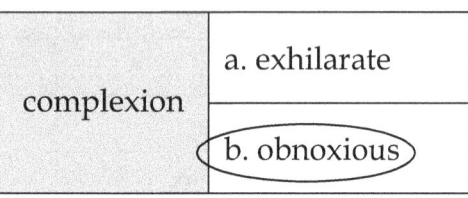

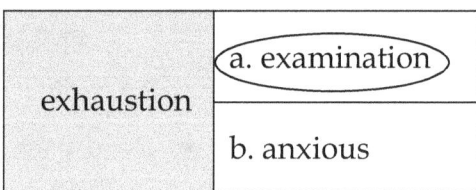

 Directions: Read each target word. Put a check (✓) under the correct column heading.
지도: 각 대상 단어를 읽으십시오. 올바른 열 제목 아래에 체크(✓)를하십시오.

Target Words	"x" has the /k/ + /s/ sounds as in the word <u>box</u>	"x" has the /z/ sound as in the word <u>xylophone</u>	"x" has the /g/ + /z/ sounds as in the word <u>exhibit</u>	"x" has the /k/ + /sh/ sounds as in the word <u>anxious</u>
1. xylography		✓		
2. complexion				✓
3. Oxford	✓			
4. exhaustion			✓	

Answer Key

 Name: _____ Date: ___/___/_____ Score: _____

The Reading Challenge

Lesson 24.2

Reading Multisyllable Words

✓ Lesson Check Point

 Directions: Read and divide each target word into syllables. Write each word and place a hyphen (-) between the syllables in the second column. Write the number of syllables in the third column. Use a dictionary or the Internet to check your answers.

지도: 각 대상 단어를 읽고 음절로 나눕니다. 각 단어를 쓰고 두 번째 열의 음절 사이에 하이픈(-)을 넣습니다. 세 번째 열에 음절 수를 쓰십시오. 사전이나 인터넷을 사용하여 답을 확인하십시오.

Target Words	Words Divided into Syllables	Number of Syllables
1. climax	cli-max	2
2. anxiety	anx-i-e-ty	4
3. waxing	wax-ing	2
4. fixation	fix-a-tion	3
5. expectant	ex-pec-tant	3
6. remixing	re-mix-ing	3
7. xylophone	xy-lo-phone	3
8. textbooks	text-books	2
9. expanded	ex-pand-ed	3
10. toxicology	tox-i-col-o-gy	5

Assessment

L Name: _____ Date: ___/___/_____ Score: _____

The Reading Challenge

Lesson 24.2

Reading Multisyllable Words

✓ **Lesson Check Point**

Directions: Read each target word. Circle the word in the row that is divided correctly into syllables. Use a dictionary or the Internet to check your answers.
지도: 각 대상 단어를 읽으십시오. 음절로 올바르게 나누어진 행에 있는 단어에 동그라미를 치십시오. 사전이나 인터넷을 사용하여 답을 확인하십시오.

Model

| oxidized | **a. ox-i-dized** ⬭ | b. oxi-d-ized | c. o-xi-dized |

1. complexion	**a. com-plex-ion** ⬭	b. com-ple-xion	c. co-mple-xion
2. auxiliary	a. au-xi-liary	b. aux-i-liary	**c. aux-il-ia-ry** ⬭
3. excitement	a. exci-te-ment	**b. ex-cite-ment** ⬭	c. exc-ite-ment
4. taxation	a. ta-xa-tion	**b. tax-a-tion** ⬭	c. tax-at-ion
5. examining	**a. ex-am-in-ing** ⬭	b. exam-i-ning	c. exa-min-ing
6. lexicon	a. le-xi-con	b. le-xic-on	**c. lex-i-con** ⬭
7. exporting	a. exp-o-rting	b. exp-or-ting	**c. ex-port-ing** ⬭
8. exclusive	a. excl-u-sive	**b. ex-clu-sive** ⬭	c. ex-clus-ive

Answer Key

 Name: _____ Date: ___/___/_____ Score: _____

Lesson 24.3

Reading and Writing

Proper and Common Nouns and Adjectives

✓ Lesson Check Point

 Directions: Read the words in the word box. Put an (X) on the line next to each word that is written incorrectly. Remember that all proper nouns and proper adjectives are capitalized. Use a dictionary or the Internet to check your answers.
지도: 단어 상자에 있는 단어를 읽으십시오. 잘못 쓰여진 각 단어 옆의 줄에 (X)를 표시하십시오. 모든 고유 명사와 고유 형용사는 대문자임을 기억하십시오. 사전이나 인터넷을 사용하여 답을 확인하십시오.

	Word Box				
X	Dr. xavier	__	Xingu River	X	xanthus
__	Xerox	X	Xylograph	__	xebec
X	X-rays	X	xanadu	__	xenophiles
__	x-axis	X	Xylophonist	__	xylem

 Directions: Read each unedited sentence and underline the word that is written incorrectly. Write each sentence correctly on the line.
지도: 편집되지 않은 각 문장을 읽고 잘못 쓰여진 단어에 밑줄을긋습 니다. 각 문장을 줄에 올바르게 쓰십시오.

Model
Xia said, "The population of xankandi is 33,000 people."
Xia said, "The population of Xankandi is 33,000 people."

1. The article noted that Mr. Xavier is a professional Xylophonist.
The article noted that Mr. Xavier is a professional xylophonist.

2. The xingu River in Brazil flows north into the Amazon River.
The Xingu River in Brazil flows north into the Amazon River.

3. I noticed that Xanthan gum is an ingredient in marshmallows.
I noticed that xanthan gum is an ingredient in marshmallows.

4. Mr. and Mrs. xing work for Xerox in the printing department.
Mr. and Mrs. Xing work for Xerox in the printing department.

Assessment

Name: _____ Date: ___/___/_____ Score: _____

Lesson 25.1

Reading Words with the Letter Y/y

✓ Lesson Check Point

Directions: Read each target word. Find the letter "y" and put a check (✓) in the column that identifies its position: beginning, within or end.
지도: 각 대상 단어를 읽으십시오. 문자"y"를 찾아 체크 표시(✓)위치를 식별하는 열에서 시작, 내부 또는 끝.

Target Words	Beginning (First Letter)	Within	End (Last Letter)
1. yeast	✓		
2. factory			✓
3. deeply			✓
4. crystals		✓	
5. gymnastic		✓	

Directions: Read each sentence and underline the words that begin with the letter "y." Write all the underlined words in alphabetical order on the lines below.
지도: 각 대상 단어를 읽으십시오. 문자"y를 찾아 체크 표시(✓)위치를식별하는 열에서 시작, 내부 또는 끝.

6. I bought a roll of yellow yarn.

7. Yesterday, Isaiah was caught yawning in class.

8. Did James watch the New York Yankees' game?

9. All the youngsters are playing in the large yard.

10. Yusef used the yardstick to measure the area of his bedroom.

Yankees'   yard   yardstick
yarn   yawning   yellow
Yesterday   York   youngsters
                  Yusef

Answer Key

 Name: _____ Date: ___/___/_____ Score: _____

Lesson 25.1

Reading Words with the Letter Y/y

✓ Lesson Check Point

 Directions: Read each target word. Circle the word in the row that has a different "y" sound than the target word.
지도: 각 대상 단어를 읽으십시오. 목표 단어와 다른"y" 소리가 나는 행의 단어에 동그라미를 치십시오.

Target Words				
1. sycamore	catalyst	analytic	hypnosis	(gigabyte)
2. yesterday	yielded	papaya	(symphony)	yonder
3. Kenya	Malaya	yogurt	(bicycles)	Maya
4. typhoon	(typical)	types	tycoon	tyrant
5. youngster	(baby)	yellow	yarn	years

 Directions: Read the words in the four boxes. Circle two words that have the same "y" sound.
지도: 네 개의 상자에 있는 단어를 읽으십시오. "y"소리가 같은 두 단어에 동그라미를 치십시오.

(goodbye)	mystery
(styling)	today

young	argyle
baby	(yogurt)

syntax	youth
(eyelids)	(analyze)

rhyme	(hypnosis)
you'll	(calypso)

(Kenya)	(Maya)
hype	hyssop

windy	(yellow)
(yardage)	syntax

Assessment

 Name: _____ Date: ___/___/_____ Score: _____

Lesson 25.2

Reading Words with a Vowel before the Letter "y"

✓ Lesson Check Point

 Directions: Read each target word. Circle the word in the column that has the same "y" sound as the target word.
지도: 각 대상 단어를 읽으십시오. 목표 단어와 같은 "y" 소리가 나는 열의 단어에 동그라미를 치십시오.

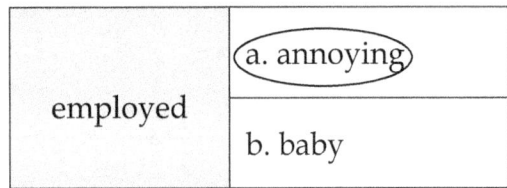
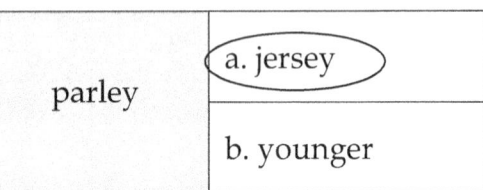
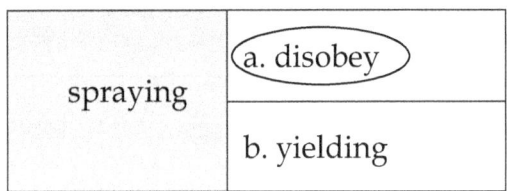
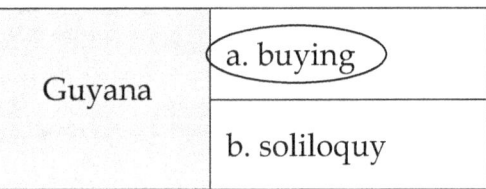

 Directions: Read each target word. Put a check (✓) under the correct column heading.
지도: 각 대상 단어를 읽으십시오. 올바른 열 제목 아래에 체크(✓)를 하십시오.

Target Words	"y" has the /y/ sound as in the word <u>yes</u>	"oy" has the /oi/ sound as in the word <u>boy</u>	"y" has the /ī/ sound as in the word <u>by</u>	"y" is silent as in the word <u>day</u>
1. employed		✓		
2. parley				✓
3. spraying				✓
4. Guyana			✓	

Answer Key

 Name: _____ Date: ___/___/_____ Score: _____

Lesson 25.3

Reading Words with the "cy" Letter Combination

✓ Lesson Check Point

 Directions: Read each target word. Find the "cy" letter combination and put a check (✓) in the column to identify its position in the word: beginning, within or end.
지도: 각 대상 단어를 읽으십시오. "cy" 문자 조합을 찾고 열에 체크(✓)를 넣어 단어에서 시작, 안에 또는 끝의 위치를 식별합니다.

Target Words	Beginning (First 2 Letters)	Within	End (Last 2 Letters)
1. cystic	✓		
2. Cynthia	✓		
3. Cyprus	✓		
4. currency			✓
5. policyholder		✓	

 Directions: Read each target word. Put a check (✓) under the correct column heading.
지도: 각 대상 단어를 읽으십시오. 올바른 열 제목 아래에 체크(✓)를하십시오.

Target Words	"cy" has the /s/ + /ĭ/ sounds as in the word <u>cylinder</u>	"cy" has the /s/ + /ī/ sounds as in the word <u>cycle</u>	"cy" has the /s/ + /ē/ sounds as in the word <u>agency</u>
6. cystic	✓		
7. Cynthia	✓		
8. Cyprus		✓	
9. currency			✓
10. policyholder			✓

Assessment

Name: _____ Date:___/___/_____ Score:_____

Lesson 25.4

Reading Words with the Final Letter "y"

✓ Lesson Check Point

Directions: Read each target word. Find the letter "y" and put a check (✓) in the column that identifies its position within the word.
지도: 각 대상 단어를 읽으십시오. 문자"y"를 찾아 체크 표시(✓)단어내에서의 위치를 식별하는 열에서.

Target Words	"y" is at the end of a one syllable word	"y" is at the end of the first syllable	"y" is at the end of a multi-syllable word
1. fry	✓		
2. happy			✓
3. melody			✓
4. cyclone		✓	
5. hydrometer		✓	

Directions: Read each target word. Put a check (✓) under the correct column heading.
지도: 각 대상 단어를 읽으십시오. 올바른 열 제목 아래에 체크(✓)를 하십시오.

Target Words	"y" has the /ē/ sound as in the word <u>agency</u>	"y" has the /ī/ sound as in the word <u>flying</u>
6. fry		✓
7. happy	✓	
8. melody	✓	
9. cyclone		✓
10. hydrometer		✓

Answer Key

 Name: _____ Date:___/___/_____ Score: _____

Lesson 25.5

Reading Words with the "yr" Letter Combination

✓ Lesson Check Point

 Directions: Read each target word. Circle the word in the column that has the same "yr" sounds as the target word.
지도: 각 대상 단어를 읽으십시오. 목표 단어와 같은 "yr" 소리가 나는 열의 단어에 동그라미를 치십시오.

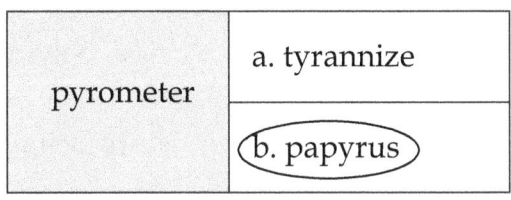
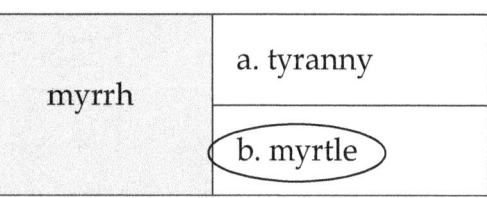
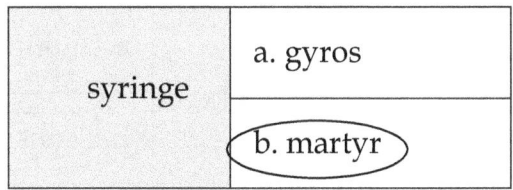
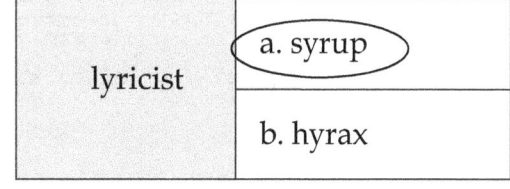

 Directions: Read each target word. Put a check (✓) under the correct column heading.
지도: 각 대상 단어를 읽으십시오. 올바른 열 제목 아래에 체크(✓)를 하십시오.

Target Words	"yr" has the /û/ + /r/ sounds as in the word myrtle	"yr" has the /ĭ/ + /r/ sounds as in the word pyramid	"yr" has the /ī/ + /r/ sounds as in the word gyro	"yr" has the /ə/ + /r/ sounds as in the word martyr
1. myrrh	✓			
2. lyricist		✓		
3. syringe				✓
4. pyrometer			✓	

Learn To Read English With Directions In Korean

Assessment

 Name: _____ Date: ___/___/_____ Score: _____

Lesson 25.6

Reading Letter "y" Words with the Schwa Vowel Sound

✓ Lesson Check Point

 Directions: Read each target word. Circle the word in the column that has the same "y" sound as the target word.
지도: 각 대상 단어를 읽으십시오. 대상 단어와"y" 소리가 같은 열의단어에 동그라미를 치십시오.

Polynesian	(a. beryl)
	b. money

vinyl	(a. polymer)
	b. facility

Polynesia	(a. vinyl)
	b. eyesore

sibyl	a. multiply
	(b. Pennsylvania)

 Directions: Read each target word. Put a check (✓) under the correct column heading.
지도: 각 대상 단어를 읽으십시오. 올바른 열 제목 아래에 체크(✓)를 하십시오.

Target Words	"y" has the /ə/ sound as in the word <u>syringe</u>	"y" does not have the /ə/ sound
1. Polynesian	✓	
2. vinyl	✓	
3. Polynesia	✓	
4. sibyl	✓	

Answer Key

 Name: _____ Date: ___/___/_____ Score: _____

Lesson 25.7

Reading Words with a Silent Letter "y"

✓ Lesson Check Point

 Directions: Read the target words in the word box. Write the words that have a silent letter "y" in the first column. Write the words that do not have a silent letter "y" in the second column.

지도: 단어 상자에 있는 대상 단어를 읽으십시오. 첫 번째 열에 묵음문자 "y"가 있는 단어를 쓰십시오. 두 번째 열에 묵음 문자 "y"가 없는 단어를 쓰십시오.

Target Word Box				
layers	obey	survey	jersey	today
years	youngster	hay	yellow	yourself
Sunday	cruelty	yummy	yours	medley
yonder	convey	yolk	Friday	youth

Letter "y" is silent	Letter "y" has the /y/ or /ē/ sound
hay	yolk
obey	years
layers	yours
jersey	youth
convey	yonder
medley	yellow
today	yummy
survey	cruelty
Friday	yourself
Sunday	youngster

Unit Y
Lesson 25.7

Learn To Read English With Directions In Korean   241   Copyrighted Material

Assessment

 Name: _____ Date: ___/___/_____ Score: _____

The Reading Challenge

Lesson 25.8

Reading Multisyllable Words

✓ Lesson Check Point

 Directions: Read and divide each target word into syllables. Write each word and place a hyphen (-) between the syllables in the second column. Write the number of syllables in the third column. Use a dictionary or the Internet to check your answers.
지도: 각 대상 단어를 읽고 음절로 나눕니다. 각 단어를 쓰고 두 번째 열의 음절 사이에 하이픈(-)을 넣습니다. 세 번째 열에 음절 수를 쓰십시오. 사전이나 인터넷을 사용하여 답을 확인하십시오.

Target Words	Words Divided into Syllables	Number of Syllables
1. yanking	yank-ing	2
2. yogurt	yo-gurt	2
3. younger	young-er	2
4. yearling	year-ling	2
5. yeasty	yeast-y	2
6. yielded	yield-ed	2
7. yesterday	yes-ter-day	3
8. youngest	young-est	2
9. yourselves	your-selves	2
10. yardsticks	yard-sticks	2

Answer Key

Name: _____ Date: ____/____/____ Score: _____

The Reading Challenge

Lesson 25.8

Reading Multisyllable Words

✓ Lesson Check Point

Directions: Read each target word. Circle the word in the row that is divided correctly into syllables. Use a dictionary or the Internet to check your answers.
지도: 각 대상 단어를 읽으십시오. 음절로 올바르게 나누어진 행에 있는 단어에 동그라미를 치십시오. 사전이나 인터넷을 사용하여 답을 확인하십시오.

Model

| yesterday | a. ye-ster-day | b. yest-er-day | c. yes-ter-day ⭕ |

1. yodeling	a. yod-e-ling	b. yod-el-ing	c. yo-del-ing ⭕
2. Yakima	a. Ya-ki-ma ⭕	b. Ya-kim-a	c. Yak-im-a
3. youngster	a. young-ster ⭕	b. you-ngst-er	c. yo-ung-ster
4. yarmulke	a. yarm-ul-ke	b. yar-mul-ke ⭕	c. ya-rmul-ke
5. yeastier	a. yeast-i-er ⭕	b. yea-sti-er	c. yeas-ti-er
6. yardstick	a. yard-stick ⭕	b. yards-tick	c. yardst-ick
7. yearly	a. yearl-y	b. yea-rly	c. year-ly ⭕
8. yogurt	a. yo-gurt ⭕	b. yog-urt	c. yo-gu-rt

Unit Y Lesson 25.8

Learn To Read English With Directions In Korean   Copyrighted Material

Assessment

Name: _____ Date: ____/___/_____ Score: _____

Lesson 25.9

Reading and Writing

Proper and Common Nouns and Adjectives

✓ Lesson Check Point

Directions: Read the words in the word box. Put an (X) on the line next to each word that is written incorrectly. Remember that all proper nouns and proper adjectives are capitalized. Use a dictionary or the Internet to check your answers.

지도: 단어 상자에 있는 단어를 읽으십시오. 잘못 쓰여진 각 단어 옆의 줄에 (X)를 표시하십시오. 모든 고유 명사와 고유 형용사는 대문자임을 기억하십시오. 사전이나 인터넷을 사용하여 답을 확인하십시오.

Word Box					
__	Yemen	__	yourself	X	yonkers
__	yippee	X	yosemite Falls	__	yearlong
X	yogyakarta	__	Yoruba	__	Yugoslavia
X	Yesterday	X	Yonder	X	Youngsters

Directions: Read each unedited sentence and underline the word that is written incorrectly. Write each sentence correctly on the line.

지도: 편집되지 않은 각 문장을 읽고 잘못 쓰여진 단어에 밑줄을 긋습니다. 각 문장을 줄에 올바르게 쓰십시오.

Model
Is the New York <u>yankees</u> your favorite baseball team?
<u>Is the New York Yankees your favorite baseball team?</u>

1. Can <u>You</u> locate the Yucatan Peninsula on the map?
<u>Can you locate the Yucatan Peninsula on the map?</u>

2. Yes, Yvette speaks both <u>yoruba</u> and English fluently.
<u>Yes, Yvette speaks both Yoruba and English fluently.</u>

3. <u>yesterday</u>, I went to a Yugoslavian restaurant for lunch.
<u>Yesterday, I went to a Yugoslavian restaurant for lunch.</u>

4. Yolanda said, "William Butler <u>yeats</u> was a famous poet and playwright."
<u>Yolanda said, "William Butler Yeats was a famous poet and playwright."</u>

Learn To Read English With Directions In Korean   Copyrighted Material

Answer Key

 Name: _____ Date: ___/___/_____ Score: _____

Lesson 26.1

Reading Words with the Letter Z/z

✓ Lesson Check Point

 Directions: Read each target word. Find the letter "z" and put a check (✓) in the column that identifies its position: beginning, within or end.
지도: 각 대상 단어를 읽으십시오. 문자"z"를 찾아 체크 표시(✓)위치를 식별하는 열에서 시작, 내부 또는 끝.

Target Words	Beginning (First Letter)	Within	End (Last Letter)
1. waltz			✓
2. whiz			✓
3. zenith	✓		
4. zealous	✓		
5. Switzerland		✓	

 Directions: Read each sentence and underline the words that begin with the letter "z." Write all the underlined words in alphabetical order on the lines below.
지도: 각 문장을 읽고"z"로 시작하는 단어에 밑줄을 긋습니다. 아래 줄에 밑줄 친 단어를 알파벳 순서로 모두 쓰십시오.

6. The <u>zebra</u> in the cartoon is <u>zany</u>.

7. Samuel stored the <u>zucchini</u> in two <u>Ziploc</u> bags.

8. The <u>zookeeper</u> is feeding the <u>zebras</u> and horses.

9. Alexander and <u>Zoë</u> went to <u>Zimbabwe</u> on vacation.

10. The <u>Zulu</u> warriors proclaimed the war chants with great <u>zeal</u>.

zany	zeal	zebra
zebras	Zimbabwe	Ziploc
zebras	zookeeper	zucchini
	Zulu	

Learn To Read English With Directions In Korean

Assessment

 Name: _____ Date: ___/___/_____ Score: _____

Lesson 26.1

Reading Words with the Letter Z/z

✓ Lesson Check Point

 Directions: Read each target word. Circle the word in the column that has the same "z" sound as the target word.
지도: 각 대상 단어를 읽으십시오. 대상 단어와 "z" 소리가 같은 열의단어에 동그라미를 치십시오.

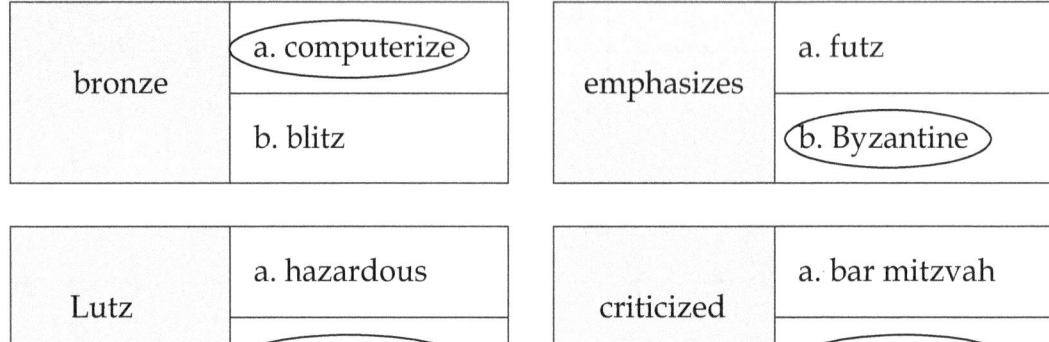

 Directions: Read each target word. Put a check (✓) under the correct column heading.
지도: 각 대상 단어를 읽으십시오. 올바른 열 제목 아래에 체크(✓)를 하십시오.

Target Words	"z" has the /z/ sound as in the word <u>zipper</u>	"z" has the /s/ sound as in the word <u>quartz</u>
1. bronze	✓	
2. emphasizes	✓	
3. Lutz		✓
4. criticized	✓	

Answer Key

Name: _____ Date: ___/___/_____ Score: _____

Lesson 26.2

Reading Words with a Silent Letter "z"

 Directions: Read the target words in the word box. Write the words that have a silent letter "z" in the first column. Write the words that do not have a silent letter "z" in the second column.

지도: 단어 상자에 있는 대상 단어를 읽으십시오. 첫 번째 열에 묵음 문자 "z"가 있는 단어를 쓰십시오. 두 번째 열에 묵음 문자"z"가 없는 단어를 쓰십시오.

Target Word Box				
embezzled	normalize	laziness	dazzling	frazzle
colonized	dizzy	fizzles	agonizing	zipper
puzzled	verbalized	nozzle	bronze	Byzantine
squeeze	jazz	amazing	dazzle	nuzzled

Letter "z" is silent

- jazz
- dizzy
- dazzle
- fizzles
- nozzle
- frazzle
- nuzzled
- puzzled
- dazzling
- embezzled

Letter "z" has the /z/ or /s/ sound

- zipper
- bronze
- amazing
- squeeze
- laziness
- agonizing
- Byzantine
- colonized
- verbalized
- normalize

Assessment

Name: _____ Date:___/___/_____ Score:_____

The Reading Challenge

Lesson 26.3

Reading Multisyllable Words

✓ Lesson Check Point

Directions: Read and divide each target word into syllables. Write each word and place a hyphen (-) between the syllables in the second column. Write the number of syllables in the third column. Use a dictionary or the Internet to check your answers.

지도: 각 대상 단어를 읽고 음절로 나눕니다. 각 단어를 쓰고 두 번째 열의 음절 사이에 하이픈(-)을 넣습니다. 세 번째 열에 음절 수를 쓰십시오. 사전이나 인터넷을 사용하여 답을 확인하십시오.

Target Words	Words Divided into Syllables	Number of Syllables
1. zinger	zing-er	2
2. Zurich	Zu-rich	2
3. zonal	zon-al	2
4. Zaire	Za-ire	2
5. zooming	zoom-ing	2
6. Zambia	Zam-bi-a	3
7. Zululand	Zu-lu-land	3
8. zigzags	zig-zags	2
9. Zimbabwe	Zim-bab-we	3
10. zealousness	zeal-ous-ness	3

Answer Key

Name: _____ Date: ___/___/_____ Score: _____

The Reading Challenge

Lesson 26.3

Reading Multisyllable Words

✓ Lesson Check Point

Directions: Read each target word. Circle the word in the row that is divided correctly into syllables. Use a dictionary or the Internet to check your answers.
지도: 각 대상 단어를 읽으십시오. 음절로 올바르게 나누어진 행에 있는 단어에 동그라미를 치십시오. 사전이나 인터넷을 사용하여 답을 확인하십시오.

Model

| zoology | (a. zo-ol-o-gy) | b. zoo-lo-gy | c. zool-o-gy |

1. Zanzibar	a. Zanz-i-bar	b. Zan-zib-ar	(c. Zan-zi-bar)
2. zealously	a. zea-lousl-y	(b. zeal-ous-ly)	c. zea-lous-ly
3. zygotic	a. zyg-o-tic	b. zyg-ot-ic	(c. zy-got-ic)
4. zestfulness	a. ze-stful-ness	(b. zest-ful-ness)	c. zes-tful-ness
5. zodiac	(a. zo-di-ac)	b. zod-i-ac	c. zo-dia-c
6. zenith	a. zen-i-th	(b. ze-nith)	c. z-en-ith
7. zoning	a. zo-ning	(b. zon-ing)	b. zo-n-ing
8. zookeeper	a. zooke-eper	b. zook-eep-er	(c. zoo-keep-er)

Learn To Read English With Directions In Korean   249   Copyrighted Material

Assessment

 Name: _____ Date: ___/___/_____ Score: _____

Lesson 26.4

Reading and Writing

Proper and Common Nouns and Adjectives

✓ Lesson Check Point

 Directions: Read the words in the word box. Put an (X) on the line next to each word that is written incorrectly. Remember that all proper nouns and proper adjectives are capitalized. Use a dictionary or the Internet to check your answers.

지도: 단어 상자에 있는 단어를 읽으십시오. 잘못 쓰여진 각 단어 옆의 줄에 (X)를 표시하십시오. 모든 고유 명사와 고유 형용사는 대문자임을 기억하십시오. 사전이나 인터넷을 사용하여 답을 확인하십시오.

Word Box					
__	zebu	__	zebra	X	zurich
__	Zambian	X	Zoology	__	zygote
X	zeus	__	zombie	__	zero
X	Zipper	X	Zenith	X	Zillion

 Directions: Read each unedited sentence and underline the word that is written incorrectly. Write each sentence correctly on the line.

지도: 편집되지 않은 각 문장을 읽고 잘못 쓰여진 단어에 밑줄 을긋습니다. 각 문장을 줄에 올바르게 쓰십시오.

Model
The steep path zigzags through the <u>zagros</u> Mountains.
<u>The steep path zigzags through the Zagros Mountains.</u>

1. Do you know that Zeanna's zip code ends with a <u>Zero</u>?
<u>Do you know that Zeanna's zip code ends with a zero?</u>

2. On Wednesday, Zachary is going to <u>zambia</u> on vacation.
<u>On Wednesday, Zachary is going to Zambia on vacation.</u>

3. In the morning, Zoey <u>Zapped</u> her breakfast in the microwave.
<u>In the morning, Zoey zapped her breakfast in the microwave.</u>

4. Mr. <u>zebulon</u> said that Zealand is the largest island in Denmark.
<u>Mr. Zebulon said that Zealand is the largest island in Denmark.</u>

Answer Key

 Name: _____ Date: ___/___/_____ Score: _____

Appendix 1.0

Introduction of the Letter A/a

✓ Lesson Check Point

 Directions: Circle the correct letter "a" pair: uppercase and lowercase letters.
지도: 올바른 문자"a" 쌍에 동그라미를 치십시오: 대문자와 소문자.

    Ae   Ao   Ea   Oa

 Directions: The uppercase letter "A" is in the first column. Look at the four letters in the row and circle the lowercase letter that matches the uppercase letter "A."
지도: 대문자"A"는 첫 번째 열에 있습니다. 행의 네 글자를 보고대문자 "A"와 일치하는 소문자에 동그라미를 치십시오.

A	(a)	e	c	o
A	x	u	q	(a)
A	c	o	(a)	u
A	e	(a)	u	c

 Directions: The lowercase letter "a" is in the first column. Look at the four letters in the row and circle the uppercase letter that matches the lowercase letter "a."
지도: 소문자"a"는 첫 번째 열에 있습니다. 행의 네 글자를 보고소문자 "a"와 일치하는 대문자에 동그라미를 치세요.

a	E	(A)	X	V
a	R	U	O	(A)
a	(A)	E	G	Z
a	U	J	(A)	E

Assessment

 Name: _____ Date:____/____/_____ Score:_____

Appendix 2.0

Introduction of the Letter B/b

✓ Lesson Check Point

 Directions: Circle the correct letter "b" pair: uppercase and lowercase letters.
지도: 올바른 문자"b" 쌍에 동그라미를 치십시오: 대문자와 소문자.

(Bb)　　　bD　　　Fb　　　Bp　　　Bd

 Directions: The uppercase letter "B" is in the first column. Look at the four letters in the row and circle the lowercase letter that matches the uppercase letter "B."
지도: 대문자"B"는 첫 번째 열에 있습니다. 행의 네 글자를 보고 대문자 "B"와 일치하는 소문자에 동그라미를 치십시오.

B	d	p	f	(b)
B	(b)	h	j	d
B	p	q	(b)	d
B	k	p	(b)	f

 Directions: The lowercase letter "b" is in the first column. Look at the four letters in the row and circle the uppercase letter that matches the lowercase letter "b."
지도: 소문자"b"는 첫 번째 열에 있습니다. 행의 네 글자를 보고 소문자"b"와 일치하는 대문자에 동그라미를 치세요.

b	(B)	Q	K	L
b	P	(B)	Q	D
b	K	D	(B)	M
b	L	M	(B)	F

Answer Key

Name: _____ Date: ___/___/_____ Score: _____

Appendix 2.0

Letter Recognition B/b

Uppercase and Lowercase Letter

✓ Lesson Check Point

Directions: Read each target word. Read the words in the row and circle the word that begins with a different letter.
지도: 각 대상 단어를 읽으십시오. 행에 있는 단어를 읽고 다른 문자로시작하는 단어에 동그라미를 치십시오.

Target Words				
1. body	brother	(pants)	boss	block
2. bow	(pepper)	book	boat	bliss
3. block	bread	blood	blow	(door)
4. blue	blink	(push)	blizzard	bus
5. bird	both	buns	(quick)	bent

Directions: Read the words in the four boxes. Circle two words that start with the uppercase and lowercase letter "b."
지도: 네 개의 상자에 있는 단어를 읽으십시오. 대문자와 소문자"b"로시작하는 두 단어에 동그라미를 치십시오.

(Big)	(big)
Rig	dig

(bag)	tag
Rag	(Bag)

(bet)	Hen
ten	(Bet)

(ban)	Dan
(Ban)	fan

Mud	(Bud)
(bud)	mud

(Boss)	Toss
toss	(boss)

Assessment

 Name: _____ Date: ___/___/_____ Score: _____

Appendix 3.0

Introduction of the Letter C/c

✓ Lesson Check Point

 Directions: Circle the correct letter "c" pair: uppercase and lowercase letters.
지도: 올바른 문자"c" 쌍에 동그라미를 치십시오: 대문자와 소문자.

    oC   Pc   Gc   Cu   (cC)

 Directions: The uppercase letter "C" is in the first column. Look at the four letters in the row and circle the lowercase letter that matches the uppercase letter "C."
지도: 대문자"C"는 첫 번째 열에 있습니다. 행의 네 글자를 보고 대문자 "C"와 일치하는 소문자에 동그라미를 치십시오.

C	g	o	(c)	d
C	o	(c)	m	b
C	(c)	q	o	x
C	(c)	g	d	o

 Directions: The lowercase letter "c" is in the first column. Look at the four letters in the row and circle the uppercase letter that matches the lowercase letter "c."
지도: 소문자"c"는 첫 번째 열에 있습니다. 행의 네 글자를 보고 소문자"c"와 일치하는 대문자에 동그라미를 치세요.

c	Q	V	(C)	G
c	(C)	O	M	D
c	O	Q	(C)	N
c	(C)	G	Q	D

Answer Key

Name: _____ Date: ___/___/_____ Score: _____

Appendix 3.0

Letter Recognition C/c

Uppercase and Lowercase Letter

✓ Lesson Check Point

Directions: Read each target word. Read the words in the row and circle the word that begins with a different letter.
지도: 각 대상 단어를 읽으십시오. 행에 있는 단어를 읽고 다른 문자로시작하는 단어에 동그라미를 치십시오.

Target Words				
1. club	(powder)	carbon	cent	change
2. child	(donut)	chip	circle	clip
3. confirm	cactus	(money)	check	click
4. compact	cargo	chance	(zebra)	clinic
5. chemical	chess	(table)	calendar	chart

Directions: Read the words in the four boxes. Circle two words that start with the uppercase and lowercase letter "c."
지도: 네 개의 상자에 있는 단어를 읽으십시오. 대문자와 소문자"c"로시작하는 두 단어에 동그라미를 치십시오.

(Carbon)	gallon
(crop)	borrow

Oil	(Cash)
(cart)	Quart

(Cram)	Draw
Goat	(clean)

Queen	(cold)
(Chain)	rain

Grasp	Pollen
(college)	(Coast)

Quick	(Curl)
Over	(cloud)

Assessment

 Name: _____ Date: ___/___/_____ Score: _____

Appendix 4.0

Introduction of the Letter D/d

✓ **Lesson Check Point**

 Directions: Circle the correct letter "d" pair: uppercase and lowercase letters.
지도: 올바른 문자"d" 쌍에 동그라미를 치십시오: 대문자와 소문자.

    Db   Dp   Fd   Bd   (Dd)

 Directions: The uppercase letter "D" is in the first column. Look at the four letters in the row and circle the lowercase letter that matches the uppercase letter "D."
지도: 대문자"D"는 첫 번째 열에 있습니다. 행의 네 글자를 보고 대문자 "D"와 일치하는 소문자에 동그라미를 치십시오.

D	t	h	k	(d)
D	l	b	(d)	t
D	f	(d)	h	b
D	(d)	k	f	t

 Directions: The lowercase letter "d" is in the first column. Look at the four letters in the row and circle the uppercase letter that matches the lowercase letter "d."
지도: 소문자"d"는 첫 번째 열에 있습니다. 행의 네 글자를 보고 소문자"d"와 일치하는 대문자에 동그라미를 치세요.

d	F	B	(D)	H
d	B	(D)	E	B
d	(D)	F	B	M
d	G	N	H	(D)

Answer Key

Name: _____ Date: ___/___/_____ Score: _____

Appendix 4.0

Letter Recognition D/d

Uppercase and Lowercase Letter

✓ **Lesson Check Point**

 Directions: Read each target word. Read the words in the row and circle the word that begins with a different letter.
지도: 각 대상 단어를 읽으십시오. 행에 있는 단어를 읽고 다른 문자로시 작하는 단어에 동그라미를 치십시오.

Target Words				
1. dance	dean	doe	(quilt)	die
2. drip	(proud)	doubt	droll	dot
3. disk	drift	(bank)	dig	drag
4. dear	does	deem	(peach)	dead
5. draws	(quest)	draft	dream	duck

 Directions: Read the words in the four boxes. Circle two words that start with the uppercase and lowercase letter "d."
지도: 네 개의 상자에 있는 단어를 읽으십시오. 대문자와 소문자 "d"로 시작하는 두 단어에 동그라미를 치십시오.

(duck)	got	(Down)	town	(dash)	Queen
(Dot)	truck	pen	(dean)	pass	(Draft)

Glove	(Dove)	Grape	pose	Ben	(den)
train	(drain)	(does)	(Drape)	(Dig)	pig

Learn To Read English With Directions In Korean   257   Copyrighted Material

Assessment

 Name: _____ Date:___/___/_____ Score: _____

Appendix 5.0

Introduction of the Letter E/e

✓ Lesson Check Point

 Directions: Circle the correct letter "e" pair: uppercase and lowercase letters.
지도: 올바른 문자"e" 쌍에 동그라미를 치십시오: 대문자와 소문자.

    eF   hE   cE   Oe   (Ee)

 Directions: The uppercase letter "E" is in the first column. Look at the four letters in the row and circle the lowercase letter that matches the uppercase letter "E."
지도: 대문자"E"는 첫 번째 열에 있습니다. 행의 네 글자를 보고대문자 "E"와 일치하는 소문자에 동그라미를 치십시오.

E	c	(e)	s	v
E	(e)	x	f	h
E	z	a	d	(e)
E	g	w	(e)	x

 Directions: The lowercase letter "e" is in the first column. Look at the four letters in the row and circle the uppercase letter that matches the lowercase letter "e."
지도: 소문자"e"는 첫 번째 열에 있습니다. 행의 네 글자를 보고소문자"e" 와 일치하는 대문자에 동그라미를 치세요.

e	H	F	(E)	X
e	(E)	W	Z	N
e	F	R	X	(E)
e	C	(E)	D	F

Answer Key

 Name: _____ Date: ___/___/_____ Score: _____

Appendix 6.0

Introduction of the Letter F/f

✓ Lesson Check Point

 Directions: Circle the correct letter "f" pair: uppercase and lowercase letters.
지도: 올바른 문자"f" 쌍에 동그라미를 치십시오: 대문자와 소문자.

    Pf   (Ff)   fH   Lf   Ef

 Directions: The uppercase letter "F" is in the first column. Look at the four letters in the row and circle the lowercase letter that matches the uppercase letter "F."
지도: 대문자"F"는 첫 번째 열에 있습니다. 행의 네 글자를 보고대문자 "F"와 일치하는 소문자에 동그라미를 치십시오.

F	k	(f)	j	t
F	l	h	(f)	p
F	b	(f)	d	h
F	(f)	t	h	l

 Directions: The lowercase letter "f" is in the first column. Look at the four letters in the row and circle the uppercase letter that matches the lowercase letter "f."
지도: 소문자"f"는 첫 번째 열에 있습니다. 행의 네 글자를 보고소문자"f" 와 일치하는 대문자에 동그라미를 치세요.

f	E	H	(F)	T
f	(F)	K	L	E
f	T	(F)	Y	E
f	U	E	(F)	B

Assessment

 Name: _____ Date:___/___/_____ Score: _____

Appendix 6.0

Letter Recognition F/f

Uppercase and Lowercase Letter

✓ Lesson Check Point

 Directions: Read each target word. Read the words in the row and circle the word that begins with a different letter.
지도: 각 대상 단어를 읽으십시오. 행에 있는 단어를 읽고 다른 문자로시작하는 단어에 동그라미를 치십시오.

Target Words				
1. fuzz	flat	frizz	(Earth)	fleet
2. fruit	friends	fresh	frost	(house)
3. flute	food	(band)	fix	false
4. fence	fluke	floor	flex	(Yard)
5. French	fume	(toys)	faith	flap

 Directions: Read the words in the four boxes. Circle two words that start with the uppercase and lowercase letter "f."
지도: 네 개의 상자에 있는 단어를 읽으십시오. 대문자와 소문자"f"로시작하는 두 단어에 동그라미를 치십시오.

bath	Hours		(fan)	heat		(Flip)	Hold
(Fad)	(fade)		Daisy	(Flint)		trap	(fat)

(flight)	Drops		(Fling)	(fake)		trees	blood
loves	(Fool)		hatch	Door		(Fear)	(flood)

Answer Key

 Name: _____ Date: ___/___/_____ Score: _____

Appendix 7.0

Introduction of the Letter G/g

✓ Lesson Check Point

 Directions: Circle the correct letter "g" pair: uppercase and lowercase letters.
지도: 올바른 문자"g" 쌍에 동그라미를 치십시오: 대문자와 소문자.

Og　　　　　Gp　　　　　gQ　　　　　(Gg)　　　　　gU

 Directions: The uppercase letter "G" is in the first column. Look at the four letters in the row and circle the lowercase letter that matches the uppercase letter "G."
지도: 대문자"F"는 첫 번째 열에 있습니다. 행의 네 글자를 보고 대문자 "F"와 일치하는 소문자에 동그라미를 치십시오.

G	p	(g)	j	y
G	y	j	p	(g)
G	(g)	y	q	t
G	p	y	(g)	j

 Directions: The lowercase letter "g" is in the first column. Look at the four letters in the row and circle the uppercase letter that matches the lowercase letter "g."
지도: 소문자"g"는 첫 번째 열에 있습니다. 행의 네 글자를 보고 소문자"g"와 일치하는 대문자에 동그라미를 치세요.

g	P	O	(G)	M
g	O	(G)	U	E
g	Q	J	O	(G)
g	U	C	(G)	O

Assessment

Name: _____ Date: ___/___/_____ Score: _____

Appendix 7.0

Letter Recognition G/g

Uppercase and Lowercase Letter

✓ Lesson Check Point

 Directions: Read each target word. Read the words in the row and circle the word that begins with a different letter.
지도: 각 대상 단어를 읽으십시오. 행에 있는 단어를 읽고 다른 문자로시작하는 단어에 동그라미를 치십시오.

Target Words				
1. gate	grape	gaze	gift	(June)
2. glue	(push)	glance	great	gloss
3. grand	guide	grab	gross	(place)
4. gum	grain	gleam	(joke)	groom
5. golf	gone	gap	globe	(down)

 Directions: Read the words in the four boxes. Circle two words that start with the uppercase and lowercase letter "g."
지도: 네 개의 상자에 있는 단어를 읽으십시오. 대문자와 소문자"g"로시작하는 두 단어에 동그라미를 치십시오.

(grade)	(Girl)
push	just

dance	(glance)
(Gong)	praise

Join	ball
(globe)	(Guest)

Plan	(great)
Queen	(Glove)

(gown)	down
juice	(Greek)

(Go)	job
(group)	praise

Answer Key

 Name: _____ Date: ___/___/_____ Score: _____

Appendix 8.0

Introduction of the Letter H/h

✓ Lesson Check Point

 Directions: Circle the correct letter "h" pair: uppercase and lowercase letters.
지도: 올바른 문자"h" 쌍에 동그라미를 치십시오: 대문자와 소문자.

    Lh   Hf   (Hh)   Ph   bH

 Directions: The uppercase letter "H" is in the first column. Look at the four letters in the row and circle the lowercase letter that matches the uppercase letter "H."
지도: 대문자"H"는 첫 번째 열에 있습니다. 행의 네 글자를 보고대문자 "H"와 일치하는 소문자에 동그라미를 치십시오.

H	f	(h)	d	t
H	(h)	l	t	f
H	t	k	l	(h)
H	d	f	(h)	p

 Directions: The lowercase letter "h" is in the first column. Look at the four letters in the row and circle the uppercase letter that matches the lowercase letter "h."
지도: 소문자"h"는 첫 번째 열에 있습니다. 행의 네 글자를 보고소문자"h" 와 일치하는 대문자에 동그라미를 치세요.

h	(H)	G	O	P
h	K	F	(H)	E
h	F	(H)	E	K
h	L	(H)	B	T

Learn To Read English With Directions In Korean   263   Copyrighted Material

Assessment

Name: _____ Date:___/___/_____ Score:_____

Appendix 8.0

Letter Recognition H/h

Uppercase and Lowercase Letter

✓ Lesson Check Point

 Directions: Read each target word. Read the words in the row and circle the word that begins with a different letter.
지도: 각 대상 단어를 읽으십시오. 행에 있는 단어를 읽고 다른 문자로시작하는 단어에 동그라미를 치십시오.

Target Words				
1. house	(touch)	harp	herb	hoist
2. herb	hiss	her	hot	(low)
3. hope	harsh	heed	(down)	hide
4. hawk	(kind)	hark	hue	had
5. helping	haste	(been)	hedge	halt

 Directions: Read the words in the four boxes. Circle two words that start with the uppercase and lowercase letter "h."
지도: 네 개의 상자에 있는 단어를 읽으십시오. 대문자와 소문자"h"로시작하는 두 단어에 동그라미를 치십시오.

Talk	lunch
(High)	(house)

Does	(have)
loud	(Hard)

(Health)	five
Trip	(hill)

(hang)	(Hall)
fresh	thanks

(heart)	Kick
look	(Hawk)

(Hide)	from
(hike)	drive

Name: _____ Date: ___/___/_____ Score: _____

Answer Key

Appendix 9.0

Introduction of the Letter I/i

✓ **Lesson Check Point**

 Directions: Circle the correct letter "i" pair: uppercase and lowercase letters.
지도: 올바른 문자"i" 쌍에 동그라미를 치십시오: 대문자와 소문자.

Li   (iI)   It   Ji   Ij

 Directions: The uppercase letter "I" is in the first column. Look at the four letters in the row and circle the lowercase letter that matches the uppercase letter "I."
지도: 대문자"I"는 첫 번째 열에 있습니다. 행의 네 글자를 보고대문자 "I"와 일치하는 소문자에 동그라미를 치십시오.

I	y	h	t	(i)
I	(i)	j	g	t
I	j	(i)	y	f
I	g	y	j	(i)

 Directions: The lowercase letter "i" is in the first column. Look at the four letters in the row and circle the uppercase letter that matches the lowercase letter "i."
지도: 소문자"i"는 첫 번째 열에 있습니다. 행의 네 글자를 보고소문자"i"와 일치하는 대문자에 동그라미를 치세요.

i	J	(I)	Y	T
i	E	D	K	(I)
i	B	(I)	N	J
i	(I)	T	F	K

Learn To Read English With Directions In Korean   Copyrighted Material

Assessment

 Name: _____ Date: ___/___/_____ Score: _____

Appendix 10.0

Introduction of the Letter J/j

✓ Lesson Check Point

 Directions: Circle the correct letter "j" pair: uppercase and lowercase letters.
지도: 올바른 문자"j" 쌍에 동그라미를 치십시오: 대문자와 소문자.

    Kj   jY   Jg   (Jj)   Lj

 Directions: The uppercase letter "J" is in the first column. Look at the four letters in the row and circle the lowercase letter that matches the uppercase letter "J."
지도: 대문자"J"는 첫 번째 열에 있습니다. 행의 네 글자를 보고대문자 "J"와 일치하는 소문자에 동그라미를 치십시오.

J	l	(j)	k	b
J	(j)	g	y	q
J	g	i	z	(j)
J	q	y	(j)	p

 Directions: The lowercase letter "j" is in the first column. Look at the four letters in the row and circle the uppercase letter that matches the lowercase letter "j."
지도: 소문자"j"는 첫 번째 열에 있습니다. 행의 네 글자를 보고소문자"j" 와 일치하는 대문자에 동그라미를 치세요.

j	(J)	V	D	G
j	L	N	E	(J)
j	H	(J)	C	O
j	O	(J)	G	T

Learn To Read English With Directions In Korean

Answer Key

 Name: _____ Date: ___/___/_____ Score: _____

Appendix 10.0

Letter Recognition J/j

Uppercase and Lowercase Letter

✓ Lesson Check Point

 Directions: Read each target word. Read the words in the row and circle the word that begins with a different letter.
지도: 각 대상 단어를 읽으십시오. 행에 있는 단어를 읽고 다른 문자로시작하는 단어에 동그라미를 치십시오.

Target Words				
1. jug	jab	jersey	jet	(years)
2. jade	job	(guest)	jack	jeep
3. jazz	jewel	jam	(love)	joke
4. junior	(back)	join	jump	jail
5. jellyfish	jolt	(young)	jar	joy

 Directions: Read the words in the four boxes. Circle two words that start with the uppercase and lowercase letter "j."
지도: 네 개의 상자에 있는 단어를 읽으십시오. 대문자와 소문자"j"로시작하는 두 단어에 동그라미를 치십시오.

(Juice)	group
(job)	youth

grow	young
(jog)	(Jet)

(Jeep)	yours
foxes	(jock)

cares	(June)
(jump)	gloss

years	gate
(Joint)	(junk)

yoke	(jean)
guess	(Joke)

Learn To Read English With Directions In Korean

Assessment

 Name: _____ Date: ___/___/_____ Score: _____

Appendix 11.0

Introduction of the Letter K/k

✓ Lesson Check Point

 Directions: Circle the correct letter "k" pair: uppercase and lowercase letters.
지도: 올바른 문자"k" 쌍에 동그라미를 치십시오: 대문자와 소문자.

    Lk   lK   (Kk)   Jk   hK

 Directions: The uppercase letter "K" is in the first column. Look at the four letters in the row and circle the lowercase letter that matches the uppercase letter "K."
지도: 대문자"K"는 첫 번째 열에 있습니다. 행의 네 글자를 보고 대문자 "K"와 일치하는 소문자에 동그라미를 치십시오.

K	k	j	g	o
K	h	k	b	p
K	n	l	k	b
K	p	d	l	k

 Directions: The lowercase letter "k" is in the first column. Look at the four letters in the row and circle the uppercase letter that matches the lowercase letter "k."
지도: 소문자"k"는 첫 번째 열에 있습니다. 행의 네 글자를 보고 소문자"k"와 일치하는 대문자에 동그라미를 치세요.

k	P	K	Y	N
k	Q	J	K	V
k	B	K	C	S
k	K	X	H	Q

Answer Key

Name: _____ Date: ___/___/_____ Score: _____

Appendix 11.0

Letter Recognition K/k

Uppercase and Lowercase Letter

✓ Lesson Check Point

Directions: Read each target word. Read the words in the row and circle the word that begins with a different letter.
지도: 각 대상 단어를 읽으십시오. 행에 있는 단어를 읽고 다른 문자로시작하는 단어에 동그라미를 치십시오.

Target Words				
1. knob	keep	kind	(tent)	knot
2. ketch	kale	krill	knit	(house)
3. karts	(frank)	key	kick	keel
4. knight	kept	(tooth)	knoll	keen
5. knock	(frame)	kelp	kedge	keg

Directions: Read the words in the four boxes. Circle two words that start with the uppercase and lowercase letter "k."
지도: 네 개의 상자에 있는 단어를 읽으십시오. 대문자와 소문자 "k"로시작하는 두 단어에 동그라미를 치십시오.

lamb	(Knows)
(kids)	Eggs

found	(kind)
Laugh	(Knock)

Enough	Friends
(Kicks)	(knot)

(Knight)	down
(kept)	Boat

(keeps)	(Knits)
Dreams	house

(knob)	drops
Vase	(Keen)

Assessment

 Name: _____ Date:____/____/_____ Score: _____

Appendix 12.0

Introduction of the Letter L/l

✓ Lesson Check Point

 Directions: Circle the correct letter "l" pair: uppercase and lowercase letters.
지도: 올바른 문자"l" 쌍에 동그라미를 치십시오: 대문자와 소문자.

      Jl   (Ll)   Lk   lF   jL

 Directions: The uppercase letter "L" is in the first column. Look at the four letters in the row and circle the lowercase letter that matches the uppercase letter "L."
지도: 대문자"L"는 첫 번째 열에 있습니다. 행의 네 글자를 보고 대문자 "L"와 일치하는 소문자에 동그라미를 치십시오.

L	j	(l)	h	t
L	k	b	f	(l)
L	f	i	(l)	h
L	(l)	j	i	f

 Directions: The lowercase letter "l" is in the first column. Look at the four letters in the row and circle the uppercase letter that matches the lowercase letter "l."
지도: 소문자"l"는 첫 번째 열에 있습니다. 행의 네 글자를 보고 소문자"l" 와 일치하는 대문자에 동그라미를 치세요.

l	(L)	H	J	K
l	T	B	(L)	J
l	(L)	J	D	N
l	J	H	(L)	B

Answer Key

Name: _____ Date: ___/___/_____ Score: _____

Appendix 12.0

Letter Recognition L/l

Uppercase and Lowercase Letter

✓ Lesson Check Point

Directions: Read each target word. Read the words in the row and circle the word that begins with a different letter.
지도: 각 대상 단어를 읽으십시오. 행에 있는 단어를 읽고 다른 문자로시작하는 단어에 동그라미를 치십시오.

Target Words				
1. light	love	(finds)	luck	Latin
2. leach	live	loaf	(hose)	leaf
3. loam	lick	(beef)	laugh	league
4. leap	(kitchen)	lime	lamb	lend
5. lenses	learn	loud	less	(dress)

Directions: Read the words in the four boxes. Circle two words that start with the uppercase and lowercase letter "l."
지도: 네 개의 상자에 있는 단어를 읽으십시오. 대문자와 소문자"l"로시작하는 두 단어에 동그라미를 치십시오.

trees	dawn
(Limp)	(lawn)

(Lid)	Trips
(land)	house

Years	(lease)
(Launch)	France

(Light)	dance
hunch	(lead)

Branch	(Lack)
friends	(leg)

(line)	(Load)
Hours	Town

Learn To Read English With Directions In Korean   271   Copyrighted Material

Assessment

 Name: _____ Date: ___/___/_____ Score: _____

Appendix 13.0

Introduction of the Letter M/m

✓ Lesson Check Point

 Directions: Circle the correct letter "m" pair: uppercase and lowercase letters.
지도: 올바른 문자"m" 쌍에 동그라미를 치십시오: 대문자와 소문자.

Nm   Mu   Zm   Mn   (Mm)

 Directions: The uppercase letter "M" is in the first column. Look at the four letters in the row and circle the lowercase letter that matches the uppercase letter "M."
지도: 대문자"M"는 첫 번째 열에 있습니다. 행의 네 글자를 보고 대문자 "M"와 일치하는 소문자에 동그라미를 치십시오.

M	n	w	(m)	u
M	(m)	n	h	b
M	w	u	(m)	v
M	(m)	n	w	x

 Directions: The lowercase letter "m" is in the first column. Look at the four letters in the row and circle the uppercase letter that matches the lowercase letter "m."
지도: 소문자"m"는 첫 번째 열에 있습니다. 행의 네 글자를 보고 소문자 "m" 와 일치하는 대문자에 동그라미를 치세요.

m	(M)	N	Z	T
m	Y	W	(M)	N
m	N	Y	W	(M)
m	Z	N	Y	(M)

Answer Key

Name: _____ Date: ___/___/_____ Score: _____

Appendix 13.0

Letter Recognition M/m

Uppercase and Lowercase Letter

✓ Lesson Check Point

Directions: Read each target word. Read the words in the row and circle the word that begins with a different letter.
지도: 각 대상 단어를 읽으십시오. 행에 있는 단어를 읽고 다른 문자로시 작하는 단어에 동그라미를 치십시오.

Target Words				
1. milk	much	maid	mug	(vain)
2. mouse	mixed	(norm)	mall	move
3. meal	(vine)	male	mock	mint
4. mind	made	(rain)	moon	might
5. munch	mumps	mince	(neck)	mood

Directions: Read the words in the four boxes. Circle two words that start with the uppercase and lowercase letter "m."
지도: 네 개의 상자에 있는 단어를 읽으십시오. 대문자와소문자 "m"로시 작 하는 두 단어에 동그라미를 치십시오.

Name	(Male)
(mild)	wear

wax	need
(Mesh)	(mink)

very	(Mill)
notch	(moan)

(munch)	noun
(Man)	yes

(mud)	(Mine)
zoo	Next

(Map)	nice
whale	(mole)

Learn To Read English With Directions In Korean   273   Copyrighted Material

Assessment

 Name: _____ Date: ___/___/_____ Score: _____

Appendix 14.0

Introduction of the Letter N/n

✓ **Lesson Check Point**

 Directions: Circle the correct letter "n" pair: uppercase and lowercase letters.
지도: 올바른 문자"n" 쌍에 동그라미를 치십시오: 대문자와 소문자.

    mN   Mn   uN   (nN)   Un

 Directions: The uppercase letter "N" is in the first column. Look at the four letters in the row and circle the lowercase letter that matches the uppercase letter "N."
지도: 대문자"N"는 첫 번째 열에 있습니다. 행의 네 글자를 보고 대문자 "N"와 일치하는 소문자에 동그라미를 치십시오.

N	u	(n)	y	m
N	(n)	h	u	z
N	y	v	(n)	u
N	v	u	x	(n)

 Directions: The lowercase letter "n" is in the first column. Look at the four letters in the row and circle the uppercase letter that matches the lowercase letter "n."
지도: 소문자"n"는 첫 번째 열에 있습니다. 행의 네 글자를 보고 소문자"n"와 일치하는 대문자에 동그라미를 치세요.

n	Z	(N)	U	M
n	(N)	Y	M	W
n	U	Z	H	(N)
n	Y	U	(N)	Z

Learn To Read English With Directions In Korean

Answer Key

Name: _____ Date: ___/___/_____ Score: _____

Appendix 14.0

Letter Recognition N/n

Uppercase and Lowercase Letter

✓ Lesson Check Point

Directions: Read each target word. Read the words in the row and circle the word that begins with a different letter.
지도: 각 대상 단어를 읽으십시오. 행에 있는 단어를 읽고 다른 문자로시 작하는 단어에 동그라미를 치십시오.

Target Words				
1. new	night	none	(moon)	neck
2. neat	(round)	nerve	noon	name
3. niche	near	(made)	norm	next
4. nook	nose	nail	neat	(went)
5. normal	(cute)	noun	nine	noise

Directions: Read the words in the four boxes. Circle two words that start with the uppercase and lowercase letter "n."
지도: 네 개의 상자에 있는 단어를 읽으십시오. 대문자와 소문자 "n"로시 하는 두 단어에 동그라미를 치십시오.

(notch)	moon	(nip)	most	mist	van
home	(None)	you	(Nose)	(Night)	(nudge)

(net)	(Nil)	verse	(Nag)	(nook)	vote
word	man	roll	(not)	(Next)	milk

Learn To Read English With Directions In Korean   275   Copyrighted Material

Assessment

 Name: _____ Date: ___/___/_____ Score: _____

Appendix 15.0

Introduction of the Letter O/o

✓ Lesson Check Point

 Directions: Circle the correct letter "o" pair: uppercase and lowercase letters.
지도: 올바른 문자 "o" 쌍에 동그라미를 치십시오: 대문자와 소문자.

Qo (Oo) Co Uo Ou

 Directions: The uppercase letter "O" is in the first column. Look at the four letters in the row and circle the lowercase letter that matches the uppercase letter "O."
지도: 대문자 "O"는 첫 번째 열에 있습니다. 행의 네 글자를 보고 대문자 "O"와 일치하는 소문자에 동그라미를 치십시오.

O	c	(o)	s	p
O	q	g	u	(o)
O	u	p	(o)	s
O	(o)	h	c	d

 Directions: The lowercase letter "o" is in the first column. Look at the four letters in the row and circle the uppercase letter that matches the lowercase letter "o."
지도: 소문자 "o"는 첫 번째 열에 있습니다. 행의 네 글자를 보고 소문자 "o"와 일치하는 대문자에 동그라미를 치세요.

o	U	J	(O)	P
o	(O)	C	U	Q
o	Q	(O)	Y	C
o	(O)	D	B	U

Answer Key

 Name: _____ Date: ___/___/_____ Score: _____

Appendix 16.0

Introduction of the Letter P/p

✓ Lesson Check Point

 Directions: Circle the correct letter "p" pair: uppercase and lowercase letters.
지도: 올바른 문자"p" 쌍에 동그라미를 치십시오: 대문자와 소문자.

Pd (Pp) Pg Pb Bp

 Directions: The uppercase letter "P" is in the first column. Look at the four letters in the row and circle the lowercase letter that matches the uppercase letter "P."
지도: 대문자"P"는 첫 번째 열에 있습니다. 행의 네 글자를 보고 대문자 "P"와 일치하는 소문자에 동그라미를 치십시오.

P	(p)	b	d	q
P	g	d	(p)	b
P	d	g	b	(p)
P	(p)	b	g	j

 Directions: The lowercase letter "p" is in the first column. Look at the four letters in the row and circle the uppercase letter that matches the lowercase letter "p."
지도: 소문자"p"는 첫 번째 열에 있습니다. 행의 네 글자를 보고 소문자"p"와 일치하는 대문자에 동그라미를 치세요.

p	Q	B	(P)	D
p	H	G	T	(P)
p	(P)	Q	D	B
p	G	(P)	B	D

Assessment

Name: _____ Date: ___/___/_____ Score: _____

Appendix 16.0

Letter Recognition P/p

Uppercase and Lowercase Letter

✓ Lesson Check Point

Directions: Read each target word. Read the words in the row and circle the word that begins with a different letter.
지도: 각 대상 단어를 읽으십시오. 행에 있는 단어를 읽고 다른 문자로시작하는 단어에 동그라미를 치십시오.

Target Words				
1. pace	price	(quest)	push	pine
2. prove	(young)	princess	plop	pink
3. purge	plunge	plus	pearl	(guest)
4. peach	(good)	pint	peek	pants
5. please	plane	(quick)	pipe	plain

Directions: Read the words in the four boxes. Circle two words that start with the uppercase and lowercase letter "p."
지도: 네 개의 상자에 있는 단어를 읽으십시오. 대문자와 소문자 "p"로 시작하는 두 단어에 동그라미를 치십시오.

(pen)	Slate	Beep	(Peep)	dull	(pull)
(Plate)	den	(pound)	keep	full	(Push)

(park)	bark	Dry	(pry)	(plum)	lunch
Dark	(Purse)	(Price)	Try	(Punch)	bunch

Learn To Read English With Directions In Korean   278   Copyrighted Material

Answer Key

 Name: _____ Date:___/___/_____ Score:_____

Appendix 17.0

Introduction of the Letter Q/q

✓ Lesson Check Point

 Directions: Circle the correct letter "q" pair: uppercase and lowercase letters.
지도: 올바른 문자"q" 쌍에 동그라미를 치십시오: 대문자와 소문자.

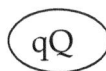   Qp   Oq   Gq   Qg

 Directions: The uppercase letter "Q" is in the first column. Look at the four letters in the row and circle the lowercase letter that matches the uppercase letter "Q."
지도: 대문자"Q"는 첫 번째 열에 있습니다. 행의 네 글자를 보고 대문자 "Q"와 일치하는 소문자에 동그라미를 치십시오.

Q	p	ⓠ	b	d
Q	j	g	ⓠ	b
Q	ⓠ	j	b	p
Q	g	b	j	ⓠ

 Directions: The lowercase letter "q" is in the first column. Look at the four letters in the row and circle the uppercase letter that matches the lowercase letter "q."
지도: 소문자"q"는 첫 번째 열에 있습니다. 행의 네 글자를 보고 소문자"q"와 일치하는 대문자에 동그라미를 치세요.

q	Ⓠ	G	O	C
q	O	S	Ⓠ	U
q	G	O	U	Ⓠ
q	C	Ⓠ	O	G

Assessment

Name: _____ Date: ___/___/_____ Score: _____

Appendix 17.0

Letter Recognition Q/q

Uppercase and Lowercase Letter

✓ Lesson Check Point

Directions: Read each target word. Read the words in the row and circle the word that begins with a different letter.
지도: 각 대상 단어를 읽으십시오. 행에 있는 단어를 읽고 다른 문자로시작하는 단어에 동그라미를 치십시오.

Target Words				
1. quaint	(pedal)	quickly	qualm	quartz
2. quit	quotes	quail	qualify	(demand)
3. quiet	quaint	(bunch)	quake	quack
4. quite	quest	quarrel	(publish)	quibble
5. quarter	quake	(dances)	Qatar	quark

Directions: Read the words in the four boxes. Circle two words that start with the uppercase and lowercase letter "q."
지도: 네 개의 상자에 있는 단어를 읽으십시오. 대문자와 소문자 "q"로시작하는 두 단어에 동그라미를 치십시오.

(quails)	(Quagmire)
project	jumbo

Octopus	(Quake)
(quarrel)	yarn

guess	(Quicken)
prefix	(quarter)

(Query)	Organ
yield	(queasy)

(quickie)	pound
(Quench)	yogurt

judge	Orchid
(quickly)	(Quota)

Answer Key

 Name: _____ Date: ___/___/_____ Score: _____

Appendix 18.0

Introduction of the Letter R/r

✓ Lesson Check Point

 Directions: Circle the correct letter "r" pair: uppercase and lowercase letters.
지도: 올바른 문자"r" 쌍에 동그라미를 치십시오: 대문자와 소문자.

    Rd   rV   Nr   (rR)   Rx

 Directions: The uppercase letter "R" is in the first column. Look at the four letters in the row and circle the lowercase letter that matches the uppercase letter "R."
지도: 대문자"R"는 첫 번째 열에 있습니다. 행의 네 글자를 보고 대문자 "R"와 일치하는 소문자에 동그라미를 치십시오.

R	v	(r)	a	g
R	y	x	c	(r)
R	(r)	v	b	f
R	p	f	(r)	c

 Directions: The lowercase letter "r" is in the first column. Look at the four letters in the row and circle the uppercase letter that matches the lowercase letter "r."
지도: 소문자"r"는 첫 번째 열에 있습니다. 행의 네 글자를 보고 소문자"r"와 일치하는 대문자에 동그라미를 치세요.

r	D	(R)	C	F
r	(R)	H	B	K
r	Q	T	(R)	V
r	J	K	G	(R)

Learn To Read English With Directions In Korean

Assessment

Name: _____ Date: ___/___/_____ Score: _____

Appendix 18.0

Letter Recognition R/r

Uppercase and Lowercase Letter

✓ Lesson Check Point

Directions: Read each target word. Read the words in the row and circle the word that begins with a different letter.
지도: 각 대상 단어를 읽으십시오. 행에 있는 단어를 읽고 다른 문자로시 작하는 단어에 동그라미를 치십시오.

Target Words				
1. rig	rate	(cares)	rhythm	rock
2. rhyme	robe	reed	range	(moon)
3. round	rain	reach	(used)	raid
4. road	(mold)	roar	rule	ream
5. renters	rare	rail	(need)	risk

Directions: Read the words in the four boxes. Circle two words that start with the uppercase and lowercase letter "r."
지도: 네 개의 상자에 있는 단어를 읽으십시오. 대문자와 소문자 "r"로시작 하는 두 단어에 동그라미를 치십시오.

need	(red)
Piece	(Roll)

cow	(rich)
part	(Ramp)

(rib)	money
name	(Rite)

(Role)	noise
(roost)	Park

mouse	(Realm)
(rouse)	peace

(Reap)	(rip)
cats	perm

Answer Key

 Name: _____ Date: ___/___/_____ Score: _____

Appendix 19.0

Introduction of the Letter S/s

✓ **Lesson Check Point**

 Directions: Circle the correct letter "s" pair: uppercase and lowercase letters.
지도: 올바른 문자"s" 쌍에 동그라미를 치십시오: 대문자와 소문자.

    Cs   Zs   (sS)   Os   cS

 Directions: The uppercase letter "S" is in the first column. Look at the four letters in the row and circle the lowercase letter that matches the uppercase letter "S."
지도: 대문자"S"는 첫 번째 열에 있습니다. 행의 네 글자를 보고 대문자 "S"와 일치하는 소문자에 동그라미를 치십시오.

S	(s)	c	z	u
S	z	g	(s)	b
S	u	(s)	o	z
S	c	z	g	(s)

 Directions: The lowercase letter "s" is in the first column. Look at the four letters in the row and circle the uppercase letter that matches the lowercase letter "s."
지도: 소문자"s"는 첫 번째 열에 있습니다. 행의 네 글자를 보고 소문자"s"와 일치하는 대문자에 동그라미를 치세요.

s	Z	(S)	U	C
s	U	X	(S)	Z
s	(S)	Z	C	O
s	Z	(S)	G	C

Assessment

Name: _____ Date: ___/___/_____ Score: _____

Appendix 19.0

Letter Recognition S/s

Uppercase and Lowercase Letter

✓ **Lesson Check Point**

Directions: Read each target word. Read the words in the row and circle the word that begins with a different letter.
지도: 각 대상 단어를 읽으십시오. 행에 있는 단어를 읽고 다른 문자로시작하는 단어에 동그라미를 치십시오.

Target Words				
1. soak	shoe	scrub	(zipper)	says
2. sight	(zero)	sauce	shrimp	some
3. slow	should	slice	slide	(homes)
4. salt	(vests)	shift	scent	skip
5. snake	sheep	(zoo)	sand	sound

Directions: Read the words in the four boxes. Circle two words that start with the uppercase and lowercase letter "s."
지도: 네 개의 상자에 있는 단어를 읽으십시오. 대문자와 소문자"s"로시작하는 두 단어에 동그라미를 치십시오.

zips	(Skull)
ponies	(soon)

crown	(Sang)
(shelf)	cones

green	zoo
(script)	(Send)

(Shawl)	zebra
combs	(scoop)

(Sense)	(ships)
grows	clips

sung	cliffs
(Scalp)	noses

Answer Key

 Name: _____ Date: ___/___/_____ Score: _____

Appendix 20.0

Introduction of the Letter T/t

✓ Lesson Check Point

 Directions: Circle the correct letter "t" pair: uppercase and lowercase letters.
지도: 올바른 문자"t" 쌍에 동그라미를 치십시오: 대문자와 소문자.

   Lt   tF   bT   Bt

(Tt) is circled.

 Directions: The uppercase letter "T" is in the first column. Look at the four letters in the row and circle the lowercase letter that matches the uppercase letter "T."
지도: 대문자"T"는 첫 번째 열에 있습니다. 행의 네 글자를 보고대문자 "T"와 일치하는 소문자에 동그라미를 치십시오.

T	(t)	l	y	j
T	h	j	f	(t)
T	l	(t)	k	d
T	b	h	(t)	g

 Directions: The lowercase letter "t" is in the first column. Look at the four letters in the row and circle the uppercase letter that matches the lowercase letter "t."
지도: 소문자"t"는 첫 번째 열에 있습니다. 행의 네 글자를 보고소문자"t" 와 일치하는 대문자에 동그라미를 치세요.

t	F	(T)	H	J
t	(T)	B	F	D
t	J	F	B	(T)
t	H	L	(T)	F

Learn To Read English With Directions In Korean

Assessment

Name: _____ Date: ___/___/_____ Score: _____

Appendix 20.0

Letter Recognition T/t

Uppercase and Lowercase Letter

✓ Lesson Check Point

Directions: Read each target word. Read the words in the row and circle the word that begins with a different letter.
지도: 각 대상 단어를 읽으십시오. 행에 있는 단어를 읽고 다른 문자로시 작하는 단어에 동그라미를 치십시오.

Target Words				
1. type	tall	tomb	thigh	(flag)
2. tired	(love)	tape	tongue	twelve
3. toad	then	(dance)	trick	trench
4. tense	tribe	tale	twist	(house)
5. torn	tail	thigh	tends	(boat)

Directions: Read the words in the four boxes. Circle two words that start with the uppercase and lowercase letter "t."
지도: 네 개의 상자에 있는 단어를 읽으십시오. 대문자와 소문자 "t"로 시작하는 두 단어에 동그라미를 치십시오.

Flame	(Tough)		King	harmony		label	(Taught)
(try)	desk		(trait)	(Taste)		Panel	(tree)

lamb	(tread)		(True)	kind		(There)	taint
food	(Teach)		dream	(twine)		house	Lady

Answer Key

 Name: _____ Date:___/___/_____ Score:_____

Appendix 21.0

Introduction of the Letter U/u

✓ Lesson Check Point

 Directions: Circle the correct letter "u" pair: uppercase and lowercase letters.
지도: 올바른 문자"u" 쌍에 동그라미를 치십시오: 대문자와 소문자.

uV   Uv   Ou   Yu   (Uu)

 Directions: The uppercase letter "U" is in the first column. Look at the four letters in the row and circle the lowercase letter that matches the uppercase letter "U."
지도: 대문자"U"는 첫 번째 열에 있습니다. 행의 네 글자를 보고 대문자 "U"와 일치하는 소문자에 동그라미를 치십시오.

U	v	(u)	o	c
U	(u)	c	x	o
U	c	o	f	(u)
U	y	(u)	c	n

 Directions: The lowercase letter "u" is in the first column. Look at the four letters in the row and circle the uppercase letter that matches the lowercase letter "u."
지도: 소문자"u"는 첫 번째 열에 있습니다. 행의 네 글자를 보고 소문자 "u"와 일치하는 대문자에 동그라미를 치세요.

u	(U)	V	F	O
u	G	X	(U)	V
u	N	O	M	(U)
u	S	(U)	R	Z

Assessment

 Name: _____ Date: ___/___/_____ Score: _____

Appendix 22.0

Introduction of the Letter V/v

✓ Lesson Check Point

 Directions: Circle the correct letter "v" pair: uppercase and lowercase letters.
지도: 올바른 문자"v" 쌍에 동그라미를 치십시오: 대문자와 소문자.

xV   (Vv)   vW   Mv   Uv

 Directions: The uppercase letter "V" is in the first column. Look at the four letters in the row and circle the lowercase letter that matches the uppercase letter "V."
지도: 대문자"V"는 첫 번째 열에 있습니다. 행의 네 글자를 보고 대문자 "V"와 일치하는 소문자에 동그라미를 치십시오.

V	(v)	w	u	o
V	x	z	(v)	l
V	w	(v)	x	u
V	(v)	a	y	w

 Directions: The lowercase letter "v" is in the first column. Look at the four letters in the row and circle the uppercase letter that matches the lowercase letter "v."
지도: 소문자"v"는 첫 번째 열에 있습니다. 행의 네 글자를 보고 소문자"v"와 일치하는 대문자에 동그라미를 치세요.

v	W	(V)	U	M
v	A	Y	(V)	X
v	(V)	W	Z	A
v	X	Y	A	(V)

Answer Key

Name: _____ Date: ___/___/_____ Score: _____

Appendix 22.0

Letter Recognition V/v

Uppercase and Lowercase Letter

✓ Lesson Check Point

 Directions: Read each target word. Read the words in the row and circle the word that begins with a different letter.
지도: 각 대상 단어를 읽으십시오. 행에 있는 단어를 읽고 다른 문자로시작하는 단어에 동그라미를 치십시오.

Target Words				
1. vain	valve	vote	vent	(west)
2. vest	verb	vice	(mouse)	void
3. vogue	(nuts)	van	vein	vex
4. versed	voice	(windy)	vamp	vow
5. viewing	vague	(wise)	vane	verse

 Directions: Read the words in the four boxes. Circle two words that start with the uppercase and lowercase letter "v."
지도: 네 개의 상자에 있는 단어를 읽으십시오. 대문자와 소문자 "v"로시작하는 두 단어에 동그라미를 치십시오.

More	(Vase)
Wall	(valid)

(Vouch)	click
mouse	(voiced)

zooms	weak
(Vile)	(vine)

(Vault)	wife
(vet)	zoo

(vetch)	(Veil)
Went	paint

noon	(Volt)
(visa)	wealth

Learn To Read English With Directions In Korean

Assessment

 Name: _____ Date:___/___/_____ Score:_____

Appendix 23.0

Introduction of the Letter W/w

✓ Lesson Check Point

 Directions: Circle the correct letter "w" pair: uppercase and lowercase letters.
지도: 올바른 문자"w" 쌍에 동그라미를 치십시오: 대문자와 소문자.

Wv	uW	wY	wZ	(Ww)

 Directions: The uppercase letter "W" is in the first column. Look at the four letters in the row and circle the lowercase letter that matches the uppercase letter "W."
지도: 대문자"W"는 첫 번째 열에 있습니다. 행의 네 글자를 보고 대문자 "W"와 일치하는 소문자에 동그라미를 치십시오.

W	v	y	z	(w)
W	x	(w)	v	y
W	k	v	(w)	x
W	(w)	x	y	z

 Directions: The lowercase letter "w" is in the first column. Look at the four letters in the row and circle the uppercase letter that matches the lowercase letter "w."
지도: 소문자"w"는 첫 번째 열에 있습니다. 행의 네 글자를 보고 소문자 "w"와 일치하는 대문자에 동그라미를 치세요.

w	(W)	X	Z	M
w	N	T	X	(W)
w	X	(W)	V	Y
w	Y	V	(W)	M

Answer Key

Name: _____ Date: ___/___/_____ Score: _____

Appendix 23.0

Letter Recognition W/w

Uppercase and Lowercase Letter

✓ Lesson Check Point

Directions: Read each target word. Read the words in the row and circle the word that begins with a different letter.
지도: 각 대상 단어를 읽으십시오. 행에 있는 단어를 읽고 다른 문자로 시작하는 단어에 동그라미를 치십시오.

Target Words				
1. way	world	witch	wall	(nine)
2. weep	(mouse)	whim	worn	waltz
3. worm	win	(verbal)	weird	waive
4. walk	(none)	wake	worse	whine
5. wife	wok	whirl	(volleyball)	worst

Directions: Read the words in the four boxes. Circle two words that start with the uppercase and lowercase letter "w."
지도: 네 개의 상자에 있는 단어를 읽으십시오. 대문자와 소문자 "w"로 시작 하는 두 단어에 동그라미를 치십시오.

(Whiz)	Violin		(week)	(Wrack)		Moon	(whisk)
Neck	(won)		Mate	Nose		Vase	(Wrath)

vest	Marble		Noodle	(Warmth)		(well)	virus
(ward)	(Wove)		(width)	Variety		Noon	(Wait)

Learn To Read English With Directions In Korean   291   Copyrighted Material

Assessment

 Name: _____ Date: ___/___/_____ Score: _____

Appendix 24.0

Introduction of the Letter X/x

✓ **Lesson Check Point**

 Directions: Circle the correct letter "x" pair: uppercase and lowercase letters.
지도: 올바른 문자"x" 쌍에 동그라미를 치십시오: 대문자와 소문자.

      (xX)   Kx   Yx   Wx   Xk

 Directions: The uppercase letter "X" is in the first column. Look at the four letters in the row and circle the lowercase letter that matches the uppercase letter "X."
지도: 대문자"X"는 첫 번째 열에 있습니다. 행의 네 글자를 보고 대문자 "X"와 일치하는 소문자에 동그라미를 치십시오.

X	y	z	(x)	v
X	(x)	y	v	c
X	w	(x)	v	y
X	z	v	m	(x)

 Directions: The lowercase letter "x" is in the first column. Look at the four letters in the row and circle the uppercase letter that matches the lowercase letter "x."
지도: 소문자"x"는 첫 번째 열에 있습니다. 행의 네 글자를 보고 소문자 "x"와 일치하는 대문자에 동그라미를 치세요.

x	(X)	V	Y	Z
x	F	(X)	V	K
x	(X)	K	Z	V
x	K	V	Y	(X)

Answer Key

Name: _____ Date: ____/____/_____ Score: _____

Appendix 24.0

Letter Recognition X/x

Uppercase and Lowercase Letter

✓ Lesson Check Point

Directions: Read each target word. Read the words in the row and circle the word that does not contain a letter "x."
지도: 각 대상 단어를 읽으십시오. 행에 있는 단어를 읽고 문자"x"가 포함되지 않은 단어에 동그라미를 치십시오.

Target Words				
1. fax	relax	(sent)	taxes	sixth
2. toxic	apex	oxen	(cry)	boxed
3. exist	(milk)	cortex	mix	expand
4. sixty	exact	(keep)	tuxedo	next
5. expel	waxy	mixed	excel	(book)

Directions: Read the words in the four boxes. Circle two words that start with the uppercase and lowercase letter "x."
지도: 네 개의 상자에 있는 단어를 읽으십시오. 대문자와 소문자"x"로 시작하는 두 단어에 동그라미를 치십시오.

(Xylem)	xylan		yours	(xylose)		horse	(Xylene)
extra	kicks		cord	(Xeric)		(xiphoid)	noun

(xyster)	vein		(Xenon)	young		knight	voice
(Xerox)	knot		house	(x-axis)		(Xebec)	(x-ray)

Learn To Read English With Directions In Korean   Copyrighted Material

Assessment

 Name: _____ Date: ___/___/_____ Score: _____

Appendix 25.0

Introduction of the Letter Y/y

✓ Lesson Check Point

 Directions: Circle the correct letter "y" pair: uppercase and lowercase letters.
지도: 올바른 문자"y" 쌍에 동그라미를 치십시오: 대문자와 소문자.

    yX   Yk   (Yy)   Xy   yF

 Directions: The uppercase letter "Y" is in the first column. Look at the four letters in the row and circle the lowercase letter that matches the uppercase letter "Y."
지도: 대문자"Y"는 첫 번째 열에 있습니다. 행의 네 글자를 보고 대문자 "Y"와 일치하는 소문자에 동그라미를 치십시오.

Y	(y)	v	a	z
Y	x	j	v	(y)
Y	z	x	(y)	k
Y	j	(y)	g	v

 Directions: The lowercase letter "y" is in the first column. Look at the four letters in the row and circle the uppercase letter that matches the lowercase letter "y."
지도: 소문자"y"는 첫 번째 열에 있습니다. 행의 네 글자를 보고 소문자"y"와 일치하는 대문자에 동그라미를 치세요.

y	X	A	(Y)	F
y	(Y)	V	X	Z
y	K	(Y)	A	X
y	J	H	X	(Y)

Answer Key

Name: _____ Date: ___/___/_____ Score: _____

Appendix 25.0

Letter Recognition Y/y

Uppercase and Lowercase Letter

✓ Lesson Check Point

Directions: Read each target word. Read the words in the row and circle the word that begins with a different letter.
지도: 각 대상 단어를 읽으십시오. 행에 있는 단어를 읽고 다른 문자로 시작하는 단어에 동그라미를 치십시오.

Target Words				
1. Yale	yak	(quiz)	yet	yam
2. yards	year	yes	y-axis	(push)
3. yahoo	(join)	yap	yours	yarn
4. yellow	yard	yeast	(groom)	yield
5. yearbook	yes	(jumps)	yacht	Yemen

Directions: Read the words in the four boxes. Circle two words that start with the uppercase and lowercase letter "y."
지도: 네 개의 상자에 있는 단어를 읽으십시오. 대문자와 소문자 "y"로 시작하는 두 단어에 동그라미를 치십시오.

quiz	goal
(y-axis)	(Yeast)

(yuck)	jazz
ground	(Yolk)

queen	(Yam)
goat	(yet)

(yards)	just
(Yours)	greet

press	(Yahoo)
(yo-yo)	guest

(Youth)	(yarn)
pride	gold

Learn To Read English With Directions In Korean   295   Copyrighted Material

Assessment

 Name: _____ Date: ___/___/_____ Score: _____

Appendix 26.0

Introduction of the Letter Z/z

✓ Lesson Check Point

 Directions: Circle the correct letter "z" pair: uppercase and lowercase letters.
지도: 올바른 문자"z" 쌍에 동그라미를 치십시오: 대문자와 소문자.

Xz   (Zz)   zY   Zs   Kz

 Directions: The uppercase letter "Z" is in the first column. Look at the four letters in the row and circle the lowercase letter that matches the uppercase letter "Z."
지도: 대문자"Z"는 첫 번째 열에 있습니다. 행의 네 글자를 보고 대문자 "Z"와 일치하는 소문자에 동그라미를 치십시오.

Z	(z)	x	n	f
Z	y	v	(z)	x
Z	g	(z)	h	y
Z	v	k	x	(z)

 Directions: The lowercase letter "z" is in the first column. Look at the four letters in the row and circle the uppercase letter that matches the lowercase letter "z."
지도: 소문자"z"는 첫 번째 열에 있습니다. 행의 네 글자를 보고 소문자 "z" 와 일치하는 대문자에 동그라미를 치세요.

z	N	A	(Z)	J
z	M	(Z)	F	N
z	(Z)	X	N	W
z	N	(Z)	W	A

Learn To Read English With Directions In Korean

Answer Key

 Name: _____ Date: ___/___/_____ Score: _____

Appendix 26.0

Letter Recognition Z/z

Uppercase and Lowercase Letter

✓ Lesson Check Point

 Directions: Read each target word. Read the words in the row and circle the word that begins with a different letter.
지도: 각 대상 단어를 읽으십시오. 행에 있는 단어를 읽고 다른 문자로시작하는 단어에 동그라미를 치십시오.

Target Words				
1. zealous	(umpire)	zip	zinc	zebra
2. zoologist	zinger	zoo	(whale)	zero
3. zillionaire	zone	(vase)	zoom	zonal
4. zoophobia	zenith	zipper	zap	(next)
5. Zimbabwe	Zurich	zodiac	Zambia	(session)

 Directions: Read the words in the four boxes. Circle two words that start with the uppercase and lowercase letter "z."
지도: 네 개의 상자에 있는 단어를 읽으십시오. 대문자와 소문자"z"로시작하는 두 단어에 동그라미를 치십시오.

usher	(Zap)
(zeal)	swim

(zonal)	sweat
under	(Zinc)

wheel	(Zoo)
vote	(zone)

visit	stone
(zero)	(Zebra)

(Zip)	zealous
sprout	violet

(zigzag)	speak
(Zenith)	west

Assessment

Your Next Step:

Learn To Read English Vowels With Directions In Korean

www.ingramcontent.com/pod-product-compliance
Lightning Source LLC
Chambersburg PA
CBHW080835230426
43665CB00021B/2853